Q: Skills for Success ③
LISTENING AND SPEAKING

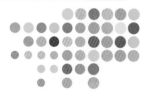

Miles Craven

Kristin D. Sherman

SERIES CONSULTANTS

Marguerite Ann Snow

Lawrence J. Zwier

VOCABULARY CONSULTANT

Cheryl Boyd Zimmerman

OXFORD

UNIVERSITY PRESS

OXFORD
UNIVERSITY PRESS

198 Madison Avenue
New York, NY 10016 USA

Great Clarendon Street, Oxford OX2 6DP UK

Oxford University Press is a department of the University of Oxford.
It furthers the University's objective of excellence in research, scholarship,
and education by publishing worldwide in

Oxford New York

Auckland Cape Town Dar es Salaam Hong Kong Karachi
Kuala Lumpur Madrid Melbourne Mexico City Nairobi
New Delhi Shanghai Taipei Toronto

With offices in

Argentina Austria Brazil Chile Czech Republic France Greece
Guatemala Hungary Italy Japan Poland Portugal Singapore
South Korea Switzerland Thailand Turkey Ukraine Vietnam

OXFORD and OXFORD ENGLISH are registered trademarks of
Oxford University Press in certain countries.

© Oxford University Press 2011

Database right Oxford University Press (maker)

No unauthorized photocopying

Any websites referred to in this publication are in the public domain and
their addresses are provided by Oxford University Press for information only.
Oxford University Press disclaims any responsibility for the content.

General Manager, American ELT: Laura Pearson
Publisher: Stephanie Karras
Associate Publishing Manager: Sharon Sargent
Managing Editors: Martin Coleman, Mary Whittemore
Associate Development Editors: Rebecca Mostov, Keyana Shaw
Director, ADP: Susan Sanguily
Executive Design Manager: Maj-Britt Hagsted
Associate Design Manager: Michael Steinhofer
Electronic Production Manager: Julie Armstrong
Production Artist: Elissa Santos
Cover Design: Molly Scanlon
Image Manager: Trisha Masterson
Image Editors: Robin Fadool and Liaht Pashayan
Production Coordinator: Elizabeth Matsumoto

ISBN: 978-0-19-475612-9 LISTENING SPEAKING 3
STUDENT BOOK PACK

ISBN: 978-0-19-475602-0 LISTENING SPEAKING 3
STUDENT BOOK

ISBN: 978-0-19-475621-1 Q ONLINE PRACTICE
STUDENT ACCESS CODE CARD

Printed in China

This book is printed on paper from certified and well-managed sources.

10 9 8 7 6 5 4 3

ACKNOWLEDGMENTS

The publisher would like to thank the following for their permission to reproduce copyrighted material: p.153, from "My Buenos Aires" by Marcos Aguinis, "My Beijing" by Peter Hessler, and "My Dubai" by Paulo Coelho, http://travel. nationalgeographic.com. Used by permission of National Geographic; p.175, from "Happiness Breeds Success ... and Money!" by Sonja Lyubomirsky, July 18, 2008, http://www.psychologytoday.com. Used by permission of Sonja Lyubomirsky.

The publishers would like to thank the following for their kind permission to reproduce photographs: Cover John Giustina/Iconica/Getty Images; Sean Justice/ Riser/Getty Images; Kirsty Pargeter/iStockphoto; Leontura/iStockphoto; Illustrious/iStockphoto; vi Marcin Krygier/iStockphoto; xii Rüstem GÜRLER/ iStockphoto; p2 David Schmidt/Masterfile; p6 Hill Street Studios/Blend Images/Corbis UK Ltd.; p7 Asia Images Group/Getty Images; p10 Imagebroker/ Alamy; p11 Digital Vision/Oxford University Press; p13 DCPhoto/Alamy; p22 Corbis/SuperStock; p26 Jason Loucas/Photolibrary Group; p29 Bon Appetit/ Alamy (ice cream); p29 Steve Cavalier/Alamy (coffee); p31 Photodisc/Oxford University Press (Stuart); p31 Photodisc/Oxford University Press (Marie); p31 Image Source/Corbis UK Ltd. (Enrique); p31 Scott Karcich/Shutterstock (cheese); p32 RubberBall/Alamy; p33 Stock Connection/SuperStock; p35 Paul Abbitt/Alamy; p38 luoman/istockphoto; p39 SoFood/Alamy (fondue); p39 Tim Hill/Alamy (paella); p40 Stockbyte/Oxford University Press; p44 Imagno/ Hulton Archive/Getty Images; p46 MBI/Alamy (family); p46 Tetra Images/ Corbis UK Ltd. (computer); p46 Bloomimage/Corbis UK Ltd. (jogging); p48 Paul Collis/Alamy (car); p48 Inmagine Asia/Corbis UK Ltd. (graduation); p49 Clive Rose/Getty Images; p51 Moodboard/Corbis UK Ltd.; p52 Michel Euler/ AP Photo/Press Association Images; p58 Corbis/Digital Stock/Oxford University Press; p64 Stuart Pearce/age fotostock; p68 Tetra Images/ Alamy; p72 Rex Features; p77 Photodisc/Oxford University Press; p80 David Madison/Corbis/Oxford University Press; p84 REUTERS/Ho New; p88 HolgerBurmeister/Alamy; p92 Moodboard/Corbis UK Ltd.; p93 Doug Wechsler/Photolibrary Group; p104 Gianni Muratore/Alamy (man); p104 Digital Vision/Oxford University Press (car); p106 Jorg Greuel/The Image Bank/Getty Images; p108 Stock Connection Blue/Alamy; p112 Mary K. Engle; p124 Masterfile; p126 Monalyn Gracia/Corbis; p128 Kurt Krieger/Corbis UK Ltd. (Rodriguez); p128 Slavoljub Pantelic/shutterstock (chair); p129 Universal Pictures/Ronald Grant Archive; p133 Harry Borden (Rines); p133 F1 Online/ Photolibrary Group (Nessie); p142 Rick Gomez/Corbis UK Ltd. (woman); p142 Neus Grandia/Oxford University Press (map); p146 Chad Ehlers/Alamy; p148 Photodisc/Oxford University Press (Rome); p148 Photodisc/Oxford University Press (Sydney); p150 The Washington Post/Getty Images; p151 Mats Rosenberg/Nordic Photos/Photolibrary Group; p154 Chad Ehlers/Alamy (Buenos Aires); p154 Panorama Media Ltd./Alamy (Beijing); p154 Images & Stories/Alamy (Dubai); p154 worldthroughthelens-travel/Alamy (skyscrapers); p166 Ron Davey/Shutterstock; p170 Photodisc/Oxford University Press; p171 Steven S Miric/Superstock/Photolibrary Group; p175 Dana Patrick/Sonja Lyubomirsky, Ph.D.; p186 REUTERS/Daniel Munoz; p188 Celia Peterson/Getty Images (texting); p188 Oxford University Press (talking); p188 Blend Images/ Alamy (writing); p190 Marion Bull/Alamy; p195 Nicole Hill/Getty Images; p198 David Noton Photography/Alamy; p201 Zooid Pictures.

Illustrations by: p4 Jing Jing Tsong; p24 Bill Smith Group; p46 Bill Smith Group; p66 Barb Bastian; p86 Barb Bastian; p106 Bill Smith Group; p115 Barb Bastian; p126 Bill Smith Group; p148 Barb Bastian; p168 Barb Bastian; p188 Bill Smith Group; p193 Jean Tuttle.

ACKNOWLEDGEMENTS

Authors

Miles Craven has a diploma in TEFLA from Bell Cambridge, U.K. He has over twenty years' experience in English language teaching, as a teacher, teacher-trainer, examiner, and materials writer. He has taught students in private language schools, British Council centers, and universities in Italy, Portugal, Spain, Hong Kong, Japan and the U.K. Miles is author or co-author of several textbooks. He has written many articles and online materials, and regularly presents at conferences and workshops. Miles also helps coordinate the Business English Programme at the Møller Centre, Churchill College, University of Cambridge. His research focuses on developing skills and strategies to help learners improve their reading, listening, and speaking abilities.

Kristin Donnalley Sherman holds an M.E. in TESL from the University of North Carolina, Charlotte. She has taught ESL/EFL at Central Piedmont Community College in Charlotte, North Carolina for more than fifteen years, and has taught a variety of subjects, including grammar, reading, composition, listening, and speaking. She has written several student books, teacher's editions and workbooks in the area of academic ESL/EFL. In addition, she has delivered trainings internationally on ESL methodology.

Series Consultants

Marguerite Ann Snow holds a Ph.D. in Applied Linguistics from UCLA. She is a Professor in the Charter College of Education at California State University, Los Angeles where she teaches in the TESOL M.A. program. She has published in *TESOL Quarterly*, *Applied Linguistics*, and *The Modern Language Journal*. She has been a Fulbright scholar in Hong Kong and Cyprus. In 2006, she received the President's Distinguished Professor award at Cal State LA. In addition to working closely with ESL and mainstream public school teachers in the U.S., she has trained EFL teachers in Algeria, Argentina, Brazil, Egypt, Japan, Morocco, Pakistan, Spain, and Turkey. Her main interests are integrated content and language instruction, English for Academic Purposes, and standards for English teaching and learning.

Lawrence J. Zwier holds an M.A. in TESL from the University of Minnesota. He is currently the Associate Director for Curriculum Development at the English Language Center at Michigan State University in East Lansing. He has taught ESL/EFL in the U.S., Saudi Arabia, Malaysia, Japan, and Singapore. He is a frequent TESOL conference presenter, and has published many ESL/EFL books in the areas of test-preparation, vocabulary, and reading, including *Inside Reading 2* for Oxford University Press.

Vocabulary Consultant

Cheryl Boyd Zimmerman is Associate Professor of TESOL at California State University, Fullerton. She specializes in second language vocabulary acquisition, an area in which she is widely published. She teaches graduate courses on second language acquisition, culture, vocabulary, and the fundamentals of TESOL, and is a frequent invited speaker on topics related to vocabulary teaching and learning. She is the author of *Word Knowledge: A Vocabulary Teacher's Handbook,* and Series Director of *Inside Reading*, both published by Oxford University Press.

REVIEWERS

We would like to acknowledge the advice of teachers from all over the world who participated in online reviews, focus groups, and editorial reviews. We relied heavily on teacher input throughout the extensive development process of the Q series, and many of the features in the series came directly from feedback we gathered from teachers in the classroom. We are grateful to all who helped.

UNITED STATES Marcarena Aguilar, North Harris College, TX; **Deborah Anholt**, Lewis and Clark College, OR; **Robert Anzelde**, Oakton Community College, IL; **Arlys Arnold**, University of Minnesota, MN; **Marcia Arthur**, Renton Technical College, WA; **Anne Bachmann**, Clackamas Community College, OR; **Ron Balsamo**, Santa Rosa Junior College, CA; **Lori Barkley**, Portland State University, OR; **Eileen Barlow**, SUNY Albany, NY; **Sue Bartch**, Cuyahoga Community College, OH; **Lora Bates**, Oakton High School, VA; **Nancy Baum**, University of Texas at Arlington, TX; **Linda Berendsen**, Oakton Community College, IL; **Jennifer Binckes Lee**, Howard Community College, MD; **Grace Bishop**, Houston Community College, TX; **Jean W. Bodman**, Union County College, NJ; **Virginia Bouchard**, George Mason University, VA; **Kimberley Briesch Sumner**, University of Southern California, CA; **Gabriela Cambiasso**, Harold Washington College, IL; **Jackie Campbell**, Capistrano Unified School District, CA; **Adele C. Camus**, George Mason University, VA; **Laura Chason**, Savannah College, GA; **Kerry Linder Catana**, Language Studies International, NY; **An Cheng**, Oklahoma State University, OK; **Carole Collins**, North Hampton Community College, PA; **Betty R. Compton**, Intercultural Communications College, HI; **Pamela Couch**, Boston University, MA; **Fernanda Crowe**, Intrax International Institute, CA; **Margo Czinski**, Washtenaw Community College, MI; **David Dahnke**, Lone Star College, TX; **Gillian M. Dale**, CA; **L. Dalgish**, Concordia College, MN; **Christopher Davis**, John Jay College, NY; **Sonia Delgadillo**, Sierra College, CA; **Marta O. Dmytrenko-Ahrabian**, Wayne State University, MI; **Javier Dominguez**, Central High School, SC; **Jo Ellen Downey-Greer**, Lansing Community College, MI; **Jennifer Duclos**, Boston University, MA; **Yvonne Duncan**, City College of San Francisco, CA; **Jennie Farnell**, University of Connecticut, CT; **Susan Fedors**, Howard Community College, MD; **Matthew Florence**, Intrax International Institute, CA; **Kathleen Flynn**, Glendale College, CA; **Eve Fonseca**, St. Louis Community College, MO; **Elizabeth Foss**, Washtenaw Community College, MI; **Duff C. Galda**, Pima Community College, AZ; **Christiane Galvani**, Houston Community College, TX; **Gretchen Gerber**, Howard Community College, MD; **Ray Gonzalez**, Montgomery College, MD; **Alyona Gorokhova**, Grossmont College, CA; **John Graney**, Santa Fe College, FL; **Kathleen Green**, Central High School, AZ; **Webb Hamilton**, De Anza College, San Jose City College, CA; **Janet Harclerode**, Santa Monica Community College, CA; **Sandra Hartmann**, Language and Culture Center, TX; **Kathy Haven**, Mission College, CA; **Adam Henricksen**, University of Maryland, MD; **Peter Hoffman**, LaGuardia Community College, NY; **Linda Holden**, College of Lake County, IL; **Jana Holt**, Lake Washington Technical College, WA; **Gail Ibele**, University of Wisconsin, WI; **Mandy Kama**, Georgetown University, Washington, DC; **Stephanie Kasuboski**, Cuyahoga Community College, OH; **Chigusa Katoku**, Mission College, CA; **Sandra Kawamura**, Sacramento City College, CA; **Gail Kellersberger**, University of Houston-Downtown, TX; **Jane Kelly**, Durham Technical Community College, NC; **Julie Park Kim**, George Mason University, VA; **Lisa Kovacs-Morgan**, University of California, San Diego, CA; **Claudia Kupiec**, DePaul University, IL; **Renee La Rue**, Lone Star College-Montgomery, TX; **Janet Langon**, Glendale College, CA; **Lawrence Lawson**, Palomar College, CA; **Rachele Lawton**, The Community College of Baltimore County, MD; **Alice Lee**, Richland College, TX; **Cherie Lenz-Hackett**, University of Washington, WA; **Joy Leventhal**, Cuyahoga Community College, OH; **Candace Lynch-Thompson**, North Orange County Community College District, CA; **Thi Thi Ma**, City College of San Francisco, CA; **Denise Maduli-Williams**, City College of San Francisco, CA; **Eileen Mahoney**, Camelback High School, AZ; **Brigitte Maronde**, Harold Washington College, IL; **Keith Maurice**, University of Texas at Arlington, TX; **Nancy Mayer**, University of Missouri-St. Louis, MO; **Karen Merritt**, Glendale Union High School District, AZ; **Holly Milkowart**, Johnson County Community College, KS; **Eric Moyer**, Intrax International Institute, CA; **Gino Muzzatti**, Santa Rosa Junior College, CA; **William Nedrow**, Triton College, IL; **Eric Nelson**, University of Minnesota, MN; **Rhony Ory**, Ygnacio Valley High School, CA; **Paul Parent**, Montgomery College, MD; **Oscar Pedroso**, Miami Dade College, FL; **Robin Persiani**, Sierra College, CA; **Patricia Prenz-Belkin**, Hostos Community College, NY; **Jim Ranalli**, Iowa State University, IA; **Toni R. Randall**, Santa Monica College, CA; **Vidya Rangachari**, Mission College, CA; **Elizabeth Rasmussen**, Northern Virginia Community College, VA; **Lara Ravitch**, Truman College, IL; **Deborah Repasz**, San Jacinto College, TX; **Andrey Reznikov**, Black Hills State University, SD; **Alison Rice**, Hunter College, NY; **Jennifer Robles**, Ventura Unified School District, CA; **Priscilla Rocha**, Clark County School District, NV; **Dzidra Rodins**, DePaul University IL; **Maria Rodriguez**, Central High School, AZ; **Maria Ruiz**, Victor Valley College, CA; **Kimberly Russell**, Clark College, WA; **Irene Sakk**, Northwestern University, IL; **Shaeley Santiago**, Ames High School, IA; **Peg Sarosy**, San Francisco State University, CA; **Alice Savage**, North Harris College, TX; **Donna Schaeffer**, University of Washington, WA; **Carol Schinger**, Northern Virginia Community College, VA; **Robert Scott**, Kansas State University, KS; **Suell Scott**, Sheridan Technical Center, FL; **Shira Seaman**, Global English Academy, NY; **Richard Seltzer**, Glendale Community College, CA; **Kathy Sherak**, San Francisco State University, CA; **German Silva**, Miami Dade College, FL; **Andrea Spector**, Santa Monica Community College, CA; **Karen Stanely**, Central Piedmont Community College, NC; **Ayse Stromsdorfer**, Soldan I.S.H.S., MO; **Yilin Sun**, South Seattle Community College, WA; **Thomas Swietlik**, Intrax International Institute, IL; **Judith Tanka**, UCLA Extension–American Language Center, CA; **Priscilla Taylor**, University of Southern California, CA; **Ilene Teixeira**, Fairfax County Public Schools, VA; **Shirl H. Terrell**, Collin College, TX; **Marya Teutsch-Dwyer**, St. Cloud State University, MN; **Stephen Thergesen**, ELS Language Centers, CO; **Christine Tierney**, Houston Community College, TX; **Arlene Turini**, North Moore High School, NC; **Suzanne Van Der Valk**, Iowa State University, IA; **Nathan D. Vasarhely**, Ygnacio Valley High School, CA; **Naomi S. Verratti**, Howard Community College, MD; **Hollyahna Vettori**, Santa Rosa Junior College, CA; **Julie Vorholt**, Lewis & Clark College, OR; **Laura Walsh**, City College of San Francisco, CA; **Andrew J. Watson**, The English Bakery; **Donald Weasenforth**, Collin College, TX; **Juliane Widner**, Sheepshead Bay High School, NY; **Lynne Wilkins**, Mills College, CA; **Dolores "Lorrie" Winter**, California State University at Fullerton, CA; **Jody Yamamoto**, Kapi'olani Community College, HI; **Ellen L. Yaniv**, Boston University, MA; **Norman Yoshida**, Lewis & Clark College, OR; **Joanna Zadra**, American River College, CA; **Florence Zysman**, Santiago Canyon College, CA;

ASIA Rabiatu Abubakar, Eton Language Centre, Malaysia; **Wiwik Andreani**, Bina Nusantara University, Indonesia; **Mike Baker**, Kosei Junior High School, Japan; **Leonard Barrow**, Kanto Junior College, Japan; **Herman Bartelen**, Japan; **Siren Betty**, Fooyin University, Kaohsiung; **Thomas E. Bieri**, Nagoya College, Japan; **Natalie Brezden**, Global English House, Japan; **MK Brooks**, Mukogawa Women's University, Japan; **Truong Ngoc Buu**, The Youth Language School, Vietnam; **Charles Cabell**, Toyo University, Japan; **Fred Carruth**, Matsumoto University, Japan; **Frances Causer**, Seijo University, Japan; **Deborah Chang**, Wenzao Ursuline College of Languages, Kaohsiung; **David Chatham**, Ritsumeikan University, Japan; **Andrew Chih Hong Chen**, National Sun Yat-sen University, Kaohsiung; **Christina Chen**, Yu-Tsai Bilingual Elementary School, Taipei; **Jason Jeffree Cole**, Coto College, Japan; **Le Minh Cong**, Vungtau Tourism Vocational College, Vietnam; **Todd Cooper**, Toyama National College of Technology, Japan; **Marie Cosgrove**, Daito Bunka University, Japan; **Tony Cripps**, Ritsumeikan University, Japan; **Daniel Cussen**, Takushoku University, Japan; **Le Dan**, Ho Chi Minh City Electric Power College, Vietnam; **Simon Daykin**, Banghwa-dong Community Centre, South Korea; **Aimee Denham**, ILA, Vietnam; **Bryan Dickson**, David's English Center, Taipei; **Nathan Ducker**, Japan University, Japan; **Ian Duncan**, Simul International Corporate Training, Japan; **Nguyen Thi Kieu Dung**, Thang Long University, Vietnam; **Nguyen Thi Thuy Duong**, Vietnamese American Vocational Training College, Vietnam; **Wong Tuck Ee**, Raja Tun Azlan Science Secondary School, Malaysia; **Emilia Effendy**, International Islamic University Malaysia, Malaysia; **Robert Eva**, Kaisei Girls High School, Japan; **Jim George**, Luna International Language School, Japan; **Jurgen Germeys**, Silk Road Language Center, South Korea; **Wong Ai Gnoh**, SMJK

Chung Hwa Confucian, Malaysia; **Peter Goosselink**, Hokkai High School, Japan; **Wendy M. Gough**, St. Mary College/Nunoike Gaigo Senmon Gakko, Japan; **Tim Grose**, Sapporo Gakuin University, Japan; **Pham Thu Ha**, Le Van Tam Primary School, Vietnam; **Ann-Marie Hadzima**, Taipei; **Troy Hammond**, Tokyo Gakugei University International Secondary School, Japan; **Robiatul 'Adawiah Binti Hamzah**, SMK Putrajaya Precinct 8(1), Malaysia; **Tran Thi Thuy Hang**, Ho Chi Minh City Banking University, Vietnam; **To Thi Hong Hanh**, CEFALT, Vietnam; **Janis Hearn**, Hongik University, South Korea; **David Hindman**, Sejong University, South Korea; **Nahn Cam Hoa**, Ho Chi Minh City University of Technology, Vietnam; **Jana Holt**, Korea University, South Korea; **Jason Hollowell**, Nihon University, Japan; **F. N. (Zoe) Hsu**, National Tainan University, Yong Kang; **Wenhua Hsu**, I-Shou University, Kaohsiung; **Luu Nguyen Quoc Hung**, Cantho University, Vietnam ; **Cecile Hwang**, Changwon National University, South Korea; **Ainol Haryati Ibrahim**, Universiti Malaysia Pahang, Malaysia; **Robert Jeens**, Yonsei University, South Korea; **Linda M. Joyce**, Kyushu Sangyo University, Japan; **Dr. Nisai Kaewsanchai**, English Square Kanchanaburi, Thailand; **Aniza Kamarulzaman**, Sabah Science Secondary School, Malaysia; **Ikuko Kashiwabara**, Osaka Electro-Communication University, Japan; **Gurmit Kaur**, INTI College, Malaysia; **Nick Keane**, Japan; **Ward Ketcheson**, Aomori University, Japan; **Montchatry Ketmuni**, Rajamangala University of Technology, Thailand; **Dinh Viet Khanh**, Vietnam; **Seonok Kim**, Kangsu Jongro Language School, South Korea; **Kelly P. Kimura**, Soka University, Japan; **Stan Kirk**, Konan University, Japan; **Donald Knight**, Nan Hua/Fu Li Junior High Schools, Hsinchu; **Kari J. Kostiainen**, Nagoya City University, Japan; **Pattri Kuanpulpol**, Silpakorn University, Thailand; **Ha Thi Lan**, Thai Binh Teacher Training College, Vietnam; **Eric Edwin Larson**, Miyazaki Prefectural Nursing University, Japan; **Richard S. Lavin**, Prefectural University of Kumamoto, Japan; **Shirley Leane**, Chugoku Junior College, Japan; **Tae Lee**, Yonsei University, South Korea; **Lys Yongsoon Lee**, Reading Town Geumcheon, South Korea; **Mallory Leece**, Sun Moon University, South Korea; **Dang Hong Lien**, Tan Lam Upper Secondary School, Vietnam; **Huang Li-Han**, Rebecca Education Institute, Taipei; **Sovannarith Lim**, Royal University of Phnom Penh, Cambodia; **Ginger Lin**, National Kaohsiung Hospitality College, Kaohsiung; **Noel Lineker**, New Zealand/Japan; **Tran Dang Khanh Linh**, Nha Trang Teachers' Training College, Vietnam; **Daphne Liu**, Buliton English School, Taipei; **S. F. Josephine Liu**, Tien-Mu Elementary School, Taipei ; **Caroline Luo**, Tunghai University, Taichung; **Jeng-Jia Luo**, Tunghai University, Taichung; **Laura MacGregor**, Gakushuin University, Japan; **Amir Madani**, Visuttharangsi School, Thailand; **Elena Maeda**, Sacred Heart Professional Training College, Japan; **Vu Thi Thanh Mai**, Hoang Gia Education Center, Vietnam; **Kimura Masakazu**, Kato Gakuen Gyoshu High School, Japan; **Susumu Matsuhashi**, Net Link English School, Japan; **James McCrostie**, Daito Bunka University, Japan; **Joel McKee**, Inha University, South Korea; **Colin McKenzie**, Wachirawit Primary School, Thailand; **William K. Moore**, Hiroshima Kokusai Gakuin University, Japan; **Hudson Murrell**, Baiko Gakuin University, Japan; **Frances Namba**, Senri International School of Kwansei Gakuin, Japan; **Keiichi Narita**, Niigata University, Japan; **Kim Chung Nguyen**, Ho Chi Minh University of Industry, Vietnam; **Do Thi Thanh Nhan**, Hanoi University, Vietnam; **Dale Kazuo Nishi**, Aoyama English Conversation School, Japan; **Louise Ohashi**, Shukutoku University, Japan; **Virginia Peng**, Ritsumeikan University, Japan; **Suangkanok Piboonthamnont**, Rajamangala University of Technology, Thailand; **Simon Pitcher**, Business English Teaching Services, Japan; **John C. Probert**, New Education Worldwide, Thailand; **Do Thi Hoa Quyen**, Ton Duc Thang University, Vietnam; **John P. Racine**, Dokkyo University, Japan; **Kevin Ramsden**, Kyoto University of Foreign Studies, Japan; **Luis Rappaport**, Cung Thieu Nha Ha Noi, Vietnam; **Lisa Reshad**, Konan Daigaku Hyogo, Japan; **Peter Riley**, Taisho University, Japan; **Thomas N. Robb**, Kyoto Sangyo University, Japan; **Maria Feti Rosyani**, Universitas Kristen Indonesia, Indonesia; **Greg Rouault**, Konan University, Japan; **Chris Ruddenklau**, Kindai University, Japan; **Hans-Gustav Schwartz**, Thailand; **Mary-Jane Scott**, Soongsil University, South Korea; **Jenay Seymour,** Hongik University, South Korea; **James Sherlock**, A.P.W. Angthong, Thailand; **Yuko Shimizu**, Ritsumeikan University, Japan; **Suzila Mohd Shukor**, Universiti Sains Malaysia, Malaysia; **Stephen E. Smith**, Mahidol University, Thailand; **Mi-young Song**, Kyungwon University, South Korea; **Jason Stewart**, Taejon International Language School, South Korea; **Brian A. Stokes,** Korea University, South Korea; **Mulder Su**, Shih-Chien University, Kaohsiung; **Yoomi Suh**, English Plus, South Korea; **Yun-Fang Sun**, Wenzao Ursuline College of Languages, Kaohsiung; **Richard Swingle**, Kansai Gaidai University, Japan; **Tran Hoang Tan**, School of International Training, Vietnam; **Takako Tanaka**, Doshisha University, Japan; **Jeffrey Taschner**, American University Alumni Language Center, Thailand ; **Michael Taylor**, International Pioneers School, Thailand; **Tran Duong The**, Sao Mai Language Center, Vietnam; **Tran Dinh Tho**, Duc Tri Secondary School, Vietnam; **Huynh Thi Anh Thu**, Nhatrang College of Culture Arts and Tourism, Vietnam; **Peter Timmins**, Peter's English School, Japan; **Fumie Togano**, Hosei Daini High School, Japan; **F. Sigmund Topor**, Keio University Language School, Japan; **Yen-Cheng Tseng**, Chang-Jung Christian University, Tainan; **Hajime Uematsu**, Hirosaki University, Japan; **Rachel Um**, Mok-dong Oedae English School, South Korea; **David Underhill**, EEExpress, Japan; **Siriluck Usaha**, Sripatum University, Thailand; **Tyas Budi Utami**, Indonesia; **Nguyen Thi Van**, Far East International School, Vietnam; **Stephan Van Eycken**, Kosei Gakuen Girls High School, Japan; **Zisa Velasquez**, Taihu International School/Semarang International School, China/Indonesia; **Jeffery Walter**, Sangji University, South Korea; **Bill White**, Kinki University, Japan; **Yohanes De Deo Widyastoko**, Xaverius Senior High School, Indonesia; **Greg Chung-Hsien Wu**, Providence University, Taichung; **Hui-Lien Yeh**, Chai Nan University of Pharmacy and Science, Tainan; **Sittiporn Yodnil**, Huachiew Chalermprakiet University, Thailand; **Shamshul Helmy Zambahari**, Universiti Teknologi Malaysia, Malaysia; **Ming-Yuli**, Chang Jung Christian University, Tainan; **Aimin Fadhlee bin Mahmud Zuhodi**, Kuala Terengganu Science School, Malaysia;

TURKEY Gül Akkoç, Boğaziçi University; **Seval Akmeşe**, Haliç University; **Deniz Balım**, Haliç University; **Robert Ledbury**, Izmir University of Economics; **Oya Özağaç**, Boğaziçi University;

THE MIDDLE EAST **Amina Saif Mohammed Al Hashamia**, Nizwa College of Applied Sciences, Oman; **Sharon Ruth Devaneson**, Ibri College of Technology, Oman; **Hanaa El-Deeb,** Canadian International College, Egypt; **Brian Gay**, Sultan Qaboos University, Oman; **Gail Al-Hafidh**, Sharjah Higher Colleges of Technology, U.A.E.; **Jonathan Hastings**, American Language Center, Jordan; **Sian Khoury**, Fujairah Women's College (HCT), U.A.E.; **Jessica March**, American University of Sharjah, U.A.E.; **Neil McBeath**, Sultan Qaboos University, Oman;

LATIN AMERICA **Aldana Aguirre**, Argentina; **Claudia Almeida**, Coordenação de Idiomas, Brazil; **Cláudia Arias**, Brazil; **Maria de los Angeles Barba**, FES Acatlan UNAM, Mexico; **Lilia Barrios**, Universidad Autónoma de Tamaulipas, Mexico; **Adán Beristain**, UAEM, Mexico; **Ricardo Böck**, Manoel Ribas, Brazil; **Edson Braga**, CNA, Brazil; **Marli Buttelli**, Mater et Magistra, Brazil; **Alessandra Campos**, Inova Centro de Linguas, Brazil; **Priscila Catta Preta Ribeiro**, Brazil; **Gustavo Cestari**, Access International School, Brazil; **Walter D'Alessandro**, Virginia Language Center, Brazil; **Lilian De Gennaro**, Argentina; **Mônica De Stefani**, Quality Centro de Idiomas, Brazil; **Julio Alejandro Flores**, BUAP, Mexico; **Mirian Freire**, CNA Vila Guilherme, Brazil; **Francisco Garcia**, Colegio Lestonnac de San Angel, Mexico; **Miriam Giovanardi**, Brazil; **Darlene Gonzalez Miy**, ITESM CCV, Mexico; **Maria Laura Grimaldi**, Argentina; **Luz Dary Guzmán**, IMPAHU, Colombia; **Carmen Koppe**, Brazil; **Monica Krutzler**, Brazil; **Marcus Murilo Lacerda**, Seven Idiomas, Brazil; **Nancy Lake**, CEL-LEP, Brazil; **Cris Lazzerini**, Brazil; **Sandra Luna**, Argentina; **Ricardo Luvisan**, Brazil; **Jorge Murilo Menezes**, ACBEU, Brazil; **Monica Navarro**, Instituto Cultural A. C., Mexico; **Joacyr Oliveira**, Faculdades Metropolitanas Unidas and Summit School for Teachers, Brazil; **Ayrton Cesar Oliveira de Araujo**, E&A English Classes, Brazil; **Ana Laura Oriente**, Seven Idiomas, Brazil; **Adelia Peña Clavel**, CELE UNAM, Mexico; **Beatriz Pereira**, Summit School, Brazil; **Miguel Perez**, Instituto Cultural Mexico; **Cristiane Perone**, Associação Cultura Inglesa, Brazil; **Pamela Claudia Pogré**, Colegio Integral Caballito / Universidad de Flores, Argentina; **Dalva Prates**, Brazil; **Marianne Rampaso**, Iowa Idiomas, Brazil; **Daniela Rutolo**, Instituto Superior Cultural Británico, Argentina; **Maione Sampaio**, Maione Carrijo Consultoria em Inglês Ltda, Brazil; **Elaine Santesso**, TS Escola de Idiomas, Brazil; **Camila Francisco Santos**, UNS Idiomas, Brazil; **Lucia Silva**, Cooplem Idiomas, Brazil; **Maria Adela Sorzio**, Instituto Superior Santa Cecilia, Argentina; **Elcio Souza**, Unibero, Brazil; **Willie Thomas**, Rainbw Idiomas, Brazil; **Sandra Villegas**, Instituto Humberto de Paolis, Argentina; **John Whelan**, La Universidad Nacional Autonoma de Mexico, Mexico

WELCOME TO **Q:**Skills for Success

Q: Skills for Success is a six-level series with two strands,
Reading and Writing **and** *Listening and Speaking*.

READING AND WRITING

LISTENING AND SPEAKING

WITH Q ONLINE PRACTICE web+

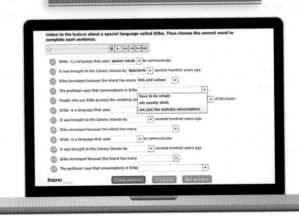

STUDENT AND TEACHER INFORMED

Q: Skills for Success is the result of an extensive development process involving thousands of teachers and hundreds of students around the world. Their views and opinions helped shape the content of the series. *Q* is grounded in teaching theory as well as real-world classroom practice, making it the most learner-centered series available.

CONTENTS

Q connects critical thinking, language skills, and learning outcomes.

LISTENING	listening for signposts
VOCABULARY	using the dictionary
GRAMMAR	types of sentences
PRONUNCIATION	intonation in different types of sentences
SPEAKING	agreeing and disagreeing

LEARNING OUTCOME

Participate in a group discussion evaluating the influence money has on happiness.

Unit QUESTION

Can money buy happiness?

PREVIEW THE UNIT

A Discuss these questions with your classmates.

How much money do you think people really need to be happy? Explain.

Do you think more money would make you happier? Why or why not?

Look at the photo. Do you think the people living in this house are happy? Why or why not?

B Discuss the Unit Question above with your classmates.

Listen to *The Q Classroom*, Track 13 on CD 3, to hear other answers.

166   UNIT 9

167

 Having the learning outcome is important because it gives students and teachers a clear idea of what the point of each task/activity in the unit is.
Lawrence Lawson, Palomar College, California

PREVIEW LISTENING 1

| Sudden Wealth

LANGUAGE SKILLS

Two listening texts provide input on the unit question and give **exposure to academic content.**

You are going to listen to a podcast that helps people learn to handle their money wisely. The article discusses people who suddenly become rich and the difficulties they face.

Which topics do you think the article will discuss? Check (✓) your ideas.

- ☐ how sudden wealth makes people happy
- ☐ how sudden wealth causes problems
- ☐ the advantages and disadvantages of sudden wealth

CRITICAL THINKING

Students **discuss** their opinions of each listening text and **analyze** how it changes their perspective on the unit question.

Q WHAT DO YOU THINK?

A. Discuss the questions in a group.

1. Which do you think comes first, happiness or money? Explain.

2. What qualities of a happy person do you think lead to better employment and financial outcomes?

Tip Critical Thinking

Question 1 of Activity B asks you to **choose** between two things. To make the best choice, you evaluate a variety of factors, including your knowledge and experience.

B. Think about both Listening 1 and Listening 2 as you discuss the questions.

1. What is the difference between sudden wealth and earning more money from a better job? Which would you prefer? Why?

2. Do you pay much attention to financial matters? Do you enjoy thinking about money, or does it make you feel stressed? Explain.

> " One of the best features is your focus on developing materials of a high "interest level."
> *Troy Hammond, Tokyo Gakugei University,*
> *International Secondary School, Japan* "

Explicit skills instruction prepares students for academic success.

LANGUAGE SKILLS

Explicit instruction and practice in listening, speaking, grammar, pronunciation, and vocabulary skills **help students achieve language proficiency.**

LEARNING OUTCOMES

Practice activities allow students to **master the skills** before they are evaluated at the end of the unit.

Listening Skill | Listening for signposts

Signposts are words and phrases that can tell you the order in which things happened. Listen for signposts to help you follow the order of events and the logic in a text.

CD 3
Track 16

Listen to these examples of signposts from Listening 1.

First, it affects how our brains work, at least for a while.
In the beginning, when we get the money, our brain identifies it as pleasure.
Then that feeling wears off.

Here are some words and phrases which are used as signposts.

At the start	In the middle	At the end
At first,	After (that),	Finally,
First,	Before (that),	In conclusion,
In the beginning,	Later,	In summary,
	Next,	
	Second,	
	Then,	

CD 3
Track 17

A. Listen to a reporter interview a secretary who suddenly acquired a lot of money. Complete the interview with the signposts you hear.

Reporter: You are one of many people in this town who suddenly acquired a lot of wealth when your company was purchased by a large software company. How has that affected your life?

Laura Green: Well, _____ it was pretty incredible. It took a
while for me to believe it. But _____ I began to realize what
it could actually do to my life. Things have changed dramatically.

Reporter: In what way?

Laura: I paid off all of my credit card debt. And sent my son to college.
Receiving this money was just fantastic! _____, I was
worried all the time.

Reporter: So your financial circumstances have improved. What else
has changed?

172   **UNIT 9** | Can money buy happiness?

Speaking Skill | Agreeing and disagreeing

There are certain phrases used for **agreeing and disagreeing**. It's important to know which phrases and expressions are appropriate for formal and informal situations. An informal conversation is very different from a formal discussion at college or at work.

Here are some phrases you can use when you want to agree or disagree in different situations.

Agreeing		Disagreeing
I agree (completely).	formal	I disagree.
That's exactly what I think.		I don't agree (at all).
That's a good point.		Sorry, but that's not my opinion.
That's right.		I don't feel the same way.
I think so too.		I don't think so.
Absolutely!		No way!
Yeah, I know!	informal	Oh, come on!

CD 3
Track 22

A. Listen to the conversations. Complete each conversation with the phrases you hear.

Ellie: What are you going to do with the money your grandfather gave you?

Sam: I'm not sure. I think I'm going to take an expensive vacation.

Ellie: Really? Don't you have a lot of school loans to pay?

Sam: _____. Maybe the vacation's not such a good idea.

Ellie: _____. Vacations are fun, but it's much more important
to pay off your debt.

Monica: I think raising the average income in countries around the world is
the best way to increase the level of happiness.

Patricia: I _____. More money might make the very poor
happier, but not everyone.

Monica: I _____. I think everyone except perhaps the very
wealthy will benefit from a higher income.

Patricia: Well, I can see we'll just have to agree to disagree.

182   **UNIT 9** | Can money buy happiness?

"" The tasks are simple, accessible, user-friendly, and very useful.
Jessica March, American University of Sharjah, U.A.E. ""

Vocabulary Skill | Using the dictionary

Definitions of similar words

Some words are similar in meaning, for instance, *creativity* and *productivity*.

> People in jobs where they can show creativity and productivity are happier than those who aren't.

Creativity and *productivity* both have to do with making things, but they are also a little different. Look at their dictionary definitions.

> **cre·a·tiv·i·ty** AWL /ˌkrieɪˈtɪvəti/ *noun* [U] the ability to make or produce new things, especially using skill or imagination: *teaching that encourages children's creativity*

> **pro·duc·tiv·i·ty** /ˌprɑdʌkˈtɪvəti; ˌproʊ-/ *noun* [U] the rate at which a worker, a company, or a country produces goods, and the amount produced: *More efficient methods will lead to greater productivity.*

All dictionary entries are taken from the *Oxford American Dictionary for learners of English.*

All dictionary entries are taken from the *Oxford American Dictionary for learners of English.*

The ***Oxford American Dictionary for learners of English*** was developed with English learners in mind, and provides extra learning tools for pronunciation, verb types, basic grammar structures, and more.

The Oxford 3000™

The Oxford 3000 encompasses **the 3000 most important words to learn in English.** It is based on a comprehensive analysis of the Oxford English Corpus, a 2 billion word collection of English text, and on extensive research with both language and pedagogical experts.

The Academic Word List AWL

The Academic Word List was created by Averil Coxhead and contains **570 words that are commonly used in academic English,** such as in textbooks or articles across a wide range of academic subject areas. These words are a great place to start if you are studying English for academic purposes.

Clear learning outcomes focus students on the goals of instruction.

LEARNING OUTCOMES

A culminating unit assignment evaluates the students' **mastery of the learning outcome.**

Unit Assignment | **Take part in a group discussion**

 In this assignment, you are going to take part in a group discussion about money and happiness. As you prepare for the discussion, think about the Unit Question, "Can money buy happiness?" and refer to the Self-Assessment checklist on page 184.

For alternative unit assignments, see the *Q: Skills for Success Teacher's Handbook.*

CONSIDER THE IDEAS

Work with a partner. Discuss the questions about money and happiness. Be sure to use the correct intonation when you ask each other questions.

What is money's influence on happiness?

What kind of person do you think would be happier with more money? Why?

Would your life be different if you had more or less money? How?

Is it more enjoyable to give or receive money? Why?

182   UNIT 9 | Can money buy happiness?

LEARNER CENTERED

Track Your Success allows students to **assess their own progress** and provides guidance on remediation.

Check (✓) the skills you learned. If you need more work on a skill, refer to the page(s) in parentheses.

LISTENING	I can listen for signposts. (p. 172)
VOCABULARY	I can use the dictionary to find the definition of similar words. (p. 178)
GRAMMAR	I can use different types of sentences. (p. 180)
PRONUNCIATION	I can use correct intonation in different sentence types. (p. 181)
SPEAKING	I can use phrases for agreeing and disagreeing. (p. 181)
LEARNING OUTCOME	I can participate in a group discussion evaluating the influence money has on happiness.

Listening and Speaking   **185**

 Students can check their learning . . . and they can focus on the essential points when they study.

Suh Yoomi, Seoul, South Korea

Q Online Practice

For the student

- **Easy-to-use:** a simple interface allows students to focus on enhancing their speaking and listening skills, not learning a new software program
- **Flexible:** for use anywhere there's an Internet connection
- **Access code card:** a *Q Online Practice* access code is included with this book. Use the access code to register for *Q Online Practice* at www.Qonlinepractice.com

For the teacher

- **Simple yet powerful:** automatically grades student exercises and tracks progress
- **Straightforward:** online management system to review, print, or export the reports they need
- **Flexible:** for use in the classroom or easily assigned as homework
- **Access code card:** contact your sales rep for your *Q Online Practice* teacher's access code

Teacher Resources

Q Teacher's Handbook gives strategic support through:
- specific teaching notes for each activity
- ideas for ensuring student participation
- multilevel strategies and expansion activities
- the answer key
- special sections on 21st Century Skills and critical thinking
- a *Testing Program CD-ROM* with a customizable test for each unit.

Oxford
Teachers' Club

For additional resources visit the
Q: Skills for Success companion website at
www.oup.com/elt/teacher/Qskillsforsuccess

Q Class Audio includes:
- listening texts
- pronunciation presentations and exercises
- *The Q Classroom*

> ❝ It's an interesting, engaging series which provides plenty of materials that are easy to use in class, as well as instructionally promising. ❞
> *Donald Weasenforth, Collin College, Texas*

UNIT	LISTENING	SPEAKING	VOCABULARY
1 First Impressions **Are first impressions accurate?** **LISTENING 1: The Psychology of First Impressions** A lecture (Psychology) **LISTENING 2: Book Review of** *Blink* **by Malcolm Gladwell** A radio program (Interpersonal Communication)	• Use prior knowledge and personal experience to predict content • Listen for main ideas • Listen for details • Make inferences to fully understand what a speaker means • Listen for opinions to understand a book review • Listen for reduced verb forms to understand everyday speech	• Make notes to prepare for a presentation or group discussion • Take turns to make a conversation go smoothly • Imply opinions to avoid stating them too directly • Use verb contractions to increase naturalness of speech	• Assess your prior knowledge of vocabulary • Use suffixes to change a word's part of speech
2 Food and Taste **What's more important: taste or nutrition?** **LISTENING 1: You Are What You Eat** A radio program (Nutrition) **LISTENING 2: Food Tasters** A podcast (Food Service)	• Use prior knowledge and personal experience to predict content • Listen for main ideas • Listen for details • Listen for causes and effects to understand relationships among ideas • Follow a summary of several ideas to match an opinion with a speaker • Identify /j/ and /w/ sounds in speech to understand links between words	• Make notes to prepare for an interview • Give advice to suggest healthy eating habits • Prepare to speak about your personal tastes to help others conduct a survey • Conduct a survey of classmates' tastes • Participate in a group discussion about results of a survey	• Assess your prior knowledge of vocabulary • Understand and use collocations of adjectives with nouns to expand vocabulary
3 Success **What can we learn from success and failure?** **LISTENING 1: Chasing Your Dreams** A lecture (Business Management) **LISTENING 2: The Benefits of Failure** A speech (Psychology)	• Use prior knowledge and personal experience to predict content • Listen for main ideas • Listen for details • Listen for opinion statements to understand a speaker's positive and negative attitudes • Match people with ideas to understand their attitudes • Listen for exact words or phrases to improve your word recognition	• Make notes to prepare for a presentation or group discussion • Ask for clarification so you understand difficult concepts • Include time for questions after a presentation so your audience can ask for clarification • Clarify what you say so others understand you better	• Assess your prior knowledge of vocabulary • Understand and use prefixes for negatives (*dis-*, *im-*, and *ir-*) and other meanings (*co-*, *re-*, *multi-*, and *anti-*) • Understand prefixes to increase comprehension • Use prefixes to expand vocabulary

GRAMMAR	PRONUNCIATION	CRITICAL THINKING	UNIT OUTCOME
• Auxiliary verbs *do, be, have*	• Use contractions with auxiliary verbs	• Assess your prior knowledge of content • Relate personal experiences to listening topics • Integrate information from multiple sources • Evaluate the truthfulness of traditional wisdom • Identify your decision-making processes • Examine your reasons for forming impressions of people	• Describe in detail an inaccurate first impression.
• Quantifiers with count/ non-count nouns	• Use linked sounds with /j/ and /w/	• Assess your prior knowledge of content • Relate personal experiences to listening topics • Integrate information from multiple sources • Identify personal tastes in food • Evaluate the healthfulness of your habits • Relate personal food preferences to those of your classmates • Evaluate classmates' reasons for food preferences	• Interview classmates to inform a group discussion on why people prefer certain foods.
• Gerunds and infinitives as the objects of verbs	• Correctly place stress on important words in sentences.	• Assess your prior knowledge of content • Relate personal experiences to listening topics • Integrate information from multiple sources • Understand, interpret, and evaluate others' attitudes toward succes and failure • Identify your attitudes toward success and failure • Consider your hopes and ambitions • Evaluate the consequences of decisions	• Discuss successful and unsuccessful personal experiences and explain what you learned from them.

UNIT	LISTENING	SPEAKING	VOCABULARY
4 New Perspectives **Q Is change good or bad?** **LISTENING 1: Changing Expectations** A talk (Finance) **LISTENING 2: An Interview with Barbara Ehrenreich** An interview (Journalism, Sociology)	• Use prior knowledge and personal experience to predict content • Listen for main ideas • Listen for details • Listen to personal stories to understand other people's experiences • Use a T-chart to take effective notes • Listen for intonation to identify a speaker's level of interest in a topic • Listen for exact words or phrases to improve your word recognition	• Make notes to prepare for a presentation or group discussion • Describe a situation using details so a listener can make inferences about an event • Ask for reasons to understand why something happened • Express reasons to explain why something happened • Use reasons to explain personal beliefs	• Assess your prior knowledge of vocabulary • Understand dictionary entries to diagram meanings in word webs
5 Responsibility **Q Are we responsible for the world we live in?** **LISTENING 1: Corporate Social Responsibility** A lecture (Business, Ecology) **LISTENING 2: Personal Responsibility** An excerpt from a college seminar (Business, Sociology)	• Use prior knowledge and personal experience to predict content • Listen for main ideas • Listen for details • Listen for supporting statements to apply a general concept to real life • Use intonation, volume, and other features to infer a speaker's attitudes • Listen for exact words in a conversation to improve your word recognition	• Take notes to prepare for a presentation or group discussion • Practice varying intonation and other features to convey your attitudes • Add tag questions to statements to find out what someone thinks • Answer tag questions using proper grammar and intonation to accurately express what you think • Lead a discussion so it proceeds smoothly, fairly, and stays on topic	• Assess your prior knowledge of vocabulary • Find the most relevant dictionary definition for a word that has many meanings
6 Advertising **Q How can advertisers change our behavior?** **LISTENING 1: Advertising Techniques** A small group presentation (Advertising) **LISTENING 2: Advertising Ethics and Standards** An interview (Business, Ethics)	• Use prior knowledge and personal experience to predict content • Listen for main ideas • Listen for details • Listen for evidence to distinguish fact from opinion • Listen for modal verbs to understand obligations, prohibitions, and recommendations • Listen for intonation to distinguish between statements and questions • Listen for exact words or phrases to improve your word recognition	• Make notes to prepare for a presentation or group discussion • Use modals to express obligation, prohibition, and recommendation • Ask questions and make statements with correct intonation to be understood clearly • Give reasons and examples to support opinions you express	• Assess your prior knowledge of vocabulary • Use context to understand the meanings of unfamiliar words or phrases

GRAMMAR	PRONUNCIATION	CRITICAL THINKING	UNIT OUTCOME
• Simple past and present perfect	• Vary intonation to show interest in a topic	• Assess your prior knowledge of content • Relate personal experiences to listening topics • Integrate information from multiple sources • Recall life experiences and assess their significance • Consider the methods used by reporters to gather information	• Participate in a group discussion emphasizing the advantages and disadvantages of change.
• Tag questions	• Use rising and falling intonation in tag questions to convey meaning	• Assess your prior knowledge of content • Relate personal experiences to listening topics • Integrate information from multiple sources • Consider social responsibility on several levels, including individual, family, and corporate responsibility • Develop skills for leadership in a small group	• State and explain your opinions about our responsibility for issues impacting our world.
• Modals that express attitude	• Correctly use intonation in *yes/no* and *wh-* questions • Use intonation to make statements into questions to express surprise	• Assess your prior knowledge of content • Relate personal experiences to listening topics • Integrate information from multiple sources • Assess your personal experiences with advertising and your responses to it • Judge real-life situations according to your ethical standards • Summarize a discussion in a group • Express and support a personal opinion	• State and support your opinions concerning the influence of advertising on our behavior.

UNIT	LISTENING	SPEAKING	VOCABULARY
7 Risk **What risks are good to take?** **LISTENING 1: Financing a Dream** A talk (Finance, Film Study) **LISTENING 2: The Truth about the Loch Ness Monster** A report (Zoology)	• Use prior knowledge and personal experience to predict content • Listen for main ideas • Listen for details • Listen for numbers to correctly understand amounts • Use the form of number expressions to distinguish between cardinal and ordinal numbers • Listen for exact words in a passage to improve your word recognition	• Make notes to prepare for a presentation or group discussion • Clearly introduce the topic of a presentation to focus an audience's attention • Use sequence expressions to clarify the order of events in a presentation • Use expressions of purpose/reason to explain actions and attitudes	• Assess your prior knowledge of vocabulary • Use a dictionary to learn about word families • Increase vocabulary by understanding word families
8 Cities **What do our cities say about us?** **LISTENING 1: Do cities have personalities?** A report (Urban studies) **LISTENING 2: Buenos Aires, Beijing, and Dubai** A description from 3 writers (Sociology)	• Use prior knowledge and personal experience to predict content • Listen for main ideas • Listen for details • Understand figurative expressions to interpret a speaker's true meaning • Listen for comments that help you match a city to a description	• Make notes to prepare for a presentation or group discussion • Use summary or recap techniques to end a presentation • Use a T-chart to take notes for a presentation	• Assess your prior knowledge of vocabulary • Understand phrasal verbs to accurately interpret statements
9 Money **Can money buy happiness?** **LISTENING 1: Sudden Wealth** A podcast (Psychology) **LISTENING 2: Happiness Breeds Success…and Money!** An interview (Personal finance, Psychology)	• Use prior knowledge and personal experience to predict content • Listen for main ideas • Listen for details • Listen for a sequence of factors to understand the stages in a process • Understand examples to relate them to larger ideas • Listen for signposts to understand the structure of a passage • Listen for exact words in a conversation to improve your word recognition	• Make notes to prepare for a presentation or group discussion • Use expressions to introduce statements of agreement and disagreement • Explain reasons to justify statements about personal preferences • Discuss with a partner attitudes about the relationship between money and happiness	• Assess your prior knowledge of vocabulary • Use a dictionary to distinguish among words that are somewhat similar in meaning
10 Keeping in Touch **Do we need technology to communicate long distance** **LISTENING 1: An Unusual Language** A lecture (Communication) **LISTENING 2: Message in a Bottle** A report (Sociology)	• Use prior knowledge and personal experience to predict content • Listen for main ideas • Listen for details • Listening for rhetorical questions to understand the structure of a lecture • Recognize definitions in a passage to understand unfamiliar vocabulary • Listen for exact words in sentences to improve your word recognition	• Take notes to prepare for a presentation or group discussion • Ask questions to confirm your understanding of definitions • Practice using idioms to increase the naturalness of your speech • Use adjectives, fixed phrases, and idioms to express emotions • Prepare a dialogue with a partner to improve your conversation skills	• Assess your prior knowledge of vocabulary • Understand idioms to accurately interpret statements • Correctly use idiomatic expressions

GRAMMAR	PRONUNCIATION	CRITICAL THINKING	UNIT OUTCOME
• Past perfect	• Correctly use contracted and uncontracted forms of *had*	• Assess your prior knowledge of content • Relate personal experiences to listening topics • Integrate information from multiple sources • Evaluate risks to determine which are justified • Reflect on your own willingness to take risks • Explain and evaluate a risk you have taken	• Give a short presentation on a risk you have taken, explaining your reasons for taking that risk.
• Separable and inseparable phrasal verbs	• Effectively link consonants and vowels	• Assess your prior knowledge of content • Relate personal experiences to listening topics • Integrate information from multiple sources • Evaluate the strengths and weaknesses of several entities • Classify items according to shared features • Assess the significance of an item's characteristics • Analyze personal preferences	• Give and recap a presentation highlighting what you like and dislike about a particular city.
• Sentence types—declarative, interrogatory, imperative, and exclamatory	• Effectively use intonation in different sentence types	• Assess your prior knowledge of content • Relate personal experiences to listening topics • Integrate information from multiple sources • Examine your attitudes toward money and happiness • Distinguish between causal relationships and correlations in research results • Support opinions with reasons an examples	• Participate in a group discussion evaluating the influence money has on happiness.
• Comparatives with adjectives	• Correctly pronounce unstressed connecting words	• Assess your prior knowledge of content • Relate personal experiences to listening topics • Integrate information from multiple sources • Reflect on personal styles of communication • Speculate about the origins of communication practices • Evaluate the effect of technology on language and communication • Decide how to resolve communication problems	• Role-play a phone call discussing an emotional event you have experienced.

UNIT 1

First Impressions

LISTENING	●	making inferences
VOCABULARY	●	suffixes
GRAMMAR	●	auxiliary verbs *do, be, have*
PRONUNCIATION	●	contractions with auxiliary verbs
SPEAKING	●	taking conversational turns

Unit QUESTION

Are first impressions accurate?

PREVIEW THE UNIT

A Discuss these questions with your classmates.

What do you notice when you meet someone for the
first time?

How important do you think first impressions are? Why?

Look at the photo. Who are the people in the photo?
What are they doing?

B Discuss the Unit Question above with your classmates.

Listen to *The Q Classroom*, Track 2 on CD 1, to hear other answers.

C Read the proverbs (sayings). Decide whether each proverb means that first impressions are accurate (A) or not accurate (N). Discuss your answers with a partner. Look up any unfamiliar words in the dictionary.

_____ 1. Don't judge a horse by its saddle. (Arabic/Chinese)

__A__ 2. Faces we see; hearts we don't know. (Spanish)

__A__ 3. What you see is what you get. (English)

__A__ 4. You must judge a man by the work of his hands. (African)

__N__ 5. Never judge a book by its cover. (English)

__A__ 6. A wheel it is and it turns around. (Greek)

__A__ 7. If it walks like a duck and quacks like a duck, it's a duck. (English)

__N__ 8. Don't think there are no crocodiles because the water is calm. (Malaysian)

D Do you have any proverbs in your culture about first impressions? What are they? Tell your partner.

E Which proverbs from Activity C do you think are the truest? Discuss your ideas with your partner.

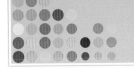

LISTENING 1 | The Psychology of First Impressions

VOCABULARY

Here are some words and phrases from Listening 1. Read the definitions.
Then complete each sentence with the correct word or phrase.

(2.2)
(3. 2)

assume *(v.)* to accept or believe that something is true *(but you don't know)*
behavior *(n.)* the way that you act or behave *action*
briefly *(adv.)* for a short time; quickly *~*
encounter *(n.)* an unexpected meeting
error *(n.)* a mistake
form an impression *(phr.)* to begin to have an idea about something
negative *(adj.)* bad or harmful
positive *(adj.)* good or useful
sample *(n.)* a small amount or example of something
trait *(n.)* a quality that forms part of your character

1. I took a(n) ___*sample*___ of the carpet home to see whether I liked the color in my living room.

2. Alberto made several ___*errors*___ on his math test because he didn't study hard enough.

3. Luisa said she wasn't feeling well, so I ___*assumed*___ she's not going out tonight.

4. The teacher went over yesterday's assignment very ___*briefly*___.
   We only spent about fifteen minutes on it, so I still have some questions.

5. When I meet new people, I watch their ___*behaviour*___ closely to see what they are like.

6. It only takes a few minutes to ___*form an impression*___ of someone you meet for the first time.

7. One ___*negative*___ thing about moving to a new place is leaving your friends and family behind.

8. Most of my good friends have one personality ___*trait*___ in common—they are all very funny.

9. Do you usually have a(n) _____positive_____ feeling about people when you meet them for the first time? I do because I think most people are good.

10. My first ____encounter____ with my new neighbors was very unpleasant. We argued about the amount of noise they were making.

PREVIEW LISTENING 1

The Psychology of First Impressions

doctor

You are going to listen to a lecture about first impressions. A psychologist explains how first impressions affect our opinion of a new person.

Check (✓) the statement about first impressions you think is true.

☐ First impressions give us a good idea of what a person is really like.
☐ We often make errors because of first impressions.

LISTEN FOR MAIN IDEAS

 CD 1
Track 3

Read the statements. Then listen to the lecture. Write *T* (true) or *F* (false).

__F__ 1. First impressions aren't important because we don't remember them.

__T__ 2. If a person is happy when we meet her, we will often think she is happy all the time.

__F__ 3. Our first impressions give us an accurate picture of the whole person.

__T__ 4. We judge other people's behavior differently from our own.

LISTEN FOR DETAILS

CD 1
Track 4

Read the sentences. Then listen again. Circle the answer that best completes each statement.

1. People _____ about what they see in a first encounter.
   a. often make mistakes
   b. never make mistakes
   c. don't care

Presentations and talks often begin with a short story or anecdote. The story is usually an example of the topic the speaker is going to talk about.

2. People assume that their first impressions tell them about _____ person.
   a. a sample of a
   b. most of a
   c. the whole

3. If we think a person is happy when we first meet her, we will think she is also _____.
   a. friendly
   b. angry
   c. boring

4. If someone else does something negative, we think it is because of _____.
   a. his personality
   b. the situation he was in
   c. how he felt that day

5. If we do something negative, we think it is because of _____.
   a. our personality
   b. the situation
   c. someone else

 ## WHAT DO YOU THINK?

Discuss the questions in a group.

1. In this lecture, the speaker says we often think that the way a person behaves when we first meet him is the way he behaves all the time. From your personal experience, do you agree or disagree? Give examples.

2. Have you ever formed a first impression of someone that was wrong? Explain.

First impressions aren't always correct.

Listening Skill | Making inferences

Making inferences means to draw conclusions about information that is not stated directly by using information that you already know or that is stated directly. Making inferences while listening can help deepen your understanding of what you hear.

CD 1 Track 5

Listen to a student talking about meeting his professor for the first time.

> When I first met my professor, he shook my hand firmly and then asked me questions about myself. He was very polite. He also was relaxed and seemed interested in what I was saying.

Even though the student does not state directly that his first impression of his professor was positive, you can infer or conclude that he did from the information he does state directly.

- He shook my hand firmly.
- He asked questions.
- He was relaxed and seemed interested.

CD 1 Track 6

A. Listen to a student talk about a first impression. Take notes in your notebook as you listen. Then answer the questions.

1. Do you think it was it a positive or negative first impression? Why? What information from your notes helped you answer?

   positive (shook hands – polite question

2. Do you think the speaker likes Lee? Why? What information from your notes helped you answer?

   yes

B. Work with a partner. Compare your answers.

CD 1 Track 7

C. Listen to the speaker's opinion of Lee. Take notes in your notebook. Compare what the speaker says about Lee with your answers in Activity B.

D. Work with a partner. Tell a story about meeting someone for the first time. Describe what she or he did and a few things you noticed. Don't say how you felt about the person. Ask your partner to infer whether your impression was positive or negative.

Book Review of *Blink* by Malcolm Gladwell

VOCABULARY

Here are some words and phrases from Listening 2. Read the sentences.
Circle the answer that best matches the meaning of each bold word or phrase.

1. I make a **conscious** effort to stay in regular contact with all my friends.
   I make time to call and email them often.
   a. accidental   b. intentional   c. occasional

2. Watching a video is an **effective** way to study someone's behavior. You can
   learn a lot from the way people move their hands.
   a. successful   b. interesting   c. unusual

3. Marcos is an **expert** at swimming. He has been doing it a long time.
   a. beginner   b. failure   c. skillful person

4. The painting was a **fake**. It was not painted by Da Vinci as the owner believed.
   a. an imitation   b. a problem   c. an original

5. When you meet new people, you should trust your **instincts**. Your first
   reaction is often correct.
   a. natural feelings   b. general knowledge   c. careful research

6. My car isn't **reliable**. There is always something wrong with it.
   a. dependable   b. expensive   c. comfortable

7. I can't **select** anyone to receive the award. There are too many good students.
   a. tell   b. call   c. choose

8. I often make **snap judgments** about things I buy. I don't like to waste time.
   a. careful decisions   b. bad decisions   c. quick decisions

9. My parents were **suspicious** when I told them the teacher did not give
   any grades for our assignment.
   a. uninterested   b. doubtful   c. excited

10. I was so focused on listening to the news this morning that I
    unconsciously poured orange juice in my coffee instead of milk.
    a. without thinking   b. without caring   c. without studying

PREVIEW LISTENING 2

Book Review of *Blink* by Malcolm Gladwell

You are going to listen to an excerpt *a piece of* from a radio show. A critic from the show is reviewing the book *Blink*, by Malcolm Gladwell. In the book, Gladwell discusses the types of decisions we make as a result of first impressions.

Check (✓) which things (if any) you could easily make a quick decision about.

☐ a book to read   ☐ a new pair of shoes

☐ a movie to see   ☐ a place to go on vacation

☐ a new car   ☐ a roommate

LISTEN FOR MAIN IDEAS

CD 1
Track 8

Listen to the book review. Circle the answer that best completes each statement according to what the critic says.

1. Malcolm Gladwell says we make decisions in _____.
   a. one way
   b. two ways
   c. many ways

2. We make _____ decisions slowly and carefully.
   a. snap
   b. conscious
   c. personal

3. Unconscious decisions are made by using _____.
   a. the situation we are in
   b. knowledge we already have
   c. new ideas

4. Snap judgments are often _____.
   a. suspicious
   b. careful
   c. reliable

LISTEN FOR DETAILS

Listen again. Match each detail with an example given in the review.

Details	Examples
_e_ 1. recognizing a fake statue	a. selecting a soccer player
_d_ 2. judging a teacher's effectiveness	b. looking at a bedroom
_b_ 3. describing someone's character	c. buying something for the kitchen
_c_ 4. an easy decision	d. watching a video
_a_ 5. a difficult decision with a lot of information	e. asking an expert

 WHAT DO YOU THINK?

A. Discuss the questions in a group.

1. Malcolm Gladwell suggests that we should make difficult decisions more quickly and with our unconscious minds. Do you agree with him? Why or why not?

2. According to Gladwell, our first impressions are often reliable. Do you think this is true? Why or why not?

B. Think about both Listening 1 and Listening 2 as you discuss the questions.

1. In Listening 1, you learned about the errors we often make with first impressions. In Listening 2, you learned that our first impressions are often accurate. Which position do you agree with more? Why?

2. In what kinds of situations do you think first impressions are usually accurate?

Tip Critical Thinking

Activity B asks you to **compare** and **contrast** Listening 1 and Listening 2. You compare ideas that are the same. You contrast ideas that are different. **Comparing** and **contrasting** can help you understand the ways in which the ideas in Listening 1 are similar to or different from the ideas in Listening 2.

We form first impressions wherever we are.

Use **suffixes** and other word endings to help you recognize parts of speech.
Recognizing the part of speech will help you guess the meaning of an unfamiliar
word. It will also help you expand your vocabulary as you notice other parts of
speech in the same word family.

Common noun suffixes: *-acy, -er/-or, -ment, -ness, -tion*

accur**acy**, research**er**, invent**or**, amuse**ment**, friendli**ness**, atten**tion**

Common verb suffixes: *-ate, -en, -ize*

stimul**ate**, strength**en**, energ**ize**

Common adjective suffixes: *-able, -al, -ful, -ive, -ous*

depend**able**, tradition**al**, care**ful**, effect**ive**, humor**ous**

Common adverb suffixes: *-ly, -ally*

particular**ly**, univers**ally**

A. Look at the new words. For each word, write the suffix, the part of
speech, and the base word from which the new word is formed.

New word	Suffix	Part of speech	Base word
1. accuracy	-acy	noun	accurate
2. assumption	tion	N	assump
3. consciously	ly	adv	conscious
4. prediction	tion	N	predict
5. effectively	-ly	adv	effective
6. instinctive	-ive	a	instinct
7. selection	-ion	N	select

B. Work with a partner. Discuss the meanings of the new words from
Activity A. Then use a dictionary to check the definitions of any words
you are not sure of.

C. Complete each sentence with the correct word from Activity A.

1. That video store offers a great _____*selection*_____ of classic movies. There are so many, it's hard to choose!

2. _____*Accuracy*_____ is really important in grammar, so you should try not to make mistakes.

3. We often make _____*assumptions*_____ about people because of the way they look. Then we sometimes discover that our first impressions were incorrect.

make assumption = assume

4. I don't pay much attention to weather reports. Their _____*predictions*_____ are usually wrong. It was supposed to be sunny yesterday, but it rained all day!

5. If an advertisement is _____*effectively*_____ designed, sales of the product will increase.

6. Many animals have a(n) _____*instinctive*_____ (natural) fear of fire and the danger it represents. They don't learn it. It's part of their nature.

7. I have to make decisions very _____*consciously*_____ when I go shopping. If I don't, I buy things I really don't need without even realizing it.

SPEAKING

> The **auxiliary verbs** *do*, *be*, and *have* are used to make questions and negative statements.
>
> Use *do* with the simple present and simple past.
>
> | **Simple present** | **Simple past** |
> |---|---|
> | **Does** he like pizza? | **Did** they bring their books? |
> | He **doesn't** like pizza. | They **didn't** bring their books. |
>
> Use *be* with the present and past continuous.
>
> | **Present continuous** | **Past continuous** |
> |---|---|
> | **Are** you reading? | **Was** Mr. Knight teaching here last year? |
> | We **aren't** reading now. | He **wasn't** teaching here last year. |
>
> Use *have* with the present perfect.
>
> **Present perfect**
> **Has** she left yet?
> Nancy **hasn't** left yet.

A. Rewrite the sentences as negative statements. Use the correct form of *do, be,* or *have* as the auxiliary verb.

1. I often make snap judgments.

   I don't often make snap judgments.

2. Bill thinks first impressions about teachers are usually accurate.

   Bill doesn't think first impression about teachers are usually accurate

3. Caterina trusted her instincts when meeting new people.

   Caterina didn't trust her instincts when meeting new ppl

4. When Reza buys something, he usually thinks about it for a long time.

   When Reza doesn't buy something, he usually doesn't thinks about it for a long time

5. Jenny is working hard this week.

   Jenny isn't working hard this week.

6. I've formed a positive impression of that company.

   I haven't formed a positive impression of that company.

B. Rewrite the sentences as questions. Use the correct form of *do*, *be*, or *have* as the auxiliary verb.

1. You have made many incorrect assumptions because of how someone looked.

   Have you made many incorrect assumptions because of how someone looked?

2. I like talking to new people on the phone.

   Do you like talking to new people on the phone?

3. Darcy is living with people she met last year.

   Is Darcy living with people she met last year?

4. Marek made lots of friends at school.

   Did Marek make lots of friends at school?

5. The experts realized the statue was a fake.

   Did the experts realize the statue was fake?

6. Patrick has selected his library books already.

   Has Patrick selected his library books already?

C. Work with a partner. Take turns asking and answering the questions from Activity B. Use auxiliary verbs in your short answers.

   A: *Do you like talking to new people on the phone?*
   B: *Yes, I do./No, I don't.*

(handwritten at top: 2 word put together)

CD 1
Track 10

Auxiliary verbs are usually unstressed and can be shortened as part of a **contraction**. Most contractions can be used in speech and informal writing, but some are only used in speech.

Listen to these examples of contractions.

Contractions used in speech or writing

She's eating now. (She is eating now.)
They're watching TV. (They are watching TV.)
Lisa's already left. (Lisa has already left.)
We've finished our work. (We have finished our work.)

Contractions used only in speech

What's it cost? (What does it cost?)
Where'd you go? (Where did you go?)
Why'd he arrive so late? (Why did he arrive so late?)

CD 1
Track 11

A. Listen to these sentences with contractions. Write the full form of the auxiliary verb.

(handwritten: OK im writing) 1. Who __s__ (is) your favorite movie star?

(handwritten: speak only) 2. Where __'d__ (did) you go on your last vacation?

(handwritten: OK write) 3. Mary __'s__ (is) going to the store.

(handwritten: write) 4. Jack __'s__ (has) gone already.

5. We __'ve__ (have) usually eaten by 6:00.   *(handwritten: vusually)*

(handwritten: speech) 6. What __'d__ (did) you do after class yesterday?

(handwritten: No write) 7. The girls _____ (have) been here before.

B. Work with a partner. Take turns saying the sentences from Activity A. Use the full form of the auxiliary verbs. Then practice saying them with contractions.

When you are speaking with someone, it is polite to take turns talking. Taking turns keeps the conversation going and shows that you are interested in what the other person is saying.

))) CD 1
Track 12

If the other person asks you a question, answer it, and add some new information. If possible, ask a question of your own. Here are some questions you can use.

What do you think?   How about you?
Do you agree?   You know?
Right?   Okay?

A. Complete the conversation with questions from the Speaking Skill box. Then practice the conversation with a partner.

Tony: Hi. I'm Tony. It's nice to meet you.

Alex: My name's Alex. Nice to meet you too. Are you a new student?

Tony: No. I've been studying here for two years.
_____How about you? / And you?_____
1

Alex: I just started this week, but so far, this class looks interesting.
_____Do you agree? / what do you think_____
2

Tony: I agree. The teacher's very effective. The book he's using looks good, too.
_____Right? / you know?_____
3

Alex: Yeah. He seems friendly and interesting.

B. Read the questions and write notes in your notebook to help you answer. Then have a conversation about each question with a partner. Keep the conversations going for at least three turns each, and signal your partner's turn by using questions from the Speaking Skill box.

1. Who was your most effective teacher when you were a child? What impressed you about him or her?   *notice*
   What was special

2. Have you ever made a bad first impression on someone else? What did you do?

In this assignment, you are going to give a talk to a partner about a first impression. As you prepare your talk, think about the Unit Question, "Are first impressions accurate?" and refer to the Self-Assessment checklist on page 20.

For alternative unit assignments, see the *Q: Skills for Success Teacher's Handbook.*

CONSIDER THE IDEAS

Which items in the chart tell you the most about new people when you are forming a first impression? Check (✓) whether you think each item is very important, important, or not important. Then compare and discuss your answers with a partner.

	Very important	Important	Not important
their level of politeness	☐	☐	☐
their clothing	☐	☐	☐
their hairstyle	☐	☐	☐
their voice	☐	☐	☐
their eye contact	☐	☐	☐
their attitude to money	☐	☐	☐
the way they drive	☐	☐	☐
their job	☐	☐	☐
their likes and dislikes	☐	☐	☐
Your own ideas:			
	☐	☐	☐
	☐	☐	☐

PREPARE AND SPEAK

A. GATHER IDEAS Complete these steps.

1. Think about a time when your first impression of someone was incorrect.

2. In your notebook, brainstorm as much as you can remember about the situation.

   write down

3. Then write what you thought about the person when you first met and how your first impression was wrong.

B. **ORGANIZE IDEAS** Use your ideas from Activity A to help you answer these questions. Do not write full sentences. Just write notes to help you remember your answers.

Who was the person? _____ A U manager _____

Where and when did you meet? ___ Electronic Store _____ 4 month ago _____

Why did you meet? _____ pay for my register _____

What was your first impression? _____ He is not nice person _____

Why did you form this impression? _ customer use gift card _____
_____ this transcation . _____
(want written above gift card)

When did you realize your first impression was wrong? _____ when 9 _____
_____ need help he help me alot . _____

What changed your mind? _____ It is not alway what 9 _____
_____ get _____

What do you think about the person now? _____ He is quit, not smile _____
_____ but he is good team . _____

C. **SPEAK** Tell your partner about your first impression of the person you chose. Refer to the Self-Assessment checklist on page 20 before you begin.

1. Use your ideas from Activity B.

2. Explain why you formed that impression and why you were wrong.

3. You can refer to your notes, but do not read exactly what you wrote.

4. Talk for at least one minute.

CHECK AND REFLECT

A. CHECK Think about the Unit Assignment as you complete the Self-Assessment checklist.

SELF-ASSESSMENT		
Yes	**No**	
☐	☐	I was able to speak easily about the topic.
☐	☐	My partner understood me.
☐	☐	I used vocabulary from the unit.
☐	☐	I used auxiliary verbs.
☐	☐	I used contractions.
☐	☐	I took turns when speaking.

B. REFLECT Discuss these questions with a partner.

What is something new you learned in this unit?

 Look back at the Unit Question. Is your answer different now than when you started this unit? If yes, how is it different? Why?

Circle the words and phrases you learned in this unit.

Nouns
accuracy AWL
assumption AWL
behavior 🔑
effectiveness *successful*
encounter 🔑 AWL
error 🔑 AWL
expert 🔑 AWL
fake
instinct
prediction AWL
sample 🔑
selection 🔑 AWL
trait

Verbs
assume 🔑 AWL
select 🔑 AWL

Adjectives
conscious 🔑
effective 🔑
instinctive
negative 🔑 AWL
positive 🔑 AWL
reliable AWL
suspicious 🔑

Adverbs
briefly 🔑
consciously
unconsciously

Phrases
form an impression
snap judgment
Do you agree?
How about you?
Okay?
Right?
What do you think?
You know?

🔑 Oxford 3000™ words
AWL Academic Word List
For more information on the Oxford 3000™ and the AWL, see page xi.

Check (✓) the skills you learned. If you need more work on a skill, refer to the page(s) in parentheses.

LISTENING ⚪	I can make inferences. (p. 8)
VOCABULARY ⚪	I can use suffixes. (p. 12)
GRAMMAR ⚪	I can use the auxiliary verbs *do*, *be*, and *have*. (p. 14)
PRONUNCIATION ⚪	I can use contractions with auxiliary verbs. (p. 16)
SPEAKING ⚪	I can take conversational turns. (p. 17)
LEARNING OUTCOME ⚪	I can describe in detail an inaccurate first impression.

LISTENING ●	listening for causes and effects
VOCABULARY ●	adjective–noun collocations
GRAMMAR ●	quantifiers with count/noncount nouns
PRONUNCIATION ●	links with /j/ and /w/
SPEAKING ●	giving advice

UNIT **2**

Food and Taste

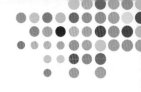

Unit QUESTION

What's more important: taste or nutrition?

PREVIEW THE UNIT

Ⓐ Discuss these questions with your classmates.

How important is food in your life? What does food mean to you?

Do you agree that if something tastes great, it's probably bad for you?

Look at the photo. What are the men doing? Why?

Ⓑ Discuss the Unit Question above with your classmates.

Listen to *The Q Classroom*, Track 13 on CD 1, to hear other answers.

23

C Read the paragraph and complete the chart.

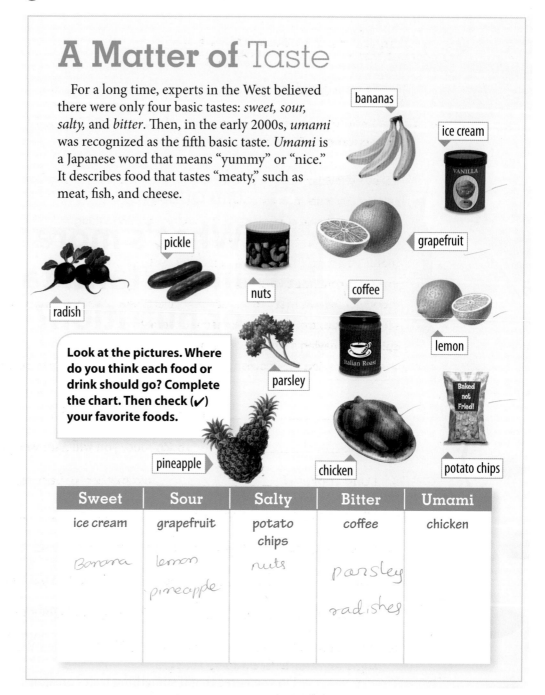

A Matter of Taste

For a long time, experts in the West believed there were only four basic tastes: *sweet, sour, salty,* and *bitter*. Then, in the early 2000s, *umami* was recognized as the fifth basic taste. *Umami* is a Japanese word that means "yummy" or "nice." It describes food that tastes "meaty," such as meat, fish, and cheese.

bananas
ice cream
pickle
grapefruit
nuts
coffee
radish
lemon
parsley
pineapple
chicken
potato chips

Look at the pictures. Where do you think each food or drink should go? Complete the chart. Then check (✓) your favorite foods.

Sweet	Sour	Salty	Bitter	Umami
ice cream	grapefruit	potato chips	coffee	chicken
Banana	lemon	nuts	parsley	
	pineapple		radishes	

D Compare your answers in a group. Do you all agree which basic taste each food has? Add some more examples to the chart.

E Check (✓) your favorite foods in the chart. Which of the five basic tastes do you like best? Who in your group shares your sense of taste?

LISTENING 1 | You Are What You Eat

VOCABULARY

Here are some words from Listening 1. Read the definitions. Then complete each sentence with the correct word.

> **balanced** *(adj.)* consisting of parts that are in correct or pleasing proportions
> **calories** *(n.)* units for measuring the energy value of food
> **concentrate** *(v.)* to give your attention or effort to something
> **consume** *(v.)* to eat or drink something
> **diet** *(n.)* the food that a person or animal usually eats
> **mix** *(v.)* to combine two or more different things
> **mood** *(n.)* the way that you feel at a particular time, such as happy or sad
> **rely on** *(phr. v.)* to depend on someone or something
> **spicy** *(adj.)* having a strong, hot flavor
> **wise** *(adj.)* having the knowledge or experience to make good and sensible decisions

1. My ____diet____ includes a lot of chicken and rice.

2. If you ____consume____ too much food, you will gain weight.

3. I can't cook, so I ____rely on____ my mother to make my meals.

4. I'm not going to eat this candy bar because it has 450 ____calories____.

5. I love chocolate because it always puts me in a good ____mood____.

6. I can't eat ____spicy____ food because it upsets my stomach.

7. Do you think it's ____wise____ to go jogging right after a big meal?

8. According to the recipe, you have to ____mix____ the flour and sugar together before adding the eggs.

9. Please don't talk to me while I'm cooking. I need to ____concentrate____.

10. A good way to stay healthy is to eat ____balanced____ meals and exercise regularly.

PREVIEW LISTENING 1

You Are What You Eat

a piece of

You are going to listen to an ~~excerpt~~ from a radio show in which Andy Patterson interviews Dr. Maureen O'Ryan, a nutrition expert. In the interview, they discuss the good and bad effects of popular foods and drinks.

Which foods in your diet do you think have good effects? Which have bad effects?

LISTEN FOR MAIN IDEAS

 CD 1 Track 14

Read the chart. Then listen to the interview. What does Dr. O'Ryan say about these foods? Check (✓) the correct answer.

	Better for you	OK in small amounts	Bad for you
1. red meat		✓	
2. white meat	✓		
3. cheese		✓	
4. coffee		✓	
5. tea	✓	✓	
6. soda			✓
7. milk chocolate			✓
8. dark chocolate		✓	

LISTEN FOR DETAILS

 CD 1 Track 15

Read the sentences. Then listen again. Circle the answer that best completes each statement.

1. Dr. O'Ryan's advice is to _____.
   a. eat anything you like
   b. always eat healthy foods
   c. eat a balanced diet

2. Red meat is good for your _____.
   a. eyesight
   b. hair and teeth
   c. bones and skin

3. Eating turkey can help you _____.
   a. feel more relaxed
   b. lose more weight
   c. have better eyesight

4. Cheese can raise your blood pressure because it contains a lot of _____.
   a. oil
   b. salt
   c. calories

5. Too much coffee can _____.
   a. make you feel stressed
   b. give you too much energy
   c. affect your heart

6. Green tea can help you _____.
   a. lose weight
   b. sleep well
   c. concentrate better

7. Calories that have no nutritional value are called _____ calories.
   a. dead
   b. empty
   c. useless

8. Drinking soda can make you feel _____.
   a. happier
   b. more tired
   c. hungrier

9. Dark chocolate _____.
   a. is good for your heart
   b. has less fat than milk chocolate
   c. can increase your blood pressure

Q WHAT DO YOU THINK?

Discuss the questions in a group.

1. Do you agree with Dr. O'Ryan's advice for a healthy diet? Why or why not?

2. Do you think people worry too much about nutrition? Give examples.

3. Do you agree that "you are what you eat"?

CD 1 Track 16

Speakers often talk about **causes** and **effects** to help explain their opinions. Listening for the linking words and phrases that connect causes (reasons) and effects (results) will help you understand a speaker's main points.

Here are some words and phrases that signal causes and effects.

I rarely cook **because** I am tired when I get home.
effect   cause

We usually eat at home **since** it's so expensive to eat out these days.
effect   cause

I never buy fish **as** I don't know how to cook it.
effect (result)   cause (reason)

The burger tasted terrible, **so** we didn't eat it.
cause   effect

phrase
Due to her healthy diet, Keiko lived to be 110 years old.
cause   effect

phr → don't eat drink soda
Because of the high calories, I never eat chocolate.
cause   effect

Note: Use *due to* and *because of* before noun phrases. Use *because, since, as,* and *so* before clauses.

CD 1 Track 17

A. Listen to the sentences. Complete each sentence with the correct word or phrase.

1. _____Since_____ *(Because of)* Dr. O'Ryan is a nutrition expert, Andy interviewed her on his radio show.

2. Eating a lot of cheese isn't good ____because of____ the large amount of salt.

3. ____Because____ Andy stopped drinking soda, he feels much healthier now.

4. Andy also wants to lose weight, ____so____ he's following Dr. O'Ryan's suggestions.

B. Listen to four statements from the radio show. Complete the chart with the causes or effects you hear. Then circle the linking words.

Cause (_reason_)   Effect (_result_)

1. (Because) it contains a natural substance which makes us feel calm, → eating turkey can actually change your mood.

2. Cheese has calcium, → (So) It's good for your teeth

Effect   Cause

1. Coffee gives you energy ← _the N. phr_ (Due to) the caffeine = because of

2. The calories in soda are what we call "empty" calories ← (Since) they have no nutrition at all

C. Think about your diet. How does what you eat affect you? For example, does it make you feel tired or awake, nervous or happy? Does the time of day make a difference? Make notes in your notebook. Then share your ideas with a partner. Be sure to use linking words and phrases when giving causes and effects.

I never eat ice cream because it makes my teeth hurt.

Sometimes I drink coffee in the morning as it helps to wake me up.

VOCABULARY

Here are some words and phrases from Listening 2. Read the sentences.
Circle the answer that best matches the meaning of each bold word or phrase.

1. Some of the best dishes are made with a variety of spices. This gives them a **complex** flavor. ≠ simple · basic
   a. complicated
   b. uninteresting
   c. important

2. That cheese smells **disgusting**. Throw it away!
   a. disappointing
   b. amazing
   c. terrible

3. Hold your nose and close your eyes, and you'll find it hard to **distinguish** between an onion and an apple.
   a. see
   b. know
   c. tell the difference

4. Scientists don't exactly know, but they **estimate** that 80 percent of what we taste is due to smell.
   a. promise
   b. agree completely
   c. calculate approximately = guess

5. Children often don't like to eat food with strong **flavors**, but they grow to like them as they get older.
   a. senses
   b. tastes
   c. feelings

6. Could you **keep an eye on** the cookies in the oven while I am out? I don't want them to burn.
   a. think about
   b. listen to
   c. check often

7. I don't eat eggs much, but **occasionally** I have an omelet.
   a. frequently
   b. never
   c. sometimes

8. You should **swallow** your vitamins with a full glass of water.
   a. try
   b. take
   c. mix

9. I don't like the **texture** of this bread—it's too hard for me.
   a. feel
   b. look
   c. taste

10. I don't take dieting **trends** seriously since they change so often.
    a. fashions
    b. meals
    c. restaurants

PREVIEW LISTENING 2

Food Tasters

You are going to listen to some podcasts from a career website. Three professional food tasters talk about their jobs. What foods do you think a food taster might taste?

cheese

Stuart

Marie

Enrique

LISTEN FOR MAIN IDEAS

CD 1
Track 19

Read the statements. Then listen to the podcasts. Write _T_ (true) or _F_ (false).

Stuart…

___T___ 1. has a degree in nutrition.

___F___ 2. started this job immediately after graduation.

___F___ 3. visits the dentist once a year.

Marie…

___F___ 4. doesn't like strong-smelling cheeses.

___F___ 5. often visits local farmers.

___T___ 6. has a degree in food science.

Enrique…

___T___ 7. has no formal qualifications.   _education_

___T___ 8. never tastes in the afternoons.

___T___ 9. doesn't consume what he tastes.

LISTEN FOR DETAILS

Listen again. Write the first letter of the person's name (S=Stuart, M=Marie, and E=Enrique) next to the correct information.

Jobs	Type of business	Locations
cheese buyer _M_	import company _E_	Los Angeles _E_
coffee taster _E_	department store _S_	London _S_
chocolate taster _S_	supermarket _M_	near Paris _M_

 ## WHAT DO YOU THINK?

A. Discuss the questions in a group.

1. Which do you like best: chocolate, cheese, or coffee? Why do you like it so much?

2. Do you think you might like to be a food taster? Why or why not?

B. Think about both Listening 1 and Listening 2 as you discuss the questions.

In Listening 1, you heard about some of the good and bad effects of chocolate, cheese, and caffeine. Talk about the professional food tasters in Listening 2. How do you think their jobs might affect their health? Who might have problems sleeping? Who might need to reduce fat and salt, and so on?

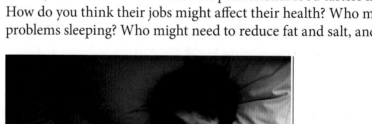

Some foods and drinks can affect your ability to sleep.

y-3

Collocations are combinations of words that are often used together. For example, certain adjectives go together with certain nouns. Using correct collocations will make your conversations sound more natural.

Here are some examples of adjective–noun collocations.

> When you eat before exercising, you should only have a **light meal**.
> There is nothing better than a **cold drink** on a hot summer day.
> I try not to eat too much **fast food**, but it's difficult because I love burgers.
> Would you like cheesecake for dessert or just some **fresh fruit**?

A. Complete each collocation with a noun from the box.

diet	drink	food	snack	steak

1. a soft _____drink_____   *has bottle*

2. junk _____food_____

3. a juicy _____steak_____

4. a balanced _____diet / meal_____

5. a quick _____snack_____

B. Complete each sentence with the correct collocation from Activity A.

1. Jim's favorite meal to cook at home is _____a juicy steak_____, served with potatoes.

2. To have _____a balanced diet_____, you need to eat lots of different kinds of foods.

3. Do you want tea, or would you like _____a soft drink_____ with lunch?

4. I used to eat chips and candy all the time. Now I hate _____quick snack_____!

5. I don't have time for a big lunch, so let's just have _____junk food_____.

C. Circle the answer that best completes each collocation.

1. James has always had a very _____ appetite.   *like to eat*
   a. healthy
   b. fit

2. Generally, I try to avoid eating a lot of fatty _____.
   a. cooking
   b. foods   *different kind of food*

3. Is all the fish on the menu deep _____?
   a. grilled
   b. fried

4. I like cooking, but I hate washing all the _____ dishes afterwards.
   a. filthy
   b. dirty

5. _____ exercise is an important part of staying healthy.
   a. Regular
   b. Steady

SPEAKING

Count nouns are the names of things we can count, for example, one egg and two bananas. **Noncount nouns** are the names of things we cannot count, such as cheese and water.

how many/how much

Use *how many* with count nouns. Use *how much* with noncount nouns.

> **How many** apples do you eat a week?
> **How much** tea do you drink a day?

too many/too much

Use *too many/too much* when there is more than you want or need.

> You can have cookies once in a while, but don't eat **too many**.
> Don't drink **too much** coffee at bedtime, or you'll never fall asleep.

enough/not enough

Use *enough/not enough* with both count and noncount nouns.

> We have **enough** food for everybody.
> We don't have **enough** chairs.

A. Complete the conversations with words and phrases from the box. Then practice the conversations with a partner.

enough	many	too many
not enough	much	too much

chilies

Mike: Hey, that smells great. What are you cooking?

Debra: Chicken with chilies and rice. Do you want to try some?

Mike: Sure… Wow! That's hot! How ___*many*___ chilies did you
          1
          put in?

Debra: Five. But they're really small. Don't you like spicy food?

Mike: Yeah, I do, but it's too hot for me!

Alain: What do you think of the soup? It's potato and onion.

Susie: Hmm. It's OK. It seems like there is something missing, though.

Alain: Maybe I didn't put in _____enough_____ salt.
2

Susie: And it's pretty thick, isn't it?

Alain: Yes. I think I used _____too many_____ potatoes.
3

Muriel: How _____much_____ sugar did you put in this coffee?
4

Angela: One teaspoon.

Muriel: That's _____not enough_____ for me! I like my coffee very sweet.
5

Angela: Well, you shouldn't have _____too much_____. You'll get fat.
6

B. Make a list of foods and drinks you like. Write *C* (Count) or *N* (Noncount) next to each item. Then discuss your favorite things to eat and drink with a partner. Be sure to use *much*, *many*, and *enough* correctly with count and noncount nouns.

Foods I like…   Drinks I like…

_____   _____

_____   _____

_____   _____

CD 1
Track 21

When certain words follow each other, additional sounds are created. These extra sounds make a natural **link** between the two words.

When a word beginning with a vowel follows a word that ends in the vowel sounds /i/, /eɪ/, or /aɪ/ (like bee, say, or eye), a /j/ sound is added between the words.

> I think Marco must **be** /j/ **Italian.**
> I can't see you tonight, but Tues**day** /j/ **is** fine.
> **I** /j/ **ate** salmon for dinner last night.

When a word beginning with a vowel follows a word that ends in the vowel sounds /u/, /o/, or /aʊ/ (like who, no and how), a /w/ sound is added between the words.

> Do **you** /w/ **eat** a balanced diet?
> Do you want to **go** /w/ **out** for lunch?
> **How** /w/ **is** your steak?

Pronouncing these linking sounds will help make your English sound more natural.

CD 1
Track 22

A. Listen to the sentences. Write /j/ or /w/ in the correct places. Then listen again and check your answers.

1. We /j/ all eat things we know we shouldn't.

2. "Empty" calories have no nutritional value at all. (w)

3. I can't drink coffee, but tea is fine. (Y)

4. Cheese has calcium, so w it's good for your teeth. (w)

5. Sometimes in the evening I'm too tired to cook. (Y)

6. Marie makes sure the cheese is ready to go w out on sale. (w)

7. Stuart thinks the appearance of chocolate can be j as (Y) important as the taste. (Y)

8. Enrique thinks people pay j a lot for coffee so they want to enjoy it.

to wen joy it   paya

CD 1
Track 23

B. Listen again. Repeat each sentence. Practice linking /j/ and /w/.

CD 1
Track 24

The words *should*, *shouldn't*, and *ought to* are used to give advice. Listen to these sentences.

According to Dr. O'Ryan, Andy **should** drink less coffee.
He **shouldn't** drink a lot of soda.
He **ought to** eat more fish.

You can sound more polite by starting a sentence with *perhaps*.

Perhaps you **should** eat more fruit and vegetables.

You can give stronger advice by adding *really*.

You **really ought to** eat more fruit and vegetables.

A. Work with a partner. Discuss your eating and drinking habits. Take turns making true statements about your diet. After each of your partner's statements, give some advice, using *should/shouldn't* or *ought to*. Remember to use count/noncount nouns correctly.

A: *I probably eat too much fast food.*
B: *You should try to eat more healthily. For example, you shouldn't eat burgers and fries for lunch. Perhaps you should eat a salad instead.*

B. Think about the advice your partner gave you. Work in a group. Share the advice you received.

I eat too much fast food, so I should try to eat more healthily. For example, I ought to eat a salad for lunch instead of a burger and fries.

In this assignment, you are going to interview three classmates about their favorite dishes. As you prepare your interview, think about the Unit Question, "What's more important: taste or nutrition?" and refer to the Self-Assessment checklist on page 42.

For alternative unit assignments, see the *Q: Skills for Success Teacher's Handbook*.

CONSIDER THE IDEAS

fondue

Work in a group. Match each dish with the country it comes from. Then discuss which dishes you have tried and whether or not you liked them.

____ 1. fondue   a. Japan

____ 2. goulash   b. Thailand

____ 3. green curry   c. Switzerland

____ 4. moussaka   d. Greece

_a_ 5. sushi   e. Mexico

_e_ 6. tacos   f. Hungary

What other dishes from around the world do you know? In your group, quiz each other on where different dishes come from.

A: *Where does paella come from?*

B: *Uh…Spain!*

Paella Valenciana

PREPARE AND SPEAK

A. **GATHER IDEAS** Make a list of your favorite dishes, either from your own country or from other cultures.

_____   _____

_____   _____

_____   _____

B. **ORGANIZE IDEAS** Choose one dish from your list in Activity A. Use the outline to help you prepare to talk about it. Do not write exactly what you are going to say. Just write notes to help you organize your ideas.

MY FAVORITE DISH

What's the name of the dish?

_____

Where is it from? _____

What are the ingredients? _____

_____

How healthy is this dish? _____

Why do you particularly like this dish? _____

_____

_____

_____

When making notes, don't write full sentences. Just write the important words.

C. SPEAK **Complete these steps. Refer to the Self-Assessment checklist on page 42 before you begin.**

1. Interview three students.

2. Ask them about their favorite dishes from Activity B, and take notes in the chart.

3. When you talk about your own favorite dish, use your notes from Activity B to help you. Do not read exactly what you wrote; just use your notes.

	Classmate 1	Classmate 2	Classmate 3
Dish			
Country			
Ingredients			
Is it healthy?			
Reasons for liking it?			

4. When you finish, discuss your interviews in a group. Do more of your classmates choose their favorite dish because of taste or nutrition? Whose favorite dish would you like to try?

CHECK AND REFLECT

A. **CHECK** Think about the Unit Assignment as you complete the Self-Assessment checklist.

SELF-ASSESSMENT		
Yes	No	
☐	☐	I was able to speak easily about the topic.
☐	☐	My classmates understood me.
☐	☐	I used vocabulary from the unit.
☐	☐	I used quantifiers with count/noncount nouns.
☐	☐	I used links with /j/ and /w/.
☐	☐	I gave advice.

B. **REFLECT** Discuss these questions with a partner.

What is something new you learned in this unit?

 Look back at the Unit Question. Is your answer different now than when you started this unit? If yes, how is it different? Why?

Circle the words and phrases you learned in this unit.

Nouns
calories
diet 🔑
flavor 🔑
mood 🔑
texture
trend 🔑 AWL

Verbs
concentrate 🔑 AWL
consume AWL
distinguish 🔑
estimate 🔑 AWL
mix 🔑

shouldn't 🔑
swallow 🔑

Adjectives
balanced
complex 🔑 AWL
disgusting 🔑
spicy 🔑
wise 🔑

Adverbs
occasionally 🔑
perhaps 🔑
really 🔑

Phrasal Verbs
rely on

Phrases
keep an eye on

Collocations
cold drink
fast food
fresh fruit
light meal

🔑 Oxford 3000™ words
AWL Academic Word List

Check (✓) the skills you learned. If you need more work on a skill, refer to the page(s) in parentheses.

LISTENING ○	I can listen for causes and effects. (p. 28)
VOCABULARY ○	I can use adjective–noun collocations. (p. 33)
GRAMMAR ○	I can use quantifiers with count/noncount nouns. (p. 35)
PRONUNCIATION ○	I can link words with /j/ and /w/ sounds. (p. 37)
SPEAKING ○	I can give advice. (p. 38)
LEARNING OUTCOME ○	I can interview my classmates on their favorite dishes and then discuss why people prefer certain foods.

LISTENING ● listening for examples
VOCABULARY ● prefixes
GRAMMAR ● gerunds and infinitives as the objects of verbs
PRONUNCIATION ● stress on important words
SPEAKING ● asking for and giving clarification

LEARNING OUTCOME

Discuss successful and unsuccessful personal experiences and explain what you learned from them.

Unit QUESTION

What can we learn from success and failure?

PREVIEW THE UNIT

Ⓐ Discuss these questions with your classmates.

What are some of the different ways a person can be successful?

In what ways do you think you are successful?

Look at the photo. What is this man trying to do? Will he be successful? Why or why not?

Ⓑ Discuss the Unit Question above with your classmates.

Listen to *The Q Classroom*, Track 25 on CD 1, to hear other answers.

45

C Look at the questionnaire. Check (✓) the three things that are most true for you. Then write reasons for each of your choices.

What does Success Mean to You?

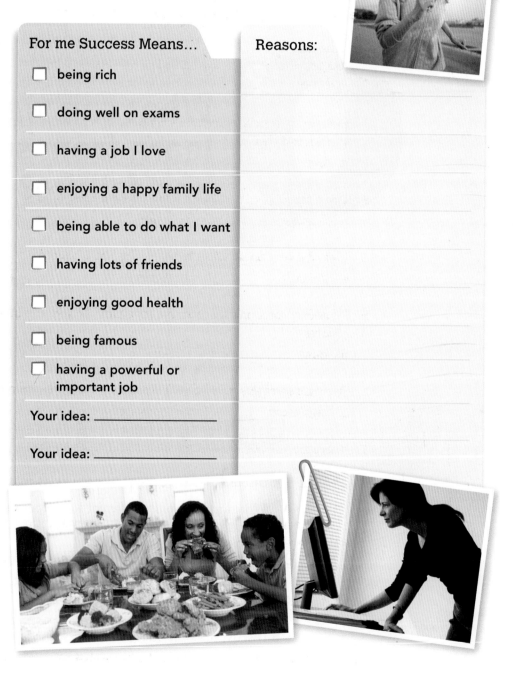

For me Success Means…	Reasons:
☐ being rich	
☐ doing well on exams	
☐ having a job I love	
☐ enjoying a happy family life	
☐ being able to do what I want	
☐ having lots of friends	
☐ enjoying good health	
☐ being famous	
☐ having a powerful or important job	

Your idea: _____

Your idea: _____

D Discuss your answers in a group. Explain the reasons for your choices.

LISTENING 1 | Chasing Your Dreams

VOCABULARY

Here are some words and phrases from Listening 1. Read the sentences. Circle the answer that best matches the meaning of each bold word or phrase.

1. It may be difficult to **achieve** your dreams, but hard work can often help you get what you want from life.

   a. reach   b. control   c. remember

2. **Determination** is important for success. You have to keep trying even when it is difficult.

   a. force   b. willpower   c. luck

3. I love my job, but the **downside** is that the salary is low.

   a. mistake   b. error   c. disadvantage

4. It can be very **frustrating** to try hard without succeeding.

   a. difficult   b. boring   c. annoying

5. "If at first you don't succeed, try, try again." This saying means "don't **give up**".

   a. quit   b. fail   c. alter

6. Peter is a salesperson now, but his **goal** is to have his own business someday.

   a. argument   b. ambition   c. challenge

7. There are various ways to **measure** success. It's not just about making lots of money.

   a. judge   b. enjoy   c. discuss

8. It's not **realistic** to expect to be successful at everything you do. No one can be good at everything.

   a. confident   b. reasonable   c. intelligent

9. Don't wash that sweater in hot water. You'll **ruin** it.

   a. break   b. injure   c. spoil

10. Sarah's new job gave her a much higher **status** within the company.

    a. position   b. activity   c. popularity

PREVIEW LISTENING 1

Chasing Your Dreams

You are going to listen to the beginning of a lecture by a college professor. The professor talks about the importance of success and what it means to be successful.

Which things do you think the professor will say are important for success? Check (✓) your answers.

☐ having clear goals
☐ trying hard
☐ never giving up
☐ being lucky

LISTEN FOR MAIN IDEAS

CD 1
Track 26

Listen to the lecture. Circle the answer that best completes each statement according to what the professor says.

1. To be successful, you _____.
   a. need to set achievable goals
   b. should never stop trying to achieve your goals

2. Achieving your goals should be _____.
   a. the most important thing in your life
   b. one of several important things in your life

3. You should try to focus on _____.
   a. only the positive aspects of success
   b. both the positive and the negative aspects of success

4. You need to _____.
   a. keep the same goals throughout your life
   b. change your goals to match different stages in your life

LISTEN FOR DETAILS

Read the statements. Then listen again. Write *T* (true) or *F* (false).

F **1.** This is the professor's first lecture on success to the class.

F **2.** She says that with hard work and determination, it is possible to achieve anything you want.

T **3.** According to the professor, trying to achieve some dreams can be a waste of time and effort.

T **4.** The professor says that trying too hard to be successful can cause problems.

T **5.** She argues that success can also bring failure.

F **6.** She gives an example of a high school friend who became very ~~famous.~~ *successful*

T **7.** She says that people often see success differently as they grow older.

WHAT DO YOU THINK?

Discuss the questions in a group.

1. Do you agree with the points the professor makes about success? Why or why not?

2. Who is the most successful person you know? In what ways is he or she successful?

3. What things do you think are more important than success?

There are many different types of success.

Listening for examples will help you understand a speaker's main points more clearly. Speakers often introduce examples with a common phrase that tells you that an example follows.

general word

| for example, | such as | To give (you) an example, |
| for instance, | Take, for example, | To illustrate this, |

consider, think *picture (show sthg)*

CD 1
Track 28

A. Listen to the lecture again. List the phrases the professor uses to introduce examples.

Let me give an example

for example

To give *you* an example

take for example

CD 1
Track 29

B. Listen to Paul talk about how his view of success has changed. List each example he gives. You do not need to write full sentences.

1. When he was younger, Paul says he was "money hungry."

sub Example: he chose job *that* pay well.

2. He also says he was concerned about status.

Example: I left one company to *work another* because job title

3. These days, Paul says being successful for him means being healthy.

for instance
Example: Jogging in the park is success to me doesn't cost anything.

4. He also says that having good friends is important to him.

Example: I see reconnecting *with* my old college friend it's great success.

C. Think about one goal you would like to achieve. Write three benefits you expect from achieving this goal.

Your goal: _my goal is to_ ----

Benefits: _g have a goal_ ---

1. _my goal is to get a degree from M=C_

2. _g have a goal to become business woman._

3. _my goal is to_

D. Work with a partner. Take turns talking about your goals and their benefits. Use phrases from the Listening Skill box when you give examples. Take notes below as you listen to your partner. Then discuss whether or not you agree with the benefits she or he expects.

Your partner's goal: _____

Benefits:

1. _____

2. _____

3. _____

VOCABULARY

Work with a partner. Here are some words from Listening 2. Circle the answer that best matches the meaning of each bold word or phrase.

1. creativity *(n.)* — (imagination)   clever   produce
2. develop *(v.)* — future   changing   (improve)
3. emphasize *(v.)* — successful   importance   (stress)
4. fear *(v.)* — scare   frightening   (be afraid) *is afraid of*
5. lack *(v.)* — missing   absence   (need)
6. permit *(v.)* — (allow)   helpful   ability
7. preparation *(n.)* — ready   (training)   educate
8. top *(adj.)* — (leading)   famously   seriousness
9. turn down *(phr. v.)* — unhelpful   acceptance   (refuse)
10. work out *(phr. v.)* — identify   (labor)   carefully *work*

PREVIEW LISTENING 2

The Benefits of Failure

Michael Jordan

You are going to listen to a short speech by a college student, Carl Simmons, who talks about the opposite of success—failure.

In what ways do you think failure can be a positive experience? Write down your ideas.

We can learn some mistake from failure and

It encourage us to become success

LISTEN FOR MAIN IDEAS

CD 1
Track 30

Listen to the speech. Check (✓) the main ideas you hear.

_____ 1. Some people prefer to fail rather than succeed.

__✓__ 2. It is sometimes necessary to fail in order to succeed.

_____ 3. Modern society doesn't accept failure.

__✓__ 4. We can learn from our failures.

__✓__ 5. Many successful people begin by failing.

LISTEN FOR DETAILS

CD 1
Track 31

Listen again. Match the people with the statements about them.

__f__ 1. The Beatles   a. "no creativity or original ideas"

__e__ 2. Michael Jordan   b. failed thousands of times before succeeding

__a__ 3. Walt Disney   c. lost a lot of money at first

__d__ 4. John Grisham   d. rejected by 16 agents and publishers

__c__ 5. Akio Morita   e. "lacked skill"

__b__ 6. Thomas Edison   f. "would never be popular"

 WHAT DO YOU THINK?

A. Discuss the questions in a group.

1. Of the people in Listening 2, who do you think overcame the biggest difficulties? Who learned the most from their failures?

2. Give an example of a time when you succeeded after failing at first. What did you learn from your mistakes?

B. Think about both Listening 1 and Listening 2 as you discuss the questions.

1. Do you think the examples in Carl Simmons' speech support the professor's ideas about success in Listening 1? Why or why not?

2. In what ways, if any, has your view of success and failure changed?

Prefixes are added to the beginning of words to change their meaning. Understanding prefixes can help you expand your vocabulary and figure out the meaning of unknown words.

Notice the use of prefixes in these examples from Listening 2.

> Being successful is not about being a **multi**millionaire.
> (**multi-** + millionaire = multimillionaire)
> Chasing an **im**possible dream, one that you can never reach, is a frustrating waste of time and energy. (**im-** + possible = impossible)

Many prefixes give the opposite meaning to words.

> **dis-** **dis**agree
> **im-** (before words beginning with *m/p*) **im**polite
> **ir-** (before words beginning with *r*) **ir**rational

These prefixes give other meanings to words.

> **co-** (together) **co**operate
> **re-** (again) **re**place, **re**write
> **multi-** (many) **multi**purpose
> **anti-** (against) **anti**war

A. Add a prefix from the Vocabulary Skill box to complete each word.

1. _re_ view (v) (A)
2. ___ responsible
3. ___ like (2-2) (v) + gerund
4. _co_ worker v+y
5. ___ perfect (3-2)
6. _anti_ social (4-3)
7. _multi_ national (5-3)
8. _dis_ honest 3-2)
9. _im_ patient (a) (7-2)
10. _ir_ regular (4-2) (irregular verb)
11. _re_ apply (3-3)
12. _multi_ media (5-3)

(handwritten margin notes:) unlike (adv) different   dislike → (gerund) (3-1) → (N)

B. Choose three words from Activity A. Write a sentence using each word.

1. _____ I review my home work.
2. _____ I work with my co-worker is very nice time
3. _____ I dislike this mouice

C. Read your sentences to a partner. Write any words you hear from Activity A in your notebook. Underline the prefixes.

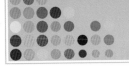

Grammar **Gerunds and infinitives as the objects of verbs**

A **gerund** is **the base form of the verb + -ing**. Gerunds can be used as the objects of certain verbs, e.g., *admit, avoid, discuss, dislike, enjoy, finish, miss, quit*.

> I enjoy **watching** tennis.
> Tara quit **studying** and went abroad for a year.

An **infinitive** is *to* + the base form of the verb. Infinitives can also be used as the objects of certain verbs, e.g., *agree, choose, decide, hope, learn, need, plan, want*.

> I hope **to become** a pilot.
> She planned **to climb** Mount Everest.

Some verbs can be followed by either a gerund or an infinitive, with no difference in meaning, e.g., *begin, hate, like, love, prefer*.

> Michael Jordan began **playing** basketball as a child.
> Michael Jordan began **to play** basketball as a child.

> He likes **competing**.
> He likes **to compete**.

A. Circle the correct verb forms to complete the conversation. If both the infinitive and the gerund are possible, circle both answers. Then practice the conversation with a partner.

Vikram: Hey, Janice. Did you hear the news? My boss agreed (giving / to give)
₁
me a promotion last month.

Janice: That's great! Well done, Vikram. So, now your life is all about work,

work, work, right?

Vikram: Yeah, but I hope (to become / becoming) vice president next year.
₂
Are you sorry you left the company?

Janice: Of course not! I love (being / to be) a stay-at-home mom. I don't miss
₃
(working / to work) in an office at all.
₄

Vikram: Hmm. I can't believe you chose (quitting / to quit). I thought you
₅
wanted (to stay / staying) at the company for at least five more years.
₆

Janice: Well, I did at one point, but I decided ((to spend) / spending) more

time with my family. I guess I figured out what was most important to me.

I don't need ((having / to have)) an important job or a huge salary to feel

successful!

B. Write answers to the questions. Then discuss your answers with a partner.

1. What is something you plan to do soon?

   I plan to go beach.

2. What is something you started to do, but didn't finish?

   I need to clean my house but I finished not yet

3. What is something you love doing, but don't have enough time for?

   I love watching TV

4. What is something you are thinking of doing next year?

   I am thinking of getting citizen

   I hope to go Burma

> Speakers usually put more **stress** on the important words in a sentence, such as *nouns, verbs, adjectives,* and *adverbs.* These words are usually louder and clearer than other words in the sentence. Listening for stressed words can help you hear and understand the most important information.

CD 1
Track 32

> Listen to these sentences from Listening 1 and Listening 2. Notice how the speakers stress the important words.
>
> You can **learn** a lot **more** from your **failures** than you **can** from your **successes**.
> **Success** for my **grandfather** is **getting** out of **bed** in the **morning**.
> **Failing** is a **good preparation** for **life**.

CD 1
Track 33

A. Listen to more sentences from Listening 2. Underline the stressed words.

1. Failure is an important stage on the road to success.

2. We shouldn't be afraid of failure, because we can learn from it.

Test

3. Failure is something to be encouraged by.

4. Don't give up too easily!

CD 1
Track 34 **B.** Listen again. Repeat the sentences. Practice stressing the important words.

CD 1
Track 35 **C.** Read the paragraph below. Underline the important words that should be stressed. Then listen to the paragraph and check your answers.

exam

> You need to experience failure and learn from it in order to really succeed. Failing is a good preparation for life. It makes you stronger and more able to overcome life's problems. Don't be scared of failure!

CD 1
Track 36 **D.** Listen again. Then read the paragraph aloud. Practice stressing the underlined words.

Speaking Skill | Asking for and giving clarification web

After you listen to a speech or presentation, you can ask questions if you need **clarification** or more information about something the speaker said. Asking questions shows that you are interested and have been paying attention.

Asking for clarification

> Sorry, I don't get what you mean.
> What do you mean exactly.
> Could you say a bit more about…?
> Can you give an example?

After giving a speech or presentation, it is a good idea to ask the audience for questions. This gives you an opportunity to clarify your most important points and make sure your audience understood them.

Giving clarification

> What I'm trying to say…
> To give you an example…
> I mean…

A. Listen to the excerpts from a discussion. Complete the excerpts wth the phrases you hear. Then practice the conversations with a partner.

Professor: So you need to make sure the success you're aiming for is achievable.

Student 1: _____₁_____.

Professor: What _____₂_____ be realistic with the goals you set for yourself.

Professor: Success in one area can bring problems in others.

Student 2: _____₃_____.

Professor: Well, _____₄_____, someone can be at the top of her career, but her family life might be in crisis as a result.

Professor: Keep your desire for success in proportion.

Student 3: _____₅_____?

Professor: Yes. I mean don't let your desire for success become greater than other important areas in your life.

Professor: Our definition of success alters with age.

Student 1: _____₆_____?

Professor: Sure. Someone of twenty might view success as being rich, but at fifty that same person might think of success as a happy family life.

B. Work with a partner. Take turns reading the statements from Listening 1 and Listening 2 aloud and asking for and giving clarification.

1. Failure is an important stage on the road to success.

    A: Sorry, I don't get what you mean.
    B: What I mean by that is we learn from our mistakes.

2. If at first you don't succeed, try, try again.

3. Success for my grandfather is simply getting out of bed in the morning.

4. Failing is a good preparation for life.

In this assignment, you are going to take part in a discussion about success and failure. As you prepare for the discussion, think about the Unit Question, "What can we learn from success and failure?" and refer to the Self-Assessment checklist on page 62.

For alternative unit assignments, see the *Q: Skills for Success Teacher's Handbook*.

CONSIDER THE IDEAS

Work in a group. Read the quotes about success and failure. Then answer the questions.

> "Success is not the key to happiness. Happiness is the key to success. If you love what you are doing, you will be successful."
>
> —*Albert Schweitzer, German philosopher*

Tip Critical Thinking

This activity asks you to **paraphrase**. **Paraphrasing**, or saying the information in your own words, helps you to understand and remember better.

What does this quote mean?

_____

Can you give an example?

_____

Do you agree or disagree with this quote? Explain.

_____

_____

> "Success is never final. Failure is never fatal. Courage is what counts."
>
> —*Winston Churchill, British statesman*

What does this quote mean?

_____

Can you give an example?

_____

Do you agree or disagree with this quote? Explain.

_____

_____

> "Many of life's failures are people who did not realize how close they were to success when they gave up."
>
> —*Thomas Edison, American inventor*

What does this quote mean?

_____

Can you give an example?

_____

Do you agree or disagree with this quote? Explain.

_____

_____

PREPARE AND SPEAK

A. GATHER IDEAS **Think about what success means to you. Complete the activities.**

1. Make a list of things you have been successful at. They can be big things, such as graduating from high school, or small things, such as cooking a delicious meal.

   _____

   _____

   _____

2. Now make a list of things you have tried, but were not successful at. Again, they can be big things, such as applying for a job, or small things, such as playing a game of tennis.

   _____

   _____

   _____

B. **ORGANIZE IDEAS** Choose one example from each list in Activity A. Complete the outline to help you prepare to discuss your ideas.

1. Something I was successful at: _____

What were some of the difficulties you experienced?

_____

_____

How has this experience affected your life?

_____

_____

What have you learned from this experience?

_____

_____

_____

2. Something I was not successful at: _____

What were some of the difficulties you experienced?

_____

_____

How has this experience affected your life?

_____

_____

What have you learned from this experience?

_____

_____

_____

C. SPEAK **Complete these steps. Refer to the Self-Assessment checklist below before you begin.**

1. Work with a partner. Take turns telling each other about your experiences.

2. Discuss which experience you learned more from. Do not read directly from your outline. Just use it to help you remember your ideas. Refer to the rubric below before you begin.

CHECK AND REFLECT

A. CHECK **Think about the Unit Assignment as you complete the Self-Assessment checklist.**

		SELF-ASSESSMENT
Yes	**No**	
☐	☐	I was able to speak easily about the topic.
☐	☐	My partner understood me.
☐	☐	I used vocabulary from the unit.
☐	☐	I used gerunds and infinitives as the objects of verbs.
☐	☐	I stressed important words.
☐	☐	I asked for and gave clarification.

B. REFLECT **Discuss these questions with a partner.**

What is something new you learned in this unit?

 Look back at the Unit Question. Is your answer different now than when you started this unit? If yes, how is it different? Why?

Track Your Success

Circle the words and phrases you learned in this unit.

Nouns
creativity AWL
determination 🔑
downside
goal 🔑 AWL
preparation 🔑
status 🔑 AWL

Verbs
achieve 🔑 AWL
develop 🔑
emphasize 🔑 AWL
fear 🔑
lack 🔑
measure 🔑 *nudge*
permit 🔑
ruin 🔑

Adjectives
frustrating
realistic 🔑
top 🔑

Phrasal Verbs
give up
turn down *refuse*
work out *labour*

Phrases
Can you give an example?
Could you go into a little more detail on…?
Could you say a bit more about…?
For example,
For instance,

Sorry, I don't get what you mean.
such as
Take for example,
To give (you) an example,
To illustrate this,
Well, what I'm getting at is…
What do you mean by…?
What I'm trying to say is…
What I mean by that is…

🔑 Oxford 3000™ words
AWL Academic Word List

Check (✓) the skills you learned. If you need more work on a skill, refer to the page(s) in parentheses.

LISTENING ○	I can listen for examples. (p. 50)
VOCABULARY ○	I can use prefixes. (p. 54)
GRAMMAR ○	I can use gerunds and infinitives as the objects of verbs. (p. 55)
PRONUNCIATION ○	I can stress important words. (p. 56)
SPEAKING ○	I can ask for and give clarification. (p. 57)
LEARNING OUTCOME ○	I can discuss successful and unsuccessful personal experiences and explain what I learned from them.

UNIT 4

New Perspectives

LISTENING ● taking notes using a T-chart
VOCABULARY ● using the dictionary
GRAMMAR ● simple past and present perfect
PRONUNCIATION ● variety of intonation to show interest
SPEAKING ● asking for and giving reasons

FRAGILE

Participate in a group discussion emphasizing the advantages and disadvantages of change.

Unit QUESTION

Is change good or bad?

PREVIEW THE UNIT

A Discuss these questions with your classmates.

Think about the biggest change in your life recently. What was it? How did it affect you?

Is there anything in your life right now that you would like to change?

Look at the photo. What is the woman doing? How do you think she feels? Why?

B Discuss the Unit Question above with your classmates.

Listen to *The Q Classroom*, Track 38 on CD 1, to hear other answers.

C Complete the questionnaire.

HOW DO YOU FEEL ABOUT Change?

1 **When I go on vacation, I prefer to...**
a. go to the same place every year.
b. go somewhere different each time.

2 **When I watch TV, I...**
a. watch the same programs every week.
b. try to find something new to watch.

3 **When I go shopping for food, I usually...**
a. buy the same things.
b. look for something different.

4 **The idea of moving to a different city makes me feel...**
a. worried.
b. excited.

5 **When it's time to have my hair cut, I prefer to...**
a. keep the same hairstyle.
b. try a different look if I feel like it.

6 **In my future career, I think I will...**
a. have the same job my whole life.
b. try a few different jobs.

7 **When it comes to my TV, cell phone, and camera, I usually...**
a. keep them until they break.
b. replace them when I want to.

8 **When I buy new clothes, I usually...**
a. choose the same style and color.
b. look for something in the latest fashion.

How well did you do?

If you chose *a* for most of your answers, you prefer things to stay the same, and perhaps feel fairly cautious about change. You know what you like, so trying new things worries you. Don't be afraid to take a few chances from time to time—you might enjoy something different.

If you chose *b* for most of your answers, you are happy to try new experiences and are open to new ideas. You love variety, but be careful—you don't need to change everything all the time! Perhaps you should think more carefully before you decide to change things.

If you chose *a* and *b* equally, you are very balanced. You welcome change sometimes, but you don't want things to change all the time. Congratulations!

D Discuss your answers in a group. Do you think the questionnaire is accurate? Why or why not? Use examples from your own life to support your opinion.

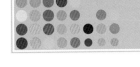
LISTENING 1 | Changing Expectations

VOCABULARY

Here are some words from Listening 1. Read the definitions. Then complete each sentence with the correct word.

> (2-2) **adapt** (v.) to change your behavior because the situation you are in has changed
> (5-2) **considerably** (adv.) a lot
> (2-1) **crisis** (n.) a time of great danger or difficulty
> (3-1) **curious** (adj.) wanting to know or learn something
> (2-2) **fulfilled** (adj.) completely satisfied and happy
> (2-1) **handle** (v.) to control or deal with someone or something
> (3-1) **justify** (v.) to give or be a good reason for something
> (3-2) **position** (n.) a job
> (3-1) **steady** (adj.) staying the same over a period of time
> (2-1) **suffer** (v.) to become worse in quality

1. When the economic ____crisis____ started, people were suddenly worried about losing their jobs.

2. Tina couldn't ____handle____ all the noise and pollution of living in a city, so she moved to the country.

3. When Brian left his small village to live in the city, it took him a few months to ____adapt____.

4. We're ____curious____ about what it would be like to live in another country. It sounds very interesting.

5. Over the years, Steve's company has developed ____steady____ and reliable relationships with many other businesses in the area.

6. I felt ____fulfilled____ as a teacher because I enjoyed helping people learn.

7. There were more than 30 applications for the ___position___ of general manager.

8. Don't you agree that keeping things the same is ___considerably___ easier than trying to change them?

9. After I borrowed money from my parents, I had to ___justify___ the purchases I made with it.

10. If you focus too much on your job, your personal relationships may ___suffer___ as a result.

Gary McBride

PREVIEW LISTENING 1

| Changing Expectations

You are going to listen to Gary McBride talk about how his life changed after leaving a high-paying job on Wall Street to work in a small town in Iowa.

Why do you think Gary wanted to do something different?

- ☐ He was bored with his job.
- ☐ He was curious about the world.

LISTEN FOR MAIN IDEAS

CD 1
Track 39

Listen to Gary McBride's talk. Check (✓) the ways in which he changed his life.

- ☐ He got married.
- ☐ He started his own business.
- ☑ He moved home. *c parents live in IOWA*
- ☑ He found more friends.
- ☑ He changed his job.
- ☐ He went to live in another country. *travel to other countries*
- ☑ He spent more time with his family.
- ☐ He became much busier.

LISTEN FOR DETAILS

Read the questions. Then listen again. Circle the correct answer.

1. Why did Gary stop working as a city trader?
   a. He lost his job.
   b. He became ill.
   c. He couldn't handle the stress.

2. What did Gary do as soon as he left his job?
   a. He looked for another job.
   b. He traveled.
   c. He moved back home.

3. Why did Gary move to Iowa?
   a. He wanted to be near his parents.
   b. He needed to find a better job.
   c. He had some good friends there.

4. How does Gary feel about his new job?
   a. It's very fulfilling.
   b. It can be difficult.
   c. The salary is too low.

5. What goal has Gary achieved?
   a. He has more time to think.
   b. He is happy.
   c. He enjoys his free time.

 ## WHAT DO YOU THINK?

Discuss the questions in a group.

1. What did Gary learn by changing his career? Do you think the lesson will last?

2. What benefits from his old job might Gary miss?

3. Do you think you could change your life completely in this way? Why or why not?

Using a **T-chart** is a simple way to separate information when you take notes. You can use a T-chart to help you see two sides of an argument, the advantages and disadvantages of a topic, or the strengths and weaknesses of an idea.

CD 1
Track 41

For example, listen to this excerpt from Gary's talk, and study the notes in the T-chart.

Life as a city trader

once to play (down side.

Advantages	Disadvantages
very well-paid	a lot of stress
designer clothes	always worried
luxury sports car	headaches/stomach problems
huge apartment	difficult to build relationships

CD 1
Track 42

A. Listen to a different excerpt from Gary's talk, as he describes his life as a home-care assistant. Complete the T-chart.

Life as a home-care assistant

Advantages	Disadvantages
he feels fulfilled	salary is considerably low
make friends	can't afford a new car
better relationship his family	can't take vacation
feels healthier	he doesn't travel any more
has time with his family	

B. Now think about a job that either you or someone you know has had. Draw a T-chart in your notebook. List the main advantages and disadvantages of that job.

C. Work with a partner. Talk about the job you chose in Activity B. Use your T-chart to help you. Do not mention the name of the job. Your partner will try to guess the job you are describing.

VOCABULARY

Here are some words and phrases from Listening 2. Read the sentences.
Circle the answer that best matches the meaning of each bold word or phrase.

(1-1)

1. It can be very difficult for people working in low-paying jobs to **cope**.
   a. manage financially
   b. build relationships
   c. be happy

(3·2)

2. After working for ten hours without a break, we were **exhausted**. *egg - zahg ted*
   a. very excited
   b. very bored
   c. very tired

3. It's hard to truly understand someone else's situation. Sometimes you need
   to experience it **firsthand**. *[2-2]*
   a. quickly
   b. directly
   c. together

(2-2)

4. You need to know all the facts before you can make an **informed** decision. *make education decision*
   a. detailed
   b. serious
   c. educated

5. Agostino is always happy. He has a **permanent** smile on his face. *(3-1)*
   a. constant
   b. occasional
   c. attractive

6. Sociologists are doing **research** on how people live in the poorest parts of *[2-1] (N) do research*
   the city.
   a. estimates
   b. practice
   c. studies

2-1

7. Many people who don't have jobs **struggle** when it is time to pay their bills.
   a. work hard
   b. have difficulty
   c. invest money

8. Many students at college don't receive money from their parents.
   They need to be able to **support themselves**.
   a. take care of themselves *to pay ur own way*
   b. live together
   c. enjoy themselves

9. When the company closed down, many of its workers became **unemployed**.
   a. jobless *to have no job*
   b. educated
   c. sick

10. I enjoy my work, but the **wages** are too low for me to make a living.
   a. benefits
   b. earnings
   c. conditions

Barbara Ehrenreich

Preview Listening 2

An Interview with Barbara Ehrenreich

write newspaper/journal

You are going to listen to a radio interview with Barbara Ehrenreich, a
well-known journalist and author. Listen to what she learned by "going
undercover"—working secretly—to do research for some of her books. Why
do you think a journalist might decide to go undercover to do research?

secretly

Listen for Main Ideas

CD 1
Track 43

Read the statements. Then listen to the interview. Write *T* (true) or *F* (false).

ask small things *unskilled jobs*

___ 1. For *Nickel and Dimed,* Ehrenreich took several low-paying jobs.

___ 2. Ehrenreich found that it wasn't so difficult to cope financially.

___ 3. For *Bait and Switch,* Ehrenreich researched unemployment among
   white-collar workers. *skilled labor*

___ 4. Ehrenreich found that life was more difficult for white-collar workers
   than unskilled workers.

___ 5. Ehrenreich is pleased that the changes she made were temporary.

___ 6. Ehrenreich didn't learn *alot* as much as she expected by going undercover
   as a reporter.

LISTEN FOR DETAILS

Read the sentences. Then listen again. Circle the answer that best completes each statement.

1. Ehrenreich worked undercover in each job for _____.
   a. one month
   b. three months
   c. six months

2. While Ehrenreich was working undercover, _____.
   a. she studied hard
   b. she had a lot of fun
   c. her life changed completely

3. Ehrenreich found that it was difficult to manage financially because _____ were so high.
   a. food prices
   b. travel expenses
   c. rents

4. Ehrenreich says that some of the jobs made her feel _____.
   a. very tired
   b. very bored
   c. very angry

5. Ehrenreich didn't expect her book *Nickel and Dimed* to be so _____.
   a. expensive
   b. popular
   c. easy to write

6. For her next book, *Bait and Switch*, Ehrenreich _____.
   a. used a false name
   b. took several top jobs
   c. didn't do any research

7. For *Bait and Switch*, Ehrenreich pretended to be an unemployed _____ executive.
   a. account
   b. human resources
   c. public relations

8. Even though Ehrenreich claimed to have _____, she couldn't find any work.

   a. letters of recommendation

   b. a lot of experience

   c. great qualifications

 WHAT DO YOU THINK?

A. Discuss the questions in a group.

1. Why do you think *Nickel and Dimed* was a best seller?

2. What qualities do you think a person needs to go undercover as Ehrenreich did? Would you like to try doing this? Why or why not?

Tip for Success

Be an active listener! Use expressions such as *Really?*, *Hmm*, *Yeah*, and *I see* to show that you are paying attention to the speaker.

B. Think about both Listening 1 and Listening 2 as you discuss the questions.

1. Think about the changes that Gary McBride and Barbara Ehrenreich experienced. How were their experiences similar? How were they different?

2. What did each person learn from change? Who do you think learned more? Explain your reasons.

 Using the dictionary web

A **word web** is a diagram that connects words. You can use a word web to show the different meanings of a word.

- Start with a word with multiple meanings, such as *get*. Write the word in the middle circle of the word web.
- Next, look up the word in the dictionary. Some dictionaries have shortcuts, words that help you find the different meanings more quickly.
- Write each shortcut word in a circle surrounding the middle circle.
- Include an example sentence to help you understand the word and show how it is used in English.

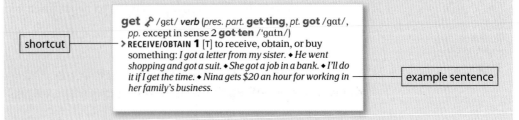

All dictionary entries are from the *Oxford American Dictionary for learners of English* © Oxford University Press 2011.

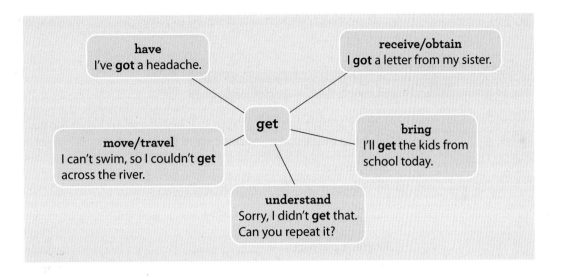

A. Read the sentences. Then write the number of each sentence below the correct shortcut in the word web. Use a dictionary to help you if necessary.

1. This town has changed a lot in recent years.

2. You need to change the light bulb in the kitchen.

3. It's quicker by bus, but you have to change twice.

4. Do you want to change before we go to the party?

5. Can you change a twenty-dollar bill?

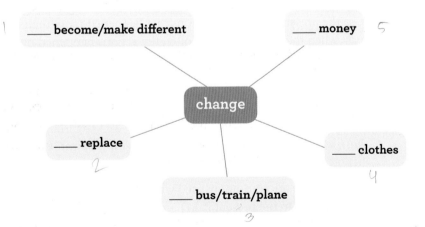

B. Work with a partner. Use a dictionary to help you build a word web with the verb *make*. Follow the steps in the Vocabulary Skill box.

SPEAKING

Grammar | **Simple past and present perfect**

Use the **simple past** for actions that began and ended in the past. For actions that began in the past and continue up to the present, use the **present perfect**.

Simple past

Genevieve **lived** in Paris two years ago.
(She no longer lives in Paris.)

Present perfect

Genevieve **has lived** in Paris for five years.
She **has lived** in Paris since she was two years old.
(She still lives in Paris.)

Use the simple past for actions that occurred at a specific time in the past. If the time an action occurred is not known or not important, use the present perfect.

Simple past

Niran **wrote** a book about Thailand last year.

Present perfect

Niran **has written** a book about Thailand.
(When he wrote the book is not important.)

Use the present perfect for actions that happened more than once in the past when the focus is on how often the actions happened rather than when they happened.

Ann loves the movie *Star Wars*. She **has seen** it four times.

Time expressions used with the simple past and present perfect

Last, ago, in, and *on* are commonly used with the simple past to show that an action was completed in the past.

For and *since* are commonly used with the present perfect to show that an action is connected to the present.

Sara started college **two years ago**.
She has been a student **for two years**.

A. Circle the correct verb forms to complete the conversation. Then practice the conversation with a partner.

Ashley: Hey, Kevin. (Did you ever travel / Have you ever traveled) abroad?
1

Kevin: Yes, I (did / have). I (went / have been) to France last year.
2　　　　　3

Ashley: Really? (Did you enjoy / Have you enjoyed) it?
4

Kevin: Yeah, it (was / has been) amazing. How about you?
5

Ashley: Oh, I (didn't go / haven't been) to Europe, but I
6

(have traveled / traveled) around South America for a month
7

a couple of years ago. It's great to see new places, isn't it?

Kevin: Yeah. It's a nice change.

Arc de Triomphe, Paris

B. Make a list of three important events that happened in your childhood. *event/hospital*

1. _when 9 was child had 9 fell down from stairs_

2. _____

3. _____

C. Make a list of three important events that have happened since your childhood.

1. _____

2. _____

3. _____

D. Work in a group. Discuss the events you listed in Activities A and B.

You can show interest while you are speaking by **varying your intonation**—making your voice rise and fall—a little more than usual. This is especially important in situations in which you need to make a good first impression, such as job interviews and meeting new people.

CD 1
Track 45

Listen to this sentence from the interview with Barbara Ehrenreich. You will hear it twice. Notice how the speaker sounds more interested the second time.

☐   Really? What exactly did you find out?

Listen to some more examples. Notice how Speaker B varies her intonation to sound interested.

A: I've never tried horseback riding.
B: You haven't? That's too bad. It's great!

A: Carol went to Australia for a month last year.
B: Did she? That sounds wonderful!

CD 1
Track 46

A. Listen twice to each sentence. Who sounds more interested, Speaker 1 or Speaker 2? Check (✓) your answers.

	Speaker 1	Speaker 2
1. I hear you're looking for a new job?	☐	☑
2. Julie and Frank just had a baby.	☑	☐
3. Michelle started at a new school on Monday.	☐	☑
4. James has been retired for over a year.	☐	☑
5. You went to London last month.	☑	☐
6. Have you ever been to Europe?	☑	☐
7. So, you learned to scuba dive as a child?	☐	☑
8. I've never lived abroad.	☑	☐

CD 1
Track 47

B. Listen again. Repeat the sentences. Use the same intonation that you hear.

To better understand someone's point of view, you can ask the person to explain the **reasons** for his or her opinion. You can also help people understand your point of view by explaining your own reasons. Here are some phrases you can use to ask for or give reasons.

Asking for reasons	Giving reasons
Why do you think/say that?	because…
What are your reasons for saying that?	because of/due to…
Can you explain why…?	The reason… is (that)…
	That's why…

To give several reasons for your point of view, you can introduce each reason with a phrase like these.

First (of all),
Also/Second,
Another reason/thing is…
Finally,

CD 1
Track 48

Listen to how the phrases are used in this conversation.

A: You know, I really don't think fishing is for me.
B: Oh yeah? **Why do you say that?**
A: Well, **first of all**, it's boring! **Also**, it's expensive to buy all the equipment, and **another thing** I hate is the smell of fish!

CD 1
Track 49

A. Listen to a conversation between two friends. Complete the conversation with the phrases you hear. Then practice the conversation with a partner.

Jez: Hi, Lisa. I haven't seen you for ages. How was your vacation in Spain?

Lisa: It was great! I tried lots of new things—horseback riding, scuba diving… I even went to a bullfight in Madrid.

Jez: What? You went to a bullfight? I'm surprised.

Lisa: Really? _____why do you say that____ ?
                                        1

Jez: _____Because_____ it's cruel, isn't it? Why would you
                    2   *very unkind*
want to watch that?

Lisa: Well, _____first of all_____, it's an important part of the culture…you know? _____Another reason is that_____ it's really popular. Lots of tourists were there. It's _____also_____ good to experience something different for a change…I think.

HW

white-water rafting

B. Work in a group. Look at the activities in the box. Discuss which activities you would like to try. Give reasons for your ideas.

bungee jumping	painting	white-water rafting
gardening	surfing	yoga
other: _____		

A: *I'd like to try white-water rafting. That sounds amazing.*

B: *Really? Why do you say that? I think it sounds scary.*

A: *Well, first of all, I love water sports, and another reason is that it looks very exciting.*

Unit Assignment | **Take part in a group discussion**

 In this assignment, you are going to take part in a group discussion about the advantages and disadvantages of change. As you prepare for the group discussion, think about the Unit Question, "Is change good or bad?" and refer to the Self-Assessment checklist on page 82.

For alternative unit assignments, see the *Q: Skills for Success Teacher's Handbook*.

CONSIDER THE IDEAS

Work in a group. Think about the following important events that can occur in people's lives. Each event represents a big change. Discuss the advantages and disadvantages that each event might have. Use phrases from the Speaking Skill box on page 79 to practice giving and asking for reasons.

changing your job	passing an exam
getting married	passing your driving test
moving away from home	starting at a new school/college

PREPARE AND SPEAK

A. GATHER IDEAS Think about the events you discussed with your group. Choose one of the events that you have experienced yourself. Then write answers to the questions.

Which event did you choose? _____

Did you experience the advantages and disadvantages you discussed with your group? What were they?

_____

_____

_____

_____

_____

What did you learn from this event?

_____

_____

_____

B. ORGANIZE IDEAS Complete the outline. Use ideas from your discussion and your notes from Activity A. Think about change in general as you answer the questions. Do not write exactly what you are going to say. Just write notes to help you organize your ideas.

What are the advantages of change?

_____

_____

_____

_____

What are the disadvantages of change?

_____

_____

_____

What can we learn from change?

_____

_____

_____

Tip for Success

When listening to your classmates, take notes of the main points each person makes. You can use these notes later when you want to ask questions.

C. SPEAK Discuss your ideas in a group. Do not read exactly what you wrote. Just use your notes. Use phrases from the Speaking Skill box on page 79 to give and ask for reasons. Remember to vary your intonation to show interest. Decide who in your group has a view of change similar to your own Refer to the Self-Assessment checklist below before you begin.

CHECK AND REFLECT

A. CHECK Think about the Unit Assignment as you complete the Self-Assessment checklist.

SELF-ASSESSMENT		
Yes	No	
☐	☐	I was able to speak easily about the topic.
☐	☐	My group understood me.
☐	☐	I used vocabulary from the unit.
☐	☐	I used the simple past and present perfect.
☐	☐	I varied my intonation to show interest.
☐	☐	I asked for reasons for someone's opinion and gave reasons for my own opinions.

B. REFLECT Discuss these questions with a partner.

What is something new you learned in this unit?

 Look back at the Unit Question. Is your answer different now than when you started this unit? If yes, how is it different? Why?

Track Your Success

Circle the words and phrases you learned in this unit.

Nouns
(2-1) crisis 🔑
(3-2) position 🔑
(2-1) research 🔑 AWL
(2-1) wages 🔑

Verbs
(2-2) adapt 🔑 AWL
(1-1) change 🔑
(1-1) cope 🔑
get 🔑
handle 🔑
(3-1) justify 🔑 AWL
(2-1) struggle 🔑
(2-1) suffer 🔑
(1-2) support (oneself) 🔑

Adjectives
curious 🔑 (3-1)
exhausted (3-2)
fulfilled (2-2)
informed (2-2)
permanent 🔑 (3-1)
steady 🔑
unemployed 🔑

Adverbs
Also, 🔑
considerably 🔑 AWL (5-2)
Finally, 🔑 AWL
First, 🔑
firsthand (2-2)
Second, 🔑 (2-1)

Phrases
Another reason/thing
  is…
Can you explain why…?
First of all,
That's why…
The reason… is (that)…
What are your reasons
  for saying that?
Why do you think/say
  that?

🔑 Oxford 3000™ words
AWL Academic Word List

Check (✓) the skills you learned. If you need more work on a skill, refer to the page(s) in parentheses.

LISTENING	○	I can take notes using a T-chart. (p. 70)
VOCABULARY	○	I can use word webs. (pp. 74–75)
GRAMMAR	○	I can use simple past and present perfect. (p. 76)
PRONUNCIATION	○	I can vary my intonation to show interest. (p. 78)
SPEAKING	○	I can ask for and give reasons. (p. 80)
LEARNING OUTCOME	●	I can participate in a group discussion and emphasize the advantages and disadvantages of change.

LISTENING	●	inferring a speaker's attitude
VOCABULARY	●	using the dictionary
GRAMMAR	●	tag questions
PRONUNCIATION	●	intonation in tag questions
SPEAKING	●	leading a group discussion

State and explain your opinions about our responsibility for issues impacting our world.

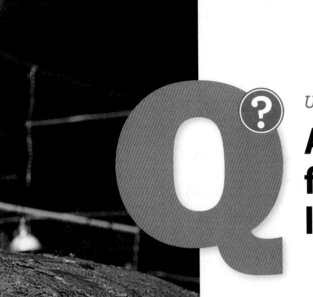

Unit QUESTION

Are we responsible for the world we live in?

PREVIEW THE UNIT

A Discuss these questions with your classmates.

Do you like to take responsibility, or do you prefer other people to take control?

Do you think you are a responsible citizen?

Look at the photo. What is the man doing? Why?

B Discuss the Unit Question above with your classmates.

Listen to *The Q Classroom*, Track 2 on CD 2, to hear other answers.

C Complete the web survey. Then work with a partner. Discuss who you think should be responsible for each activity.

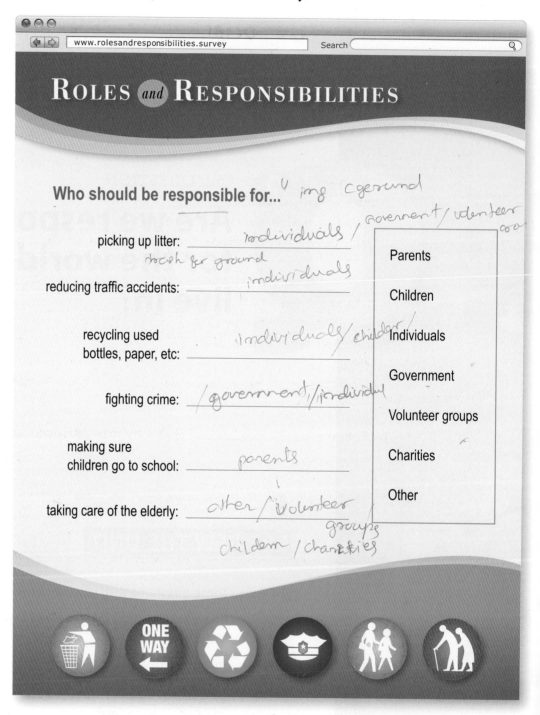

www.rolesandresponsibilities.survey   Search

ROLES *and* RESPONSIBILITIES

Who should be responsible for... *img cgeround*

picking up litter: _____ *individuals / Goverment / volenteer goa*

doesh for ground

reducing traffic accidents: _____ *individuals*

recycling used
bottles, paper, etc: _____ *individuals/ childer*

fighting crime: _____ */government, individul*

making sure
children go to school: _____ *parents*

taking care of the elderly: _____ *other / volenteer groups*
children / charities

Parents

Children

Individuals

Government

Volunteer groups

Charities

Other

D Work in a group. Discuss your ideas from Activity C. Give reasons for your answers. Then discuss how responsible you personally feel for each activity. Give examples of ways you take responsibility.

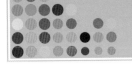

LISTENING

LISTENING 1 | Corporate Social Responsibility

VOCABULARY

Here are some words from Listening 1. Read the definitions. Then complete each sentence with the correct word.

(3-1) **benefit** (n.) an extra payment or service that is given to an employee in addition to his/her salary

(3-2) **consumer** (n.) a person who buys things or uses services

(2-2) **demand** (v.) to ask for something in a way that shows you expect to get it *strongly*

(3-2) **developed** (adj.) having advanced political or economic systems and a high standard of living

(1-1) **fair** (adj.) right, according to what people generally accept as right = equal

(1-1) **fine** (n.) money you pay for breaking a law or rule *Punishment*

(2-2) **ignore** (v.) to pay no attention to someone or something

(2-1) **impact** (n.) an effect or impression = effect

(2-2) **pollute** (v.) to make air, rivers, and oceans dirty and dangerous

(2-1) **profit** (n.) the money that you make when you sell something for more than it cost you

1. As a(n) _____consumer_____, I always try to buy products from companies I know well.

2. Most people agree that companies should pay their workers a(n) _____fair_____ wage.

3. There are laws protecting workers. Most companies follow these laws, but some companies _____ignore_____ them.

4. The company accepted responsibility for the accident and paid a large _____fine_____.

5. Some companies only care about money. Making a(n) _____profit_____ is more important to them than anything else.

6. Private health care is just one _____benefit_____ that some companies give their workers.

7. Angry workers around the world are starting to ___demand___ more rights.

8. I think companies that ___pollute___ rivers with chemicals should be closed down.

9. People these days are more aware of the ___impact___ of pollution on the environment.

10. ___Developed___ countries have a responsibility to help the global community.

PREVIEW LISTENING 1

Corporate Social Responsibility

You are going to listen to a lecture to a group of business students. The professor starts by defining "corporate social responsibility" and then discusses its importance in today's world. What do you think "corporate social responsibility" means?

LISTEN FOR MAIN IDEAS

CD 2
Track 3

Read the statements. Then listen to the lecture. Write *T* (true) or *F* (false) according to what the professor says.

__T__ 1. These days, more people are concerned about the impact companies have on the world we live in.

__F__ 2. The issue of corporate social responsibility affects only a small number of people.   *all of us*

__F__ 3. Companies in developed countries act more responsibly than those in developing countries.

__T__ 4. Pressure on companies to act more responsibly comes from several areas.

__T__ 5. It's often difficult to decide who is responsible for the actions of a company.

__F__ 6. It's not possible for companies to be socially responsible and to make a profit.

LISTEN FOR DETAILS

CD 2
Track 4

Read the sentences. Then listen again. Circle the answer that best completes each statement.

1. The professor says it's understandable that companies _____.
   a. want to make a profit
   b. find it difficult to be socially responsible

   worried

2. He adds that people in developed countries don't seem to be concerned about _____.
   a. the conditions of workers elsewhere
   b. the price they pay for products

3. He suggests that consumers are starting to demand _____.
   a. cheaper products
   b. fair pay for workers

4. The professor points out that governments are putting pressure on companies to _____.
   a. reduce pollution
   b. provide health care for their workers

5. He thinks that stopping child labor is something that _____.
   a. is not difficult to do
   b. we are all responsible for

WHAT DO YOU THINK?

Discuss the questions in a group.

Tip for Success

In discussion activities, always try to use words you have studied in the unit. This will help you learn the words and remember them in the future.

1. How important is it for companies to be socially responsible? What are the benefits?

2. Who do you think is more responsible for the actions of a company: the company itself or the individual decision-makers?

3. Which companies do you think are socially responsible?

guess

final

CD 2
Track 5

You can learn a lot about **a speaker's attitude** by noticing the way he talks. Someone who speaks slowly or sometimes hesitates before speaking might be nervous. Someone who raises her voice could be angry. Someone who is bored or uninterested might speak in a low voice with level intonation.

Listen to this excerpt from the lecture. Notice that the professor raises his voice. This indicates he feels passionately about the topic and is perhaps a little angry.

> We are all happy to buy our clothes more cheaply, but do we stop to think where they were made and who made them?

Listen to this conversation. Notice that Speaker A speaks in a low voice with level intonation, expressing a lack of interest. Speaker B speaks slowly and hesitates. This shows he is nervous.

> **A:** It's the neighbor again. What does he want this time?
> **B:** Excuse me. Would you mind turning down the music, please?
> **A:** Yeah, sure.

CD 2
Track 6

A. Listen to these sentences. Match each sentence with the speaker's attitude.

___c___ 1. Did you know that this is a nonsmoking area?   a. uninterested

___b___ 2. I don't know why Simon's always late for work.   b. angry

___a___ 3. Yeah. That garbage has been there for a week.   c. nervous

CD 2
Track 7

B. Listen to each conversation. Check (✓) the word that describes how the woman feels.

4 - 2

1. ☐ uninterested   ☑ angry   ☐ nervous
2. ☑ uninterested   ☐ angry   ☐ nervous
3. ☐ uninterested   ☐ angry   ☑ nervous

only practice

C. Work with a partner. Take turns reading the sentences. Practice sounding angry, uninterested, or nervous. Your partner will try to identify how you feel.

1. Someone's left the front door open again.

2. I think there's something wrong with the engine.

3. Heather hasn't finished the report yet.

LISTENING 2 | Personal Responsibility

VOCABULARY

Here are some words from Listening 2. Read the sentences. Then write each bold word or phrase next to the correct definition.

1. My mother told me it's not **appropriate** to wear torn jeans to the event.

2. Amy's parents worry, so they always **check up on** her.

3. Sometimes I feel **guilty** when I don't tell my parents where I'm going.

4. My parents are always busy, so I'm glad to **help out** around the house.

5. Who is **in charge of** health and safety in your school?

6. You shouldn't let other people **influence** you all the time. You need to make your own decisions.

7. Do you agree it's wrong to **lie**, even if the truth can hurt?

8. A teacher's main **obligation** is to help students learn.

9. It's not very **sensible** to run across a busy road.

10. It's important to have good friends you can **trust**.

a. ___check up on___ (phr. v.) to make sure someone is behaving well

b. ___trust___ (v.) to believe someone is honest and reliable

c. ___guilty___ (adj.) responsible for doing something wrong

d. ___sensible___ (adj.) showing the ability to act in a reasonable way

e. ___influence___ (v.) to have an effect on

f. ___obligation___ (n.) something that you must do because it is your duty or because you promised to do it

g. ___lie___ (v.) to say something that you know is not true

h. ___help out___ (adj.) responsible for something

i. ___in charge of___ (phr. v.) to assist by doing useful jobs

j. ___appropriate___ (adj.) suitable or right for a particular situation, person, or use

PREVIEW LISTENING 2

| Personal Responsibility

You are going to listen to an excerpt from a college seminar. The students are discussing the issue of personal responsibility. Think about the things you are responsible for in your daily life. What are your most important responsibilities?

LISTEN FOR MAIN IDEAS

CD 2
Track 8

Listen to the seminar. Circle the answer that best completes each statement.

1. _____ of the students feel it is important to help out at home.
   a. All   b. Some   c. None

2. The students seem to be _____ that their parents check up on them.
   a. pleased   b. annoyed   c. proud

3. The students feel their parents don't _____ them enough.
   a. trust   b. listen to   c. support

4. According to the professor, the amount of responsibility parents give their children might depend on their _____.
   a. behavior   b. attitude   c. age

5. The students do not _____ at what age children are responsible.
   a. know   b. agree   c. understand

LISTEN FOR DETAILS

CD 2
Track 9

Listen to the first part of the seminar again. Match the responsibility with the student.

__c__ 1. taking out the garbage   a. Neil

__a__ 2. looking after a little sister   b. Michael

__c__ 3. recycling   c. Naomi

__b__ 4. doing the dishes   d. Maria

__b__ 5. washing the car

__d__ 6. looking after family pets

Q WHAT DO YOU THINK?

A. Discuss the questions in a group.

1. How much responsibility does your family give you? Are you content with this much responsibility?

2. At what age do you think someone becomes responsible for his or her actions (for example, behaving well in public, doing chores, or handling money)? Explain.

B. Think about both Listening 1 and Listening 2 as you discuss the questions.

1. What should companies do to protect the environment? In what ways should individuals be responsible for the environment? Who has more responsibility?

2. In what ways do you take responsibility for the environment? Give examples.

| Vocabulary Skill | Using the dictionary | |

Finding the correct meaning

Words listed in a dictionary often have several meanings. To choose the correct meaning, first identify the part of speech (*noun, verb, adjective*, etc.). Then read all the definitions and example sentences. Finally, choose the meaning that best matches the context.

For example, read this conversation.

> **Frank:** Look, Sylvie. I found this gold ring in the park. It fits me perfectly!
>
> **Sylvie:** You're not going to keep it are you? That's wrong! Turn it into the police.

W*rong* can be a verb, noun, adjective, or adverb. Here, *wrong* is an adjective. W*rong (adj.)* in this dictionary has four different meanings. By considering the context and comparing examples, you will find that the most appropriate definition is Number 4—"not good or right."

> **wrong¹** /rɔŋ/ *adj.* **1** not true or not correct; not right: *the wrong answer* ♦ *You have the wrong number* (= on the telephone). ♦ *I think you're wrong about that.* **ANT right 2** not the best; not suitable: *That's the wrong way to hold the bat.* ♦ *I think she married the wrong man.* **ANT right 3** (not before a noun) **(with sb/sth)** causing problems or difficulties; not as it should be: *You look upset. Is something wrong?* ♦ *What's wrong with the car this time?* ♦ *She has something wrong with her leg.* **4 wrong (to do sth)** bad or against the law; not good or right: *It's wrong to tell lies.* ♦ *The man said that he had done nothing wrong.*

All dictionary entries are from the *Oxford American Dictionary for learners of English*
© Oxford University Press 2011.

A. Read the sentences. Use a dictionary. Follow the steps in the Vocabulary Skill box on page 93 to identify the correct meaning of each bold word. Then write the definition.

1. People living in a **just** society should respect the law.

   (adjective) fair and right, reasonable

2. Complaints against dishonest politicians have reached a **peak** in the last few years.

   _____

3. If it doesn't stop raining soon, I think we should **abandon** the idea of going for a walk.

   _____

4. I don't have **outstanding** bills. I paid them all on Wednesday.

   _____

5. People in positions of authority shouldn't **abuse** their power.

   _____

6. Terri lives a very **moral** life. She's a good example for her children.

   _____

7. Companies that continue to pollute the environment **risk** getting heavy fines.

   _____

8. In any relationship, it's important to be **open** and supportive.

   _____

B. Choose five words from Activity A and write your own sentences in your notebook. Then compare your sentences with a partner.

Final Exam

Grammar | Tag questions

Tag questions are common in everyday conversation. You can use a tag question to keep a conversation going by asking a person for her opinion about a situation.

Tag questions are formed by adding a short *yes/no* question at the end of a statement.

If the statement is positive, the tag question is negative.

◻ Telling a lie **is** wrong, **isn't it?**

If the statement is negative, the tag question is positive.

◻ They **aren't** responsible for the accident, **are they?**

The subject of a tag question is the pronoun form of the subject of the statement.

⌐ **You**'re telling the truth, aren't **you?**
  John went to school today, didn't **he?**
⌐ **Your parents** are strict, aren't **they?**

There are nice ppl in this class, aren't there?

The verb in a tag question is a form or part of the main verb in the statement.

If the statement contains an auxiliary verb or modal, use the auxiliary verb or modal in the tag question.

⌐ They**'re** very responsible parents, **aren't** they?
  All employees **should** get benefits, **shouldn't** they?
⌐ You **haven't** told your parents where you are, **have** you?

If the statement does not contain an auxiliary verb or modal, use a form of *do* in the tag question.

⌐ Your parents **trust** you, **don't** they?
⌐ The workers **got** benefits, **didn't** they?

A. Use tag questions to complete the conversations. Then practice the conversations with a partner.

1. A: You're a responsible person, _____ *aren't you* _____?

   B: Yes, I am.

2. A: Richard never keeps his promises, _____ *doesn't he* _____?
   doezy

   B: No, he doesn't.

3. A: They didn't tell the truth, ___did they___?

   B: No, they didn't.

4. A: It's important to help other people, ___Isn't it___?

   B: Yes, it is.

5. A: Susan should see her mother more often, ___shouldn't she___?

   B: Yes, she should.

6. A: Abed and Gary haven't called, ___have they___?

   B: No, they haven't.

7. A: Valerie came to class with a cold, ___did'n't she___?

   B: Yes, she did.

8. A: We can't help you, ___can we___?

   B: Yes, you can. Would you mind picking up those books?

B. Complete the sentences. Use tag questions. Then add three more sentences with tag questions of your own.

1. You haven't cheated on an exam, ___have you___?

2. Children should help their parents with household chores,
   ___shouldn't they___?

3. ___you should come to the class ontime, shouldn't you___?

4. ___you don't cook every day. do you?___?

5. ___The escalater is out of order. isn't it___?

C. Work with a partner. Take turns asking and answering the questions from Activity B.

The **intonation** you use in tag questions is very important. Use falling intonation on the tag question when you think you know the answer and you are asking for confirmation. Use rising intonation on the tag question when you are not certain of the answer.

Asking for confirmation

CD 2
Track 10

Telling a lie is always wrong, isn't it? ~down~   We can trust Jeff, can't we?

Uncertain of the answer

Telling a lie is always wrong, isn't it?   We can trust Jeff, can't we?

CD 2
Track 11

A. Listen to the sentences. Does the intonation rise or fall on each tag question? Check (✓) your answers.

	Rise	Fall
1. You're responsible for this, aren't you?	☑	☐
2. It's not my fault, is it?	☑	☐
3. The government should do something, shouldn't they?	☐	☑ *check*
4. Tina's late again, isn't she?	☐	☑

CD 2
Track 12

B. Listen to the sentences. Does the speaker know the answer or not? Check (✓) your answers.

fall   raising

	Knows the answer	Doesn't know the answer
1. You don't really believe that, do you?	☐	☑
2. Mike hasn't given us any help, has he?	☑	☐
3. The company accepted responsibility for the accident, didn't it?	☐	☑
4. Taxes have gone up again, haven't they?	☑	☐

KS

CD 2
Track 11
Track 12

C. Listen again to the sentences from Activities A and B. Repeat the sentences. Use the same intonation that you hear.

D. Work with a partner. Take turns reading the sentences from Activities A and B. Your partner will listen carefully and decide whether your intonation rises or falls.

| Speaking Skill | Leading a group discussion | |

When discussing a topic in a group, it is important to choose one person to **lead the discussion**. The role of the leader is to guide the flow of the discussion. The leader

- starts the discussion
- gets comments from the members of the group
- keeps the discussion on topic
- ends the discussion

Here are some phrases you can use when you are leading a discussion.

Starting the discussion

The topic I'd like to discuss today is…
Today, we're going to discuss…
Our topic today is…

Getting comments from different people

What do you think, Massoud?
Kelly, what's your opinion?
Do you have anything to add, Charlene?

Keeping on topic

I think we need to return to the topic. What is your view on…?
Sorry, but can we keep to the topic?
Let's get back on topic.

Ending the discussion

That's all we have time for today.
To sum up, then, (summarize the main points)

A. Listen to this excerpt from a discussion on recycling. Complete the discussion with the phrases you hear. Then practice the discussion in a group of four.

Leader: OK, so today _____ recycling, and exactly

1

who should be responsible. Brad, _____?

2

Brad: Well, I think that basically as individuals we can't change much. It's the

government that has to take action.

Leader: I see. _____, Seline?

3

Seline: I don't agree. We all need to do what we can. I mean, just one person

can't do much…but everyone in the world acting together can change a lot!

It's the same with raising money for charity. When everyone gives a little

money, you can raise millions!

Brad: Yes. My brother ran a marathon for charity last year and…

Leader: Sorry, but _____? Susan,

4

_____?

5

Susan: Well, I probably agree with Brad. Recycling is such a big problem—

you need the government to act, really.

Leader: OK, so _____, Susan and Brad feel the

6

government should take responsibility, while Seline thinks individuals

should lead the way.

B. Work with a partner. Continue the discussion from Activity A, using your own ideas.

In this assignment, you are going to take part in a group discussion. As you prepare for the group discussion, think about the Unit Question, "Are we responsible for the world we live in?" and refer to the Self-Assessment checklist on page 102.

For alternative unit assignments, see the *Q: Skills for Success Teacher's Handbook*.

CONSIDER THE IDEAS

Work in a group. Make a list of issues that affect your world (for example, pollution, crime, use of the Internet, etc.). Write your responsibilities concerning these issues below.

_____

_____

_____

_____

_____

PREPARE AND SPEAK

A. **GATHER IDEAS** Read the statements. Check (✓) the ones you agree with.

☐ Individuals, not governments, are responsible for the society we live in.

☐ Censorship is wrong. We should all be able to choose which movies we watch, games we play, or music we listen to.

☐ The content and use of the Internet need to be controlled.

☐ Global warming is something that only governments can fight effectively.

☐ Responsibility to your family is more important than anything else.

☐ It is OK for parents to spy on their children.

☐ Stealing is always wrong.

☐ We should all give money to support charities.

This activity asks
you to **support your
ideas**. When you
support your ideas,
you give reasons,
examples, or details
that help you prove
your point. This helps
you see strengths
and weaknesses
in your thinking.

B. ORGANIZE IDEAS Choose two statements from Activity A that you agree
with and one that you disagree with. Complete the outline to help you
prepare to give your opinion.

Agree

Statement: _____

Reasons: _____

_____

_____

Agree

Statement: _____

Reasons: _____

_____

_____

Disagree

Statement: _____

Reasons: _____

_____

_____

When taking part in
a group discussion,
encourage other
speakers by paying
close attention. You
might also want
to take notes of
any good ideas.

C. SPEAK Have a group discussion about whether or not we are
responsible for the world we live in. Refer to the Self-Assessment
checklist on page 102 before you begin.

1. Choose a leader for your discussion. The leader can begin the discussion
   by asking about your responses to the statements in Activity A.

2. When an issue you have written about in Activity B comes up for
   discussion, give your opinion and explain your reasons.

3. You can refer to your notes, but do not read exactly what you wrote.

4. Use tag questions to hold your listeners' interest.

5. Give each student a turn as group leader.

CHECK AND REFLECT

A. CHECK **Think about the Unit Assignment as you complete the Self-Assessment checklist.**

SELF-ASSESSMENT		
Yes	No	
☐	☐	I was able to speak easily about the topic.
☐	☐	My group understood me.
☐	☐	I used vocabulary from the unit.
☐	☐	I used tag questions.
☐	☐	I used intonation in tag questions.
☐	☐	I led a group discussion.

B. REFLECT **Discuss these questions with a partner.**

What is something new you learned in this unit?

 Look back at the Unit Question. Is your answer different now than when you started this unit? If yes, how is it different? Why?

Circle the words and phrases you learned in this unit.

Nouns
benefit 🔑 AWL
consumer 🔑 AWL
fine
impact 🔑 AWL
obligation
peak 🔑
profit 🔑

Verbs
abandon 🔑 AWL
abuse 🔑
demand 🔑
ignore 🔑 AWL
influence 🔑
lie 🔑
pollute
risk 🔑
trust 🔑

Adjectives
appropriate 🔑 AWL
developed
fair 🔑
guilty 🔑
in charge of
just
moral 🔑
open 🔑
outstanding 🔑
sensible 🔑
wrong 🔑

Phrasal Verbs
check up on
help out

Phrases
Do you have anything
    to add?

I think we need to
    return to the topic.
Let's get back on topic.
Our topic today is…
Sorry, but can we keep
    to the topic?
That's all we have time
    for today.
The topic I'd like to
    discuss today is…
To sum up, then,
Today, we're going to
    discuss…
What do you think?

🔑 Oxford 3000™ words
AWL Academic Word List

Check (✓) the skills you learned. If you need more work on a skill, refer to the page(s) in parentheses.

LISTENING ⚪	I can infer a speaker's attitude. (p. 90)
VOCABULARY ⚪	I can use a dictionary to find the correct meanings of words. (p. 93)
GRAMMAR ⚪	I can use tag questions. (p. 95)
PRONUNCIATION ⚪	I can use intonation in tag questions. (p. 97)
SPEAKING ⚪	I can lead a group discussion. (p. 98)
LEARNING OUTCOME ⚪	I can state and explain my opinions about our responsibility for issues impacting our world.

UNIT 6

Advertising

LISTENING	identifying fact and opinion
VOCABULARY	context clues to identify meaning
GRAMMAR	modals expressing attitude
PRONUNCIATION	intonation in questions
SPEAKING	giving and supporting your opinions

LEARNING OUTCOME

State and support your opinions concerning the influence of advertising on our behavior.

Unit QUESTION

How can advertisers change our behavior?

PREVIEW THE UNIT

A Discuss these questions with your classmates.

When you watch television, do you watch the commercials? If not, what do you do during the commercial breaks?

How often do you click on Internet ads? Did you ever buy anything after seeing an ad on the Internet?

Look at the photo. What is the man doing? How do you think he feels?

B Discuss the Unit Question above with your classmates.

Listen to *The Q Classroom*, Track 14 on CD 2, to hear other answers.

C Complete the questionnaire.

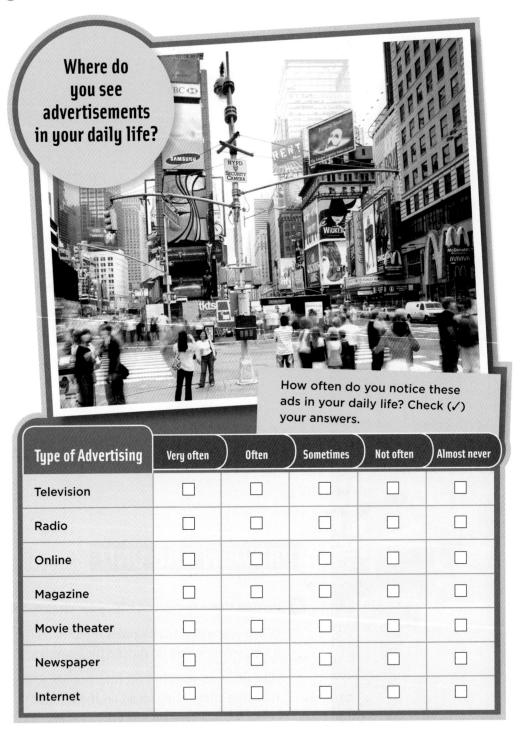

Where do you see advertisements in your daily life?

How often do you notice these ads in your daily life? Check (✓) your answers.

Type of Advertising	Very often	Often	Sometimes	Not often	Almost never
Television	☐	☐	☐	☐	☐
Radio	☐	☐	☐	☐	☐
Online	☐	☐	☐	☐	☐
Magazine	☐	☐	☐	☐	☐
Movie theater	☐	☐	☐	☐	☐
Newspaper	☐	☐	☐	☐	☐
Internet	☐	☐	☐	☐	☐

D Compare your answers with a partner. What are the advantages and disadvantages of each type of advertising? Which types do you pay most attention to?

LISTENING 1 | Advertising Techniques

VOCABULARY

Here are some words and phrases from Listening 1. Read the sentences. Circle the answer that best matches the meaning of each bold word or phrase.

1. I don't like negative advertising. I can't understand its **appeal**.
   a. attraction
   b. title
   c. product

2. This **brand** of toothpaste is the best one on the market.
   a. design
   b. management
   c. kind

3. The ad **campaign** was expensive, but it didn't produce great results.
   a. promotion
   b. sample
   c. poster

4. Many ads **claim** that products have fantastic benefits, but don't give any proof.
   a. imagine
   b. state
   c. suppose

5. We need to come up with a **jingle** that people will like and sing along to.
   a. concept
   b. message
   c. song

6. Everyone wore T-shirts showing the company's new **logo** of a jumping tiger.
   a. product
   b. design
   c. example

Keep a small
notebook with you
for new words and
phrases. Check
your notes when
you get home.

7. That company won the award for the most **memorable** ad of the year. People were still talking about it months afterwards.

   a. current

   b. unforgettable

   c. exciting

8. Advertisers use several techniques to **persuade** consumers to buy certain products.

   a. support

   b. instruct

   c. convince

9. Ads often try to **relate to** us on an emotional level.

   a. reply to

   b. connect with

   c. help

10. The **slogan** for the new sports car will be "Live life to the max."

   a. advertising phrase

   b. news story

   c. pop song

PREVIEW LISTENING 1

Advertising Techniques

You are going to listen to a group of students giving a presentation about advertising on local radio. They are explaining various advertising techniques used in the ads they heard.

What kinds of products do you expect to hear advertised on the radio? Think of three products and write them down.

_____

_____

_____

LISTEN FOR MAIN IDEAS

CD 2
Track 15

Listen to the presentation. Match the ad with the technique it uses.

____ 1. Ben's Diner

____ 2. Seattle Security

____ 3. Robertson's Black

____ 4. Sparks Body Refresher

____ 5. Arizona Rodeo

a. links the product with positive ideas

b. claims the product is very popular

c. gives key information over and over again

d. focuses on feelings and emotions

e. makes people laugh

LISTEN FOR DETAILS

CD 2
Track 16

Read the statements. Then listen again. Write _T_ (true) or _F_ (false).

____ 1. There is no charge for a security assessment from Seattle Security.

____ 2. Robertson's Black is a chocolate bar made in Switzerland.

____ 3. The Arizona Rodeo takes place next Saturday.

____ 4. The rodeo starts at noon.

____ 5. There is no charge for teenagers at Ben's Diner.

____ 6. The special offer at Ben's Diner is available all week.

____ 7. There are three varieties of Sparks Body Refresher.

 ## WHAT DO YOU THINK?

Discuss the questions in a group.

1. Which radio ads in Listening 1 do you like most? Why?

2. Which advertising technique do you think is the most effective? Explain your reasons.

3. Think of a radio ad you have heard recently. What product was it advertising? Which technique did it use? How effective do you think it was?

When you listen, it is important to identify what is a **fact** and what is someone's **opinion**.

A fact is something that is always true and can be proved.

> Paris is the capital of France.
> Soccer matches last 90 minutes.

An opinion is something that cannot be proved. People might disagree about an opinion.

> Paris is the most romantic city in the world.
> Soccer is a great game for young children.

 CD 2
Track 17

A. Listen to these statements from the radio ads you heard in Listening 1. Decide whether each statement is a fact or an opinion. Circle your answers.

1. fact / opinion

2. fact / opinion

3. fact / opinion

 CD 2
Track 18

B. Now listen to statements from another ad describing a personal computer. Decide whether each statement is a fact or an opinion. Circle your answers.

 Tip for Success

The next time you listen to the radio, focus on the ads. Listen carefully, and try to identify what is fact and what is opinion.

1. fact / opinion

2. fact / opinion

3. fact / opinion

4. fact / opinion

5. fact / opinion

6. fact / opinion

| **Advertising Ethics and Standards**

VOCABULARY

Here are some words and phrases from Listening 2. Read the definitions. Then complete each sentence with the correct word or phrase.

> **aimed at** *(phr.)* directed at something or at a particular person or group
> **competitor** *(n.)* a person, company, product, etc., that is competing against others
> **deliberately** *(adv.)* done in a way that was planned; on purpose
> **evidence** *(n.)* the facts or signs that make you believe that something is true
> **injury** *(n.)* harm done to a person's body, especially in an accident
> **mislead** *(v.)* to make someone have the wrong idea or opinion
> **monitor** *(v.)* to check, record, or watch something regularly for a period of time
> **refund** *(n.)* a sum of money that is returned to you
> **regulations** *(n.)* official rules that control how something is done
> **withdraw** *(v.)* to remove something or take something away

1. The product didn't work, so the company had to give customers a(n) _____.

2. Advertisers may be given heavy fines if they _____ the public.

3. Ads for games are usually _____ children.

4. If a product causes _____ to customers, then the fines can be very large.

5. Sometimes companies have to _____ their products from the market because of faults.

6. It's important to _____ ads to check they are fair.

7. Unfortunately, our main _____ has a very good ad campaign at the moment.

8. The company claims that this ad resulted in more sales, but there isn't any _____ of that.

9. Companies that _____ give false information should

   pay a fine.

10. In the United States, each state decides its own advertising

    _____.

Mary Engle

PREVIEW LISTENING 2

Advertising Ethics and Standards

You are going to listen to an interview with Mary Engle, associate director for advertising practices in the U.S. Federal Trade Commission (FTC). She explains some of the ways in which advertising is controlled. In what ways do you think companies that break advertising rules can be punished?

LISTEN FOR MAIN IDEAS

CD 2
Track 19

Read the statements. Then listen to the interview. Write *T* (true) or *F* (false) according to what Mary Engle says.

____ 1. The FTC makes sure ads don't break the law.

____ 2. Today there are fewer controls on advertising than in the past.

____ 3. The FTC focuses mainly on health advertising.

____ 4. Advertisers follow different regulations, depending on where the ad appears.

____ 5. The FTC only checks ads on TV and radio.

____ 6. The FTC can take various steps to stop advertisers that break the rules.

____ 7. Monitoring advertising today is more difficult than in the past.

____ 8. The way companies advertise has not changed much over the years.

LISTEN FOR DETAILS

CD 2
Track 20

Read the sentences. Then listen again. Circle the answer that best completes each statement.

1. The "truth-in-advertising" laws mean that advertisers shouldn't _____.
   a. advertise to children
   b. mislead the public
   c. make claims without providing evidence

2. As an example of untruthful advertising in the past, Engle mentions _____.
   a. weight loss products
   b. beauty products
   c. health food products

3. Engle says the main aim of the FTC is to make sure advertisers _____.
   a. don't overcharge people
   b. act responsibly
   c. don't criticize other companies

4. The FTC doesn't allow ads that might cause people to suffer physical or _____ harm.
   a. emotional
   b. personal
   c. financial

5. The FTC can only regulate _____ advertising.
   a. national
   b. state
   c. local

6. Engle gives an example of a fast food chain that broke the rules because _____.
   a. it claimed its food was healthy
   b. its food was too expensive
   c. its food made people ill

7. The FTC punished the fast food chain by _____.
   a. telling the company to withdraw the ad
   b. closing the company
   c. fining the company

8. Deliberately putting a funny video on the Internet that features a product is called _____.
   a. sub-viral marketing
   b. product placement
   c. Web promotion

WHAT DO YOU THINK?

A. Discuss the questions in a group.

1. Do you think product placement is a successful form of advertising? Explain your opinion. What product placement ads have you seen?

2. Which groups in society do you think are easy for advertisers to influence (children, teenagers, men, or women, for example)? Should advertising regulations be made stronger to protect these groups?

Tip Critical Thinking

Question 2 of Activity B asks you to **evaluate** how truthful certain ad claims are. When you evaluate, you put your knowledge and opinions together.

B. Think about both Listening 1 and Listening 2 as you discuss the questions.

1. What claims do advertisers make to influence people to buy their products (for example, "it's cheap," "it's healthy," etc.)? Make a list of examples from ads in this unit and from other ads you know.

2. Look at the claims you listed above. What products are likely to make these claims? Name one product for each claim and say whether that claim is usually truthful or not.

Vocabulary Skill | **Context clues to identify meaning**

When you hear a word or phrase you don't know, it is sometimes possible to determine the meaning from the **context**. Try to identify the part of speech, and think about the words that surround it. Use this information to help you figure out what the word means.

> This magazine has a **circulation** of 100,000 a month.

Circulation is a noun. You can tell it refers to the number of copies of the magazine sold per month.

> We advertise a lot in music magazines and video games because teenagers are our main **target**.

Target is a noun. You can tell it refers to the type of people that the ad is aimed at.

> **Infomercials** can mislead people into thinking they are watching a TV program.

Infomercial is the subject of the sentence and therefore a noun. You can see that it includes parts of two words you know: **info**rmation and com**mercial**. The context tells you that it refers to a type of TV program: an infomercial is a long commercial advertising a product.

A. Read the sentences. Underline the context clues that help you determine the meaning of each bold word. Compare your ideas with a partner.

1. That ad is <u>so big</u> and <u>colorful</u>. It's very **eye-catching**.

2. That radio station plays the same ads all day. It's **tedious** to hear them over and over.

3. Commercials in **prime time** are the most expensive because the largest number of people watch TV then.

4. We really need a more aggressive marketing strategy to **push** this product if we want it to sell more.

5. The ads for that movie are everywhere, but you shouldn't believe the **hype**. I saw it, and it's terrible.

6. The song was so **catchy** I couldn't stop humming it for days.

B. Write each word from Activity A next to its correct definition. Compare your answers with your partner.

1. _____: to make something especially noticeable or attractive, so people will buy it

2. _____: interesting or attractive to look at

3. _____: the most popular time to watch TV

4. _____: advertising that makes something seem better than it is

5. _____: easy to remember (normally refers to music)

6. _____: boring and lasting a long time

Grammar | Modals expressing attitude

Modal verbs are special *auxiliary verbs* that help to express the attitude of the speaker. They are followed by the base form of the verb.

Prohibition:	They **must not** mislead anyone.
	They **can't** say anything false.
Strong obligation:	Ads **have to** be truthful.
	Ads **must** tell the truth.
Recommendation:	You **should** tell the FTC if an ad is misleading.
	You **shouldn't** believe everything you hear.
	There's another ad for that new restaurant. We **ought to** try it.
No obligation:	Advertisers **don't have to** send ads for approval.

Note: **Must/must not** are more common in writing than in conversation.

 CD 2
Track 21

A. Listen to the conversation. Circle the modal verbs you hear. Then practice the conversation with a partner.

Yvonne: Oh, look at that ad. Those poor animals! How can they show them suffering like that? I think it's terrible!

Martin: Really? I think it's quite effective. They're trying to get your attention, you know.

Yvonne: Well, they (<u>don't have to / can't</u>) do it that way! It's not necessary,
₁ and it's upsetting.

Martin: You (<u>must not / don't have to</u>) look at it if you don't want to.
₂

Yvonne: That's not the point. That kind of advertising makes me really angry. I'm sure there's a law that says they (<u>don't have to / can't</u>) use animals
₃ like that.

Martin: Maybe you (<u>should / have to</u>) complain, then.
₄

Yvonne: Yes, I think I will. They (<u>shouldn't / don't have to</u>) be allowed to
₅ do that!

B. Discuss these questions in a group. Use modals to express your attitude when possible.

1. What do you think about ads that might make people angry?

2. Are there any types of advertising that should not be allowed?

Pronunciation | ***Part 1* Intonation in questions** web+

Intonation is different for ***yes/no* questions** than it is for ***wh-* questions** (questions that begin with *who, what, when, where, why, which,* or *how*). The intonation rises at the end of *yes/no* questions. It falls at the end of *wh-* questions.

CD 2
Track 22

Here are some examples from the interview with Mary Engle.

***Yes/no* questions**

Is there an advertising standards code?

Are the rules the same in other countries?

***Wh-* questions**

How do you find ads that break the rules?

What areas do you focus on in particular?

CD 2
Track 23

A. Listen to the questions. Does the intonation rise or fall at the end? Circle your answers.

1. Do you spend a lot of money on advertising?   rise / fall

2. What do you think of that ad?   rise / fall

3. Is that ad misleading?   rise / fall

4. Does it have a special offer?   rise / fall

5. Why is there so much hype these days?   rise / fall

CD 2
Track 24

B. Listen again. Repeat the questions. Use the same intonation that you hear.

Statements as questions

Sometimes a statement is spoken with rising intonation to make it a question. This often happens if the speaker is surprised by what he has just heard.

CD 2
Track 25

Listen to how the intonation changes these statements into questions.

Statements

There are no federal regulations.

They're going to withdraw the product.

Questions

There are no federal regulations?

They're going to withdraw the product?

CD 2
Track 26

C. **Listen to the sentences. Are they spoken as statements or questions? Circle the correct answer and complete each sentence with a period or question mark.**

1. There are no federal regulations __?__   statement / (question)

2. The company is giving a refund to all its
   customers ____   statement / question

3. You're going to withdraw the product ____   statement / question

4. That ad is really annoying ____   statement / question

5. There used to be no controls ____   statement / question

6. The rules aren't the same in other countries ____   statement / question

7. Viral marketing is becoming more popular ____   statement / question

CD 2
Track 27

D. **Listen again. Then practice with a partner. Take turns saying different sentences from Activity C and deciding whether each sentence is a statement or a question.**

It is often useful to support your opinion by giving reasons and examples.
Here are some phrases you can use when you want to give your opinion.

Giving opinions

I (don't) think (that)
In my opinion/view,
If you ask me,
As far as I'm concerned,

Here are some phrases you can use to support your opinion.

Supporting opinions

because/as
For example,
For instance,
To give you an example,

In my opinion, there's too much advertising on TV these days. **To give you an example**, a movie I watched last night had ads almost every ten minutes! **If you ask me**, they shouldn't show ads in the middle of movies on TV.

 CD 2
Track 28

A. Listen to this conversation about an ad. Complete the conversation with the phrases that you hear. Then practice the conversation with a partner.

Hugo: Hey. Look at this ad. It's got six famous people in it!

Beatrice: So what? _____, they should spend less on these

  ¹
expensive ads and lower the price of their clothes.

Hugo: Hmm. But I like seeing famous people in ads _____ it

  ²
makes it kind of cool.

Beatrice: _____, there are better ways to advertise things.

  ³
_____, they could have some facts and statistics or

  ⁴
something. You know, some information…

Hugo: But it's an ad, right? _____, an ad should get people's

  ⁵
attention, and using famous people does that.

Beatrice: Well, I guess it's eye-catching, but I'm not sure how effective it is.

B. Work with a partner. What do you think of ads that feature famous people? Are they effective? Discuss these questions. Use phrases from the Speaking Skill box to give and support your opinions.

 In this assignment, you are going to discuss the Unit Question, "How can advertisers change our behavior?" with a partner. Then you will summarize your discussion in a group and explain your own opinion. As you prepare for your discussion, refer to the Self-Assessment checklist on page 122.

For alternative unit assignments, see the *Q: Skills for Success Teacher's Handbook.*

CONSIDER THE IDEAS

Work with a partner. Choose one of these topics and discuss your ideas. Use the questions to help you. Be sure to use the correct intonation when you ask each other questions.

Advertising and children

What kinds of products are advertised to children?

What types of advertising are often used?

How are ads aimed at children different from ads aimed at adults?

Should the regulations for ads aimed at children be different?

Should advertising to children be banned?

Health ads

What kinds of health products are advertised?

What kind of person is influenced by health ads?

Are you influenced by health ads?

Should the regulations for health ads be stricter?

Should the advertising of unhealthy products (fast food, tobacco, etc.) be banned?

Status

What kinds of products are advertised as "high class"?

Who do you think is the target for these kinds of status ads?

Are the claims made by status ads misleading?

Why are so many people influenced by this type of advertising?

Are you influenced by this type of advertising?

PREPARE AND SPEAK

A. GATHER IDEAS Take notes on the topic you discussed in the Consider the Ideas activity. Write as much as you can remember from your discussion and add any new ideas that you think of.

_____

_____

_____

_____

_____

_____

B. ORGANIZE IDEAS Choose the most important ideas from your notes in Activity A. Then complete the outline. Do not write exactly what you are going to say. Just write notes to help you organize your ideas.

My topic: _____

Main ideas we discussed:

_____

_____

_____

_____

My opinion: _____

_____

Reasons for my opinion:

_____

_____

_____

C. **SPEAK** Have a group discussion about how advertisers can influence our behavior. Refer to the Self-Assessment checklist below before you begin.

1. Take turns presenting your ideas from Activity B.

2. You can refer to your notes, but do not read exactly what you wrote.

3. Give each student a turn as group leader.

CHECK AND REFLECT

A. **CHECK** Think about the Unit Assignment as you complete the Self-Assessment checklist.

SELF-ASSESSMENT		
Yes	No	
☐	☐	I was able to speak easily about the topic.
☐	☐	My partner and group understood me.
☐	☐	I used vocabulary from the unit.
☐	☐	I used modals expressing attitude.
☐	☐	I used correct intonation in questions.
☐	☐	I gave and supported my opinion.

B. **REFLECT** Discuss these questions with a partner.

What is something new you learned in this unit?

 Look back at the Unit Question. Is your answer different now than when you started this unit? If yes, how is it different? Why?

Circle the words and phrases you learned in this unit.

Nouns
appeal 🔑
brand 🔑
campaign 🔑
circulation
competitor
evidence 🔑 AWL
hype
infomercial
injury 🔑 AWL
jingle
logo
refund
regulations 🔑 AWL
slogan
target 🔑 AWL

Verbs
claim 🔑
mislead
monitor 🔑 AWL
persuade 🔑
push 🔑
withdraw 🔑

Adjectives
catchy
eye-catching
memorable
tedious

Adverbs
deliberately 🔑

Phrases
aimed at
As far as I'm concerned,
because/as
For example,
For instance,
I (don't) think (that)
If you ask me,
In my opinion,
In my view,
prime time
relate to
To give you an example,

🔑 Oxford 3000™ words
AWL Academic Word List

Check (✓) the skills you learned. If you need more work on a skill, refer to the page(s) in parentheses.

LISTENING	I can identify fact and opinion. (p. 110)
VOCABULARY	I can can identify meaning from context. (p. 114)
GRAMMAR	I can use modals expressing attitude. (p. 116)
PRONUNCIATION	I can use correct intonation in questions. (pp. 117–118)
SPEAKING	I can give and support my opinions. (p. 119)
LEARNING OUTCOME	I can state and support my opinions concerning the influence of advertising on our behavior.

UNIT 7

Risk

LISTENING	identifying amounts; cardinal and ordinal numbers
VOCABULARY	word families
GRAMMAR	past perfect
PRONUNCIATION	contraction of *had*
SPEAKING	giving a short presentation

LEARNING OUTCOME

Give a short presentation on a risk you have taken, explaining your reasons for taking that risk.

Unit QUESTION

What risks are good to take?

PREVIEW THE UNIT

(A) Discuss these questions with your classmates.

What are some risks that people take? Why do they take them?

What kinds of risks are OK to take? What kinds are not? Why?

Look at the photo. What is happening? Do you think this is a risk? Why or why not?

(B) Discuss the Unit Question above with your classmates.

Listen to *The Q Classroom*, Track 29 on CD 2, to hear other answers.

125

C Look at the questionnaire. Check (✓) your answers. Then read the answers below to find out if you are a risk taker.

Are you
a risk taker?

Have you ever:	Yes I have	No, but I might	No, I never will
1 moved to a new country?	☐	☐	☐
2 quit a job without having a new one?	☐	☐	☐
3 gone to a movie by yourself?	☐	☐	☐
4 gone on vacation without a place to stay?	☐	☐	☐
5 bought something you couldn't afford?	☐	☐	☐
6 done something others might think crazy?	☐	☐	☐
7 slept outside without a tent?	☐	☐	☐
8 done karaoke in public?	☐	☐	☐
9 made a promise that might be difficult to keep?	☐	☐	☐
10 ridden on the back of a motorcycle?	☐	☐	☐

Rate your answers

If you answered mostly yes: You like to take many different kinds of risks. You may get a thrill by taking risks. Life is fast and exciting. Sometimes, the risk will be worth it, but you could get into trouble.

If you answered mostly no: You play it safe. You are uncomfortable with risks. Your idea of a good time is staying home and reading a book. The good thing is that you will avoid trouble. On the other hand, you may not be as successful as some risk takers.

If your answers were mostly in the middle column or included some of each: You are middle-of-the-road. You are willing to take some risks, but not too many. You're careful, but willing to put yourself in uncomfortable situations if it's worth it.

D Discuss the answers in a group. Do you agree with the description of you? Why or why not? Give examples.

LISTENING 1 | Financing a Dream

VOCABULARY

Here are some words from Listening 1. Read the definitions. Then complete the paragraph below with the correct word.

> **audience** *(n.)* the group of people who are watching or listening to a play, concert, speech, or the television
>
> **credit** *(n.)* the system of buying goods or services and not paying for them until later
>
> **debt** *(n.)* the state of owing money
>
> **embarrass** *(v.)* to make someone feel uncomfortable or shy
>
> **expose** *(v.)* to show something that is usually hidden
>
> **financial** *(adj.)* connected with money
>
> **funds** *(n.)* a sum of money that is collected for a particular purpose
>
> **income** *(n.)* the money you receive regularly as payment for your work
>
> **model** *(n.)* a person or thing that is a good example to copy
>
> **threaten** *(v.)* to put at risk or in danger

Learning about Money the Hard Way

When I went to college, I didn't know anything about

_____ matters. I didn't have very much money. I wasn't
    1

working, so I didn't have a regular _____ . I started buying
                                            2

things on _____ . That way I could buy whatever I wanted
              3

without paying right away. Soon, I was $25,000 in _____ .
                                                        4

When my parents found the bill, they were very upset. They offered to

give me the _____ I needed to pay it. They didn't want to
                  5

_____ me, but told me I needed to be more responsible.
    6

I finally repaid them, but it took a long time. Now I work for a bank

and give talks to college students about managing their money. I try

to _____ the problems they can have if they owe a lot of
      7

money when they are in school. I explain that what I did was not a good

_____ to follow. The students in the _____

8   9

are always interested in the topic. They usually don't know that owing so

much money can _____ their future happiness.

10

Robert Rodriguez

PREVIEW LISTENING 1

Financing a Dream

You are going to listen to a film critic talking about the different ways filmmakers have raised money for their movies.

Write down two financial risks a filmmaker might take in order to make a movie.

_____

_____

LISTEN FOR MAIN IDEAS

CD 2
Track 30

Listen to the film critic's talk. Check (✓) the risks filmmakers took when making their movies.

What RISKS do filmmakers take?

1. charging large amounts of money on credit cards ⭕
2. getting fired from a job ⭕
3. going into personal debt ⭕
4. selling their homes ⭕
5. causing family problems ⭕
6. using personal income ⭕

DIRECTOR

LISTEN FOR DETAILS

CD 2
Track 31

Listen again. Match the filmmaker with the type of financing.

___ 1. Spike Lee

___ 2. Robert Townsend

___ 3. Robert Rodriguez

___ 4. Peter Jackson

___ 5. Matt Harding

a. income from a job

b. payments from drug testing trials

c. credit card

d. own savings

e. money from a chewing gum company

Spike Lee (on right) at a movie location

 WHAT DO YOU THINK?

Discuss the questions in a group.

1. Why do you think these filmmakers had to take the risks they did?

2. Do you have any dreams or goals that might require you to take risks? What are they? What are some of the risks you might have to take to achieve them?

3. What careers do you think involve a lot of risk? Why?

Identifying amounts

When listening to amounts of money, first listen for the amounts (*fifty*, *one hundred*, *two thousand*, *million*, *billion*). Then listen for the units or currency (*dollars*, *euros*, *pounds*). It is important to remember that the way you say and hear amounts of money is different from the way you write them or see them when reading. For example, you will read and write *$300*, but you will hear *three hundred dollars*.

CD 2 Track 32

Listen to these examples.

$500	$200,000
£1,000	£5,000,000
€10,000	€12,000,000,000

CD 2 Track 33

Listen to this excerpt from Listening 1 and pay attention to the amounts you hear. Notice that the $, £, or € sign is always written to show amounts of money, but it is not always spoken, especially after the first reference.

In the 1990s, when Kevin Smith made a comedy, he did it for just $27,000. And then Robert Rodriguez made *El Mariachi*, a movie about a singer, for only $7,000.

CD 2 Track 34

Using amounts as adjectives

It was a **fifty-dollar** shirt
The **three-hundred-pound** football player needed a larger uniform.
The **four-hundred-seat** theater was too small for the crowd.
It's a **fifteen-minute** bus ride to my office.

When you write an amount as an adjective before a noun, use hyphens between each word of the adjective. Notice that it is not in the plural.

✓ A five-hundred-dollar TV.
✗ A five-hundred-dollars TV.

CD 2 Track 35

A. Listen to the sentences. Complete the sentences with the amounts you hear. Do not write the dollar sign ($). Write out the amounts in words. If the amount is an adjective, use hyphens.

1. Spike Lee made his first movie for the very low cost of

   _____.

2. The cheapest tickets are _____.

3. The _____ bag of sugar is _____.

4. The _____ theater was too small for the crowd.

5. That store sells _____ shoes.

6. We took a _____ survey online.

7. My suitcase weighs over _____.

8. Maria found a _____ bill on the sidewalk.

B. Work with a partner. Take turns asking and answering questions about the sentences in Activity A.

A: *How much did Spike Lee's movie cost?*
B: *It cost a hundred and eighty thousand dollars.*

Part 2 **Identifying amounts; cardinal and ordinal numbers** web+

Identifying cardinal and ordinal numbers

Some **ordinal** numbers sound very different from **cardinal** numbers (*first/one, second/two, third/three*). Most sound very similar except they end in a **-th** sound (*sixteen/sixteenth, thirty/thirtieth*).

CD 2
Track 36

Listen to these cardinal and ordinal numbers. Pay attention to the **-th** sound at the end of most ordinal numbers.

cardinal	ordinal	cardinal	ordinal
one	first	seven	seventh
two	second	twenty	twentieth
three	third	thirty-four	thirty-fourth
five	fifth	forty-six	forty-sixth

CD 2
Track 37

C. Listen to the sentences. Check (✓) the sentence you hear.

1. ☐ The seven tests can be taken this week.
   ☐ The seventh test can be taken this week.

2. ☐ The nine students left an hour ago.
   ☐ The ninth student left an hour ago.

3. ☐ I ate the fifteen cookies.
   ☐ I ate the fifteenth cookie.

4. ☐ Did you receive the six emails I sent you?

   ☐ Did you receive the sixth email I sent you?

5. ☐ Push the four buttons.

   ☐ Push the fourth button.

CD 2
Track 38 **D. Listen again. Repeat the sentences. Then take turns saying and identifying the sentences from Activity C with a partner.**

LISTENING 2 | The Truth about the Loch Ness Monster

VOCABULARY

Here are some words from Listening 2. Read the sentences. Then write each bold word next to the correct definition.

1. Marie Curie was the first person to **discover** the elements polonium and radium.

2. My uncle's dream is to **invent** a new machine and make lots of money from it.

3. For your next paper, I want you to **investigate** a topic that is interesting to you.

4. The police were unable to **locate** the stolen painting.

5. Until recently, the nature of the planet Mars has been a **mystery**.

6. On my **previous** trip to Italy, I went to Venice, but I'm not going there this time.

7. Columbus was able to **prove** the earth was round.

8. That university has a very good **reputation**.

9. Dr. Arnesen enjoys his job so much, he says he never wants to **retire**.

10. Some of life's problems are too difficult for people to **solve** on their own.

a. _____ (v.) to find the exact position of someone or something

b. _____ (v.) to find a way of dealing with a problem or situation

c. _____ (adj.) coming or happening before or earlier

d. _____ (v.) to try to find out all the facts about something

e. _____ (v.) to think of or make something for the first time

f. _____ (v.) to stop working, usually because you have reached a certain age

g. _____ (n.) the opinion that people in general have about someone or something

h. _____ (v.) to use facts or evidence to show something is true

i. _____ (n.) a thing that you cannot understand or explain

j. _____ (v.) to find or learn something that no one knew or had found before

PREVIEW LISTENING 2

The Truth about the Loch Ness Monster

Bob Rines

You are going to listen to a report about a scientist named Bob Rines and his search for Nessie, the Loch Ness Monster, in Scotland. Listen to what he has risked to find out if the monster exists.

What kind of risks do you think scientists might take? Check (✓) your ideas.

☐ financial risks
☐ health risks
☐ physical risks
☐ risks to their social relationships
☐ risks to their reputation

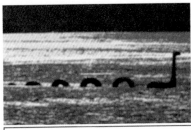
The Loch Ness Monster

LISTEN FOR MAIN IDEAS

CD 2
Track 39

Read the statements. Then listen to the report. Write *T* (true) or *F* (false).

____ 1. Rines has spent many years trying to find the Loch Ness Monster.

____ 2. Although Rines has never seen Nessie himself, he believes the reports.

____ 3. Rines has risked his reputation as a scientist because he believes the monster exists.

____ 4. Rines was fired from his job at MIT because of his work on the monster.

____ 5. So far, Rines' work hasn't produced anything useful.

____ 6. Rines has been a success in many of the things he has tried.

LISTEN FOR DETAILS

Read the questions. Then listen again. Circle the correct answer.

1. What is Loch Ness?
   a. a large freshwater lake
   b. an inland sea
   c. a large river

2. When did Rines first start believing in the Loch Ness Monster?
   a. June 1972
   b. May 1968
   c. May 2008

3. Which job has Rines had?
   a. architect
   b. doctor
   c. lawyer

4. What was discovered by one of Rines' inventions?
   a. another monster
   b. the *Titanic*
   c. how dolphins do tricks

5. What did Rines train dolphins to do?
   a. carry cameras
   b. communicate with Nessie
   c. swim for a long time

6. What did Rines invent?
   a. a submarine
   b. a device with an underwater camera
   c. a perfume

7. Why does Rines think that no one has found Nessie?
   a. We don't have the technology.
   b. Nessie is dead.
   c. The water is too deep.

 **WHAT DO YOU THINK?**

A. Discuss the questions in a group.

1. Why do you think Rines is willing to risk so much to solve this mystery? Do you think Rines is different from most people? If so, how?

2. What other mysteries have you heard about? Why do people find them so interesting?

B. Think about both Listening 1 and Listening 2 as you discuss the questions.

1. Do you think most people would rather risk their money or their reputation? Explain.

2. Can you imagine taking risks like the people you heard about? Why? Why not?

Vocabulary Skill | **Word families**

One way to increase your vocabulary is to understand **word families**. Word families consist of words that come from the same root and are related in form. They usually include several different parts of speech. For example, a noun may have an adjective and a verb form. The ending of the word often indicates the part of speech.

> **in·vent** /ɪnˈvɛnt/ *verb* [T] **1** to think of or make something for the first time: *Who invented the sewing machine?* ◆ *When was the camera invented?* **2** to say or describe something that is not true: *I realized that he had invented the whole story.* ▶ **in·ven·tor** /ɪnˈvɛntər/ *noun* [C]
>
> **in·ven·tion** /ɪnˈvɛnʃn/ *noun* **1** [C] a thing that has been made or designed by someone for the first time: *The microwave oven is a very useful invention.* **2** [U] the action or process of making or designing something for the first time: *Books had to be written by hand before the invention of printing.* **3** [C, U] telling a story or giving an excuse that is not true: *This story is apparently a complete invention.*
>
> **in·ven·tive** /ɪnˈvɛntɪv/ *adj.* having new and interesting ideas ▶ **in·ven·tive·ness** *noun* [U]

When you look up new words in the dictionary, look at the other words in the same word family. By doing this, you can add several new words to your vocabulary.

Another benefit of understanding word families is that when you see new words that look similar to words you already know, you can use your knowledge to figure out their meaning.

| Listening and Speaking   **135**

Tip Critical Thinking

The chart in Activity A **categorizes** words by their part of speech. **Categorizing** is placing things into different groups. It can help you see similarities within groups and differences between groups.

A. Work with a partner. Complete the word family chart with any forms of the words you know. Use a dictionary to check your answers.

Verb	Noun	Adjective	Adverb
invent	inventor	inventive	inventively
		creative	
discover			
embarrass			
		financial	
locate			
prove		proven	
solve			

B. Complete each sentence with an appropriate word from Activity A. You may need to change the form.

1. Children are often _____ in the ways they play.

2. I can't _____ this math problem.

3. I wish I could _____ beautiful works of art like Georgia O'Keeffe.

4. Independent filmmakers _____ their films in different ways: from credit cards to private investors to personal savings.

5. The _____ to the problem is at the back of the book.

6. Having too much credit card debt can lead to _____ disaster.

7. Bob Rines has never found real _____ that Nessie existed.

8. We decided not to buy the house because of its _____. It was too close to the freeway.

9. I can't _____ he took my money, but I think he did.

10. I spilled coffee all over the table and myself at the fancy restaurant last night—it was so _____!

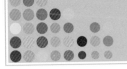

Use the **past perfect** to show the relationship between two events or actions that happened in the past. Use the past perfect to describe the first event or action that happened. Use the **simple past** to describe the second event or action.

Past perfect *(1st event)*	**Simple past** *(2nd event)*
I **had driven** for five hours.	I **went** straight to bed without dinner.

Past perfect *(1st event)*	**Simple past** *(2nd event)*
The concert **had** already **started**.	We **arrived** late.

Use the past perfect with past time clauses that begin with *when*, *before*, *by the time*, and *until*.

Past perfect *(1st event)*	**Simple past** *(2nd event)*
He **had been** at work for hours	<u>when</u> we **called** him.
Paul **had driven** for an hour	<u>before</u> he **noticed** he had a flat tire.
They **had** already **eaten** dinner	<u>by the time</u> I **got** home.
I **hadn't heard** anything about it	<u>until</u> I **read** the paper this morning.

Note: The past perfect is often used with the adverbs *already*, *yet*, *never*, *ever*, and *just*.

A. Read the pairs of sentences. Write 1 next to the sentence that happened first. Write 2 next to the sentence that happened second. Then write one sentence. Use the past time clause in parentheses.

1. Bob Rines worked on a sonar system. __1__
   He started teaching at MIT. __2__

   (before) __Bob Rines had worked on a sonar system before he started__
   __teaching at MIT.__

2. I hadn't heard about the Loch Ness monster. ____
   I read the article. ____

   (until) _____

3. It started to rain. ____
   We finished hiking. ____

   (before) _____

4. Mari picked up the phone. ____
It stopped ringing. ____

(by the time) _____

5. My sister told me. ____
I didn't realize my sweater was on backwards. ____

(until) _____

6. Hilario left his house. ____
His mother called. ____

(when) _____

7. I drank the cup of coffee. ____
I realized it wasn't mine. ____

(before) _____

8. We arrived at the airport. ____
Our plane had departed. ____

(by the time) _____

B. Complete the sentences with information that is true for you. Then take turns reading your sentences with a partner.

1. I _____ when I got home yesterday.

2. I _____ until I started taking this class.

3. I _____ by the time I graduated from high school.

4. I _____ by the year 2000.

5. I _____ before I _____.

The contraction *'d* is frequently used instead of *had* in affirmative statements with the past perfect. Noticing *had* and the contraction *'d* can help you better understand the order of past events.

**CD 2
Track 41**

Listen to these examples. The speaker joins *'d* to words that follow beginning with vowel sounds and certain consonant sounds (*l*, *r*). Notice that *'d* is not stressed.

> I**'d** already finished the test when the teacher collected our papers.
> He**'d** eaten at that restaurant before.
> We**'d** often talked about getting married.
> You**'d** left when we got there.
> She**'d** written her email before she received mine.

Do not use a contraction with questions. Notice that *had* is not stressed in these questions.

> **Had** you heard from him by the time you left?
> **Had** everyone finished the test by 2:00?

The contraction with negatives is *hadn't*.

> I **hadn't** finished my phone call by the time the train arrived.
> They **hadn't** gone to the movies before they ate dinner.

**CD 2
Track 42**

A. Listen to the sentences. Check (✓) the sentence you hear.

1. ☐ He worked at a bookstore.
   ☐ He'd worked at a bookstore.

2. ☐ We left when it started raining.
   ☐ We'd left when it started raining.

3. ☐ They answered the questions.
   ☐ They'd answered the questions.

4. ☐ I've eaten my lunch.
   ☐ I'd eaten my lunch.

5. ☐ You've already taken the test.
   ☐ You'd already taken the test.

6. ☐ She didn't work there.
   ☐ She hadn't worked there.

7. ☐ It hasn't started to rain.
   ☐ It hadn't started to rain.

8. ☐ Has he found it?
   ☐ Had he found it?

9. ☐ Have you called Alex?
   ☐ Had you called Alex?

CD 2
Track 43

B. **Listen again. Repeat the sentences. Then take turns saying and identifying the sentences from Activity A with a partner.**

Giving a short presentation

When you give a short presentation in class or at work, start by introducing your topic clearly.

Here are some phrases you can use to introduce your topic.

I want to talk about…
My topic is…
This presentation is on…
I'm going to talk about…

During your presentation, it is important to use words and phrases that help your audience understand the order of events and the reasons for them.

Here are some words and phrases you can use to help your audience follow and understand your presentation.

Order of events	Purpose/reason
First,	so…
Second,	so that…
After that,	in order to…
Then,	The reason I took this risk was…
Before	
By the time	

A. Listen to this presentation. Complete the sentences with the words and phrases you hear.

Learning Japanese

_____ 1 a time I took a risk and it turned out well. I'd always wanted to learn to speak Japanese. When I was in high school, I started to take classes in Japanese. _____ 2 I graduated from college, I had studied the language for eight years, but I still couldn't speak it very well, _____ 3 I decided to go to Japan to study. I didn't know anyone there. My grandmother had died the year before, _____ 4 I used the money she had left me for the trip. _____ 5 I left, I'd done some research on language schools. I stayed in Japan for three months and met some great people there. My Japanese improved a lot. _____ 6 I finally returned to my country, I had become fluent.

Tip for Success

At the end of a presentation, let your intonation fall so your listeners know you are finished.

B. Check (✓) the risks you have taken to learn English. Add some of your own ideas.

☐ join a club or sports team where people speak English
☐ take classes in other subjects with native English speakers
☐ move to a new city or country
☐ meet and talk to native speakers
☐ travel in English-speaking countries
☐ (your idea) _____
☐ (your idea) _____

C. Work with a partner. Take turns talking about the risks you checked in Activity B. Use words and phrases from the Speaking Skill box on page 140.

In this assignment, you are going to give a one-minute presentation on a risk you have taken. As you prepare your presentation, think about the Unit Question, "What risks are good to take?" and refer to the Self-Assessment checklist on page 144.

For alternative unit assignments, see the *Q: Skills for Success Teacher's Handbook.*

CONSIDER THE IDEAS

 CD 2
Track 45

Listen to one woman talk about a risk she took and the reasons why she took it. Take notes as you listen. Then discuss the questions with a partner.

The Pantheon in Rome

A map of Rome

What had her life been like before?

What did she risk by leaving?

Do you think it was a good risk to take? Why or why not?

What do you think happened when she arrived in Rome?

PREPARE AND SPEAK

A. **GATHER IDEAS** Think about the experience of the speaker in the Consider the Ideas Activity. Have you had a similar experience? What risks in your own life do you feel were good to take? Make a list.

_____

_____

_____

B. **ORGANIZE IDEAS** Choose one risk from your list in Activity A. Prepare to talk about it. Use the outline to help you organize your ideas.

The risk you took: _____

The reason why you took this risk:

_____

_____

_____

_____

_____

Describe what happened:

_____

_____

_____

_____

_____

_____

_____

_____

What did you learn or gain from this experience?

_____

_____

_____

_____

_____

_____

C. SPEAK Give a one-minute presentation to your group or class about a risk you have taken. Refer to the Self-Assessment checklist below before you begin.

1. Use an appropriate phrase to introduce your topic.

2. Use your notes from Activity B to help you, but do not read exactly what you wrote.

3. Try to talk continuously for the entire minute.

CHECK AND REFLECT

A. CHECK Think about the Unit Assignment as you complete the Self-Assessment checklist.

SELF-ASSESSMENT		
Yes	No	
☐	☐	I was able to speak easily about the topic.
☐	☐	My group or class understood me.
☐	☐	I used vocabulary from the unit.
☐	☐	I used the past perfect and simple past.
☐	☐	I used contractions of *had*.
☐	☐	I used phrases to introduce my topic, explain the order of events, and give reasons for events.

B. REFLECT Discuss these questions with a partner.

What is something new you learned in this unit?

Look back at the Unit Question. Is your answer different now than when you started this unit? If yes, how is it different? Why?

Circle the words and phrases you learned in this unit.

Nouns
audience 🔑
credit 🔑 AWL
debt 🔑
funds 🔑 AWL
income 🔑 AWL
model 🔑
mystery 🔑
reputation 🔑

Verbs
discover 🔑
embarrass 🔑

expose 🔑 AWL
invent 🔑
investigate 🔑 AWL
locate 🔑 AWL
prove 🔑
retire 🔑
solve 🔑
threaten 🔑

Adjectives
financial 🔑 AWL
previous 🔑 AWL

Phrases
I'm going to talk
   about…
I want to talk about…
in order to
My topic is…
This presentation is
   on…

🔑 Oxford 3000™ words
AWL Academic Word List

Check (✓) the skills you learned. If you need more work on a skill, refer to the page(s) in parentheses.

LISTENING	●	I can identify amounts; cardinal and ordinal numbers. (pp. 130–131)
VOCABULARY	●	I can use word families. (p. 135)
GRAMMAR	●	I can use the past perfect. (p. 137)
PRONUNCIATION	●	I can use the contraction of *had*. (p. 139)
SPEAKING	●	I can give a short presentation. (p. 140)
LEARNING OUTCOME	●	I can give a short presentation on a risk I have taken, explaining my reasons for taking that risk.

LEARNING OUTCOME

Give and recap a presentation highlighting what you like and dislike about a particular city.

Unit QUESTION

What do our cities say about us?

PREVIEW THE UNIT

Ⓐ Discuss these questions with your classmates.

Does the city you live in suit your personality? Why or why not?

What cities in the world do you think you might want to live in? Why?

Look at the photo. What city is it? What do you know about this city?

Ⓑ Discuss the Unit Question above with your classmates.

 Listen to *The Q Classroom*, **Track 2** on **CD 3**, to hear other answers.

C Match each city with the correct description. Then check your answers.

What do you know about these Famous Cities?

1 Bangkok, Thailand _____ **a.** One of the best places to celebrate the New Year before the rest of the world, with amazing fireworks and boats with light displays.

2 Copenhagen, Denmark _____ **b.** One of the best places to create art by taking a class in painting or sculpture, or visit one of the many art galleries.

3 Muscat, Oman _____ **c.** One of the best places to buy traditional silver jewelry, Arabian coffee pots, and shawls. The stalls at the Muttrah souk are filled with all sorts of interesting things to buy.

4 Rome, Italy _____ **d.** One of the best places to drink espresso at an outdoor café. Then you can visit the Colosseum or one of the famous museums.

5 Sydney, Australia _____ **e.** One of the best places to ride a bicycle on the many paths around the city. If you don't have your own bicycle, you can borrow one.

6 San Miguel de Allende, Mexico _____ **f.** One of the best places to shop at local markets, including the Chatuckak Market, for silk, jewelry, or just about anything you want at very low prices.

Check Your Answers: 1.f 2.e 3.c 4.d 5.a 6.b

More information about your Answers:

a: The New Year arrives in Sydney, Australia, before most of the rest of the world. Their celebration is the second largest in the world.

b: Many artists live in San Miguel de Allende, but also many tourists come to the town to take art classes.

c: Muscat, Oman is also a great place to go scuba diving or dolphin watching.

d: Like in many cities in Italy, Rome has very good espresso coffee.

e: About one-third of the residents in Copenhagen ride bikes to work.

f: The prices are very low in Bangkok, and the markets also have goods of high quality.

5–6 answers correct: You are a famous cities superstar!

3–4 answers correct: Great Job!

1–2 answers correct: Nice try! You will learn a lot in this unit.

D Discuss these questions with your group.

1. What do you like or dislike about the city you live in?

2. Which city has made the biggest impression on you? Was it negative or positive? Why?

LISTENING

LISTENING 1 | Do Cities Have Personalities?

VOCABULARY

Here are some words and phrases from Listening 1. Read the definitions.
Then complete each sentence with the correct word or phrase.

> **agreeable** *(adj.)* pleasant, nice
>
> **attract** *(v.)* to cause someone to go somewhere
>
> **conscientious** *(adj.)* careful to do something correctly and well
>
> **hand in hand** *(phr.)* usually happening together; closely connected
>
> **innovation** *(n.)* the introduction of new things or ideas
>
> **mobile** *(adj.)* able to move or be moved easily
>
> **region** *(n.)* a part of the country or the world
>
> **satisfy** *(v.)* to have or do what is necessary for something
>
> **surroundings** *(n.)* everything that is near or around you; environment
>
> **tend to** *(phr.)* to usually do or be something

1. The city of Bangalore, India, is in a(n) _____ that is known for technology jobs.

2. It's important to like where you live, since your _____ affect your happiness.

3. Some cities like Seoul or Vancouver are centers for creativity and _____. There are lots of artists and other creative people in these cities.

4. Young people especially are very _____ and don't mind traveling to find a job.

5. In manufacturing jobs, you often have to work closely and get along with other people, so being _____ is an important quality.

6. Before you can even be considered for some jobs, you need to _____ certain basic requirements.

7. Famous sites such as the Taj Mahal and the Colosseum

_____ millions of visitors every year.

8. You can depend on an employee who is _____ to
always do a good job.

9. A strong economy usually goes _____ with low
unemployment. When the economy is doing well, there are lots of jobs.

10. Generally speaking, people with similar personalities

_____ like similar jobs.

Richard Florida

PREVIEW LISTENING 1

Do Cities Have Personalities?

You are going to listen to a report about Professor Richard Florida's ideas on
why people choose to live where they do.

Do you think people with similar personalities choose to live in the same
place? Check (✓) your answer.

☐ yes   ☐ no

LISTEN FOR MAIN IDEAS

CD 3
Track 3

**Read the statements. Then listen to the report. Write _T_ (true) or _F_ (false)
according to what Professor Florida says.**

____ 1. Richard Florida thinks it doesn't really matter where you live.

____ 2. Richard Florida thinks that choosing where you live may be the
most important decision you make.

____ 3. People with similar personalities often live in the same city.

____ 4. Creative people are not more likely to live in one place over another.

____ 5. Changes in the economy may influence where people live.

____ 6. The patterns that Richard Florida talks about are only in the
United States.

Tip for Success

Listen for phrases
that show the
speaker is introducing
someone else's ideas:
_X thinks, X believes,
according to X,_ and
in X's opinion.

LISTEN FOR DETAILS

Listen again. Match the city or group of cities with the kind of work it is known for according to the report.

_____ 1. Boston, San Francisco, Seoul

_____ 2. Atlanta

_____ 3. Chicago

_____ 4. Los Angeles and Wellington, New Zealand

_____ 5. New York, London, Hong Kong

_____ 6. Guadalajara and Shanghai

a. finance

b. sales

c. manufacturing

d. technology

e. automobile production

f. film production

 WHAT DO YOU THINK?

Discuss the questions in a group.

1. Do you agree with Richard Florida's opinion that people with similar personalities tend to live in certain cities? Why or why not?

2. Think about a city you know. What types of jobs and people is it known for? Does it fit Richard Florida's theory?

People move to cities for different reasons.

Literal language refers to words or phrases that mean exactly what they say. **Figurative** language refers to using language in a different way, using comparisons.

☐ The building was **crying out** to be painted.

The building is compared to a person complaining. It needed paint very badly.

☐ Ideas can **take off** in the right environment.

Ideas are compared to a bird or an airplane. Ideas can be free to develop.

CD 3
Track 5

Listen to this excerpt from Listening 1.

☐ These cities are **magnets** for people who are curious, but who may also like to work alone. The location may **spark** their innovation.

Magnets attract things made of iron. Cities are compared to magnets, but in this case, they attract people, not iron.

Spark means to set fire to, so the location is being compared to the cause of a fire—it starts their imaginations working.

Understanding figurative meaning will help you better understand television and radio, formal speeches, and everyday idioms.

A. Read the sentences in the box, in which the bold words are used with their literal meaning. Then compare the sentences below, in which the same words are used with a figurative meaning. Complete the comparisons that follow. Discuss your answers with a partner.

> Plants **grow** well in sunlight.
> Your **heart** beats, sending blood throughout your body.
> The rocket took off from the **launching pad** this morning.
> I planted some **seeds** a few weeks ago, and I already have flowers.

1. Tall apartment buildings **grow** from the hills surrounding the city.

    (Apartment buildings are compared to _____plants_____.)

2. Music is the **heart** of Nashville, Tennessee, so it attracts lots of

    musicians and music lovers. (Nashville, Tennessee, is compared to a(n)

    _____.)

3. Boston is known for its innovation in technology. The city is seen by many as a **launching pad** for new ideas in the field. (New ideas are compared to _____.)

4. The **seeds** of independence in Argentina were planted in Buenos Aires. (Independence is compared to _____.)

CD 3
Track 6 **B. Listen to the sentences. Complete each sentence with the word you hear. Then complete the comparison.**

1. My mother is the _____ of our family.

   A *family* is compared to a(n) _____.

2. I'm not sure what I am going to do, but I have the

   _____ of an idea.

   An *idea* is compared to a(n) _____.

3. The vending machine _____ all of my money.

   The *machine* is compared to a(n) _____.

4. I can't believe it's so late. The time just _____ by.

   Time is compared to a(n) _____.

LISTENING 2 | Buenos Aires, Beijing, and Dubai

VOCABULARY

Work with a partner. Here are some words from Listening 2. Circle the answer that best matches the meaning of each bold word.

1. **artificial** *(adj.)*	falsely	manufacture	(man-made)
2. **celebrate** *(v.)*	excellent	honor	success
3. **character** *(n.)*	behave	attractive	personality
4. **direct** *(adj.)*	truth	honest	communicate
5. **lively** *(adj.)*	interest	exciting	bore
6. **precise** *(adj.)*	exact	confusion	clarify

7.	**provide** (*v.*)	give	loss	equipped
8.	**reveal** (*v.*)	hidden	secretly	uncover
9.	**update** (*v.*)	revision	modernize	incorrect
10.	**value** (*n.*)	acceptable	belief	think

PREVIEW LISTENING 2

Buenos Aires, Beijing, and Dubai

You are going to listen to three writers give descriptions of cities they know well—Buenos Aires, Beijing, and Dubai. What do you know about these cities?

LISTEN FOR MAIN IDEAS

CD 3
Track 7

Listen to the descriptions of the three cities. Match the cities with their descriptions.

Buenos Aires

Beijing

Dubai

_____ _____ 1. Buenos Aires

_____ _____ 2. Beijing

_____ _____ 3. Dubai

a. a city where the people work for success

b. a city where an old village is near very modern buildings

c. a city of cultural innovation

d. a city of change, but where the character of the people remains the same

e. a city of music and art

f. a city where the maps are constantly changing

LISTEN FOR DETAILS

Read the sentences. Then listen again. Write *BA* (Buenos Aires), *B* (Beijing), or *D* (Dubai) next to each sentence.

_____ 1. Many musicians and writers come to this city.

_____ 2. This city has the tallest skyscraper in the world.

_____ 3. Fifteen million people live in this city.

_____ 4. The writer Jorge Luis Borges set his stories in this city.

_____ 5. The people are very direct and have strong opinions.

_____ 6. It's hard to walk through the city if you don't know your way.

_____ 7. The tango comes from this city.

_____ 8. There is a man-made island in this city.

WHAT DO YOU THINK?

Tip Critical Thinking

Question 1 of Activity A asks you to **relate** what you have learned to your own life. **Relating** information to your own experience makes the information more meaningful and helps you remember it.

A. Discuss the questions in a group.

1. Which of the three cities suits *your* personality the best? Explain your reasons.

2. Which city reminds you most of a place you have lived? Why?

B. Think about both Listening 1 and Listening 2 as you discuss the questions.

1. Do you think cities have particular characters or personalities? If so, do you think the people who live in a certain city share that city's personality?

2. Think about the statement, "The difference between cities is only on the surface. Underneath they are all the same." Do you agree or disagree? Give examples from Listening 1 and Listening 2 to support your opinion.

A **phrasal verb** is a combination of a verb and a **particle**. The particle can be either a preposition or an adverb. Phrasal verbs have a different meaning than the verb and particle do individually.

> I **looked into** the room, but couldn't see my friend.
> I don't know the answer to your question, but I'll **look into** it.

In the first sentence, *look* has its literal meaning: to *use your eyes to see*. The preposition *into* does not change the meaning of the verb.

In the second sentence, *look into* is a phrasal verb that means to *research* or *investigate*. The particle *into* changes the meaning of the verb.

A. Read the sentences. Circle the answer that best matches the meaning of each bold phrase. Then check (✓) the sentences that have phrasal verbs.

☐ 1. I **came to** San Francisco when I was twenty.
   a. arrived in
   b. woke up

☐ 2. I **came to** a few hours after the operation.
   a. arrived in
   b. woke up

☐ 3. Can you **bring up** some coffee?
   a. start talking about
   b. carry upstairs

☐ 4. Don't **bring up** that topic when you speak to Sandra. It upsets her.
   a. start talking about
   b. carry upstairs

☐ 5. Don't **go out**. It's raining.
   a. go outside
   b. do something social

☐ 6. Ann and I often **go out** on Friday nights.
   a. go outside
   b. do something social

☐ 7. I don't like to **deal with** student problems. I send them to the student counselor.
  a. trade with
  b. handle

☐ 8. The United States began to **deal with** China again in the 1970s, which was good for both economies.
  a. trade with
  b. handle

☐ 9. In the movie, the machine **turned into** a person.
  a. made a turn into
  b. became

☐ 10. After we **turned into** our driveway, we realized we had a flat tire.
  a. made a turn into
  b. became

B. Complete each sentence with a phrasal verb from Activity A.

1. The man in the accident was unconscious, but he

   _____ after a few minutes.

2. Tokyo and London are very exciting cities. They have many fun places

   where you can _____ and have a good time.

3. I have a question about the assignment that I want to

   _____ in class today.

4. I think some cities can _____ tourists better

   than others.

5. Now that the city is safer and cleaner, I think it will

   _____ a popular place for tourists to visit.

Phrasal verbs are made up of a **verb** and a **particle**. Some examples of particles are *in, out, off, up, over, away,* and *along*. Phrasal verbs can be categorized as **separable** or **inseparable**.

Separable phrasal verbs can be separated by noun objects. The noun object can go after the verb and the particle or between the verb and the particle.

> Please **hand in** your tests.
> Please **hand** your tests **in**.
> Call me after you **drop off** the kids.
> Call me after you **drop** the kids **off**.

Separable phrasal verbs must be separated when using object pronouns (*me, you, him, her, it, them*).

> ✓ When you've finished your assignments, please **hand** them **in**.
> ✗ When you've finished your assignments, please **hand in** them.

> ✓ If you don't know a word, you can **look** it **up** in a dictionary.
> ✗ If you don't know a word, you can **look up** it in the dictionary.

Here are some examples of separable phrasal verbs.

> drop off   hand in   point out   sum up
> find out   look up   put away   talk over

Inseparable phrasal verbs cannot be separated by noun or pronoun objects.

> ✓ The secretary **went over** her notes after the meeting.
> ✗ The secretary **went** her notes **over** after the meeting.

> ✓ The secretary **went over** them after the meeting.
> ✗ The secretary **went** them **over** after the meeting.

Here are some examples of inseparable phrasal verbs.

> call for   deal with   go over   look into
> call on   get over   look after   run into

A. Rewrite the sentences. Use object pronouns.

1. Have you looked up the train times yet?

   Have you looked them up yet?

2. We usually run into Tina at the gym.

   _____

3. Linda and Victor talked over their presentation idea before class.

   _____

4. Hong hasn't gotten over her cold yet.

   _____

5. Will you look after my cat while I'm in São Paulo?

   _____

6. I didn't put away the dishes after dinner.

   _____

B. Answer the questions. Use object pronouns when possible. Then take turns asking and answering the questions with a partner.

1. Where did you look up the meanings of new words?

   _____

2. Who did you hand in your homework to this week?

   _____

3. Who pointed out the difference between phrasal verbs and regular verbs?

   _____

4. When did you go over your homework?

   _____

5. Did you talk over Activity B with a partner?

   _____

CD 3
Track 9

When a word ends with a *consonant*, and the next word begins with a *vowel*, the consonant is **linked** to the following vowel without a pause. This is very common in phrasal verbs, since many particles begin with vowels.

Listen to the examples.

> Please **put away** your books.
>
> I hope you **get over** the flu soon.
>
> Can you **look after** my camera for a moment?
>
> Did you **find out** what happened?

Remember that some words, such as *come*, end in a silent *e*. The ending consonant sound is still linked to the vowel at the beginning of the next word.

> Can you **come over** this evening?

CD 3
Track 10

A. **Listen to the sentences. Then repeat them.**

1. Can you look after my apartment when I'm in Paris?

2. I'd like to bring up a topic for discussion.

3. I need to look up some information about Cape Town.

4. Would you point out my mistakes?

5. The plane is about to take off.

B. **Work with a partner. Practice asking and answering the questions. Remember to link the consonant to the vowel in the phrasal verbs.**

1. Do you put away the dishes in your home?

2. Who did you run into yesterday?

3. Did the teacher call on you today?

4. What is the fastest way to get over a cold?

5. Did you drop off your clothes at the dry cleaners?

Speakers often **recap**, or summarize, their main points at the end of a presentation. One way to recap or summarize is to use one final sentence to capture the main points of a presentation.

> To summarize, Vancouver is an interesting place to live.
> To recap, many cities have their own personalities.

Here are some words and phrases you can use to recap a presentation.

> In summary,   To summarize,
> To recap,   Basically,
> To sum up,

Recapping is a good way to make sure your listeners remember your main ideas.

 CD 3 Track 11

A. Listen to this presentation about the American city of Charlotte. Take notes using the T-chart.

Advantages	Disadvantages

B. Work with a partner. Take turns summarizing the advantages and disadvantages according to your T-chart.

CD 3 Track 12

C. Now listen to a summary of the presentation. Check (✓) the information in your chart that you hear in the summary. Add any information you missed.

In this assignment, you are going to give a short presentation about a city you know and recap your ideas at the end. As you prepare your presentation think about the Unit Question, "What do our cities say about us?" and refer to the Self-Assessment checklist on page 164.

For alternative unit assignments, see the *Q: Skills for Success Teacher's Handbook*.

CONSIDER THE IDEAS

Look at the list of things you might consider when choosing where to live. Circle the three things that are most important to you. Then discuss your answers and reasons with a partner.

attractions (museums, famous places, etc.)	parks and green space
buildings/architecture	restaurants
city's personality	shopping
entertainment (art, music, sports)	transportation
location	type of business/work

PREPARE AND SPEAK

A. **GATHER IDEAS** Choose a city you know, and brainstorm a list of things you like and don't like about it. Write your notes in the T-chart.

City: _____

I like	I don't like
the location	the traffic

B. **ORGANIZE IDEAS** Choose your best ideas from Activity A. Then complete the outline. Give reasons for your opinions.

City: _____

I like:

1. _The location_____ because ____it's near the beach and____

_I love to swim._____

2. _____ because _____

_____

3. _____ because _____

_____

I don't like:

1. _____ because _____

_____

2. _____ because _____

_____

3. _____ because _____

_____

Tip for Success

Pause slightly after you finish your presentation and before you begin your recap. This is a helpful signal for your audience.

Recap/Summary:

_____

_____

C. **SPEAK** Present your ideas about the city to your classmates. Use your ideas from Activity B, but do not read directly from it. Refer to the Self-Assessment checklist on page 164 before you begin.

CHECK AND REFLECT

A. CHECK Think about the Unit Assignment as you complete the Self-Assessment checklist.

SELF-ASSESSMENT		
Yes	No	
☐	☐	I was able to speak easily about the topic.
☐	☐	My classmates understood me.
☐	☐	I used vocabulary from the unit.
☐	☐	I used phrasal verbs.
☐	☐	I linked consonants and vowels when speaking.
☐	☐	I recapped the main ideas of my presentation.

B. REFLECT Discuss these questions with a partner.

What is something new you learned in this unit?

 Look back at the Unit Question. Is your answer different now than when you started this unit? If yes, how is it different? Why?

Track Your Success

Circle the words and phrases you learned in this unit.

Nouns
character 🔑
innovation AWL
region 🔑 AWL
surroundings 🔑
value 🔑

Verbs
attract 🔑
celebrate 🔑
provide 🔑
reveal 🔑 AWL
satisfy 🔑
update

Adjectives
agreeable
artificial 🔑
conscientious
direct

lively 🔑
mobile 🔑
precise 🔑 AWL

Phrasal Verbs
bring up
call for
call on
come over
come to
cry out for
deal with
drop off
find out
get over
go out
go over
hand in

look after
look into
look up
point out
put away
run into
sum up
take off
talk over
turn into

Phrases
hand in hand
In summary,
tend to
To recap,
To sum up,
To summarize,

🔑 Oxford 3000™ words
AWL Academic Word List

Check (✓) the skills you learned. If you need more work on a skill, refer to the page(s) in parentheses.

LISTENING ⚪	I can understand figurative meaning. (p. 152)
VOCABULARY ⚪	I can use phrasal verbs. (p. 156)
GRAMMAR ⚪	I can use separable and inseparable phrasal verbs. (p. 158)
PRONUNCIATION ⚪	I can link consonants and vowels. (p. 160)
SPEAKING ⚪	I can recap a presentation. (p. 161)
LEARNING OUTCOME ⚪	I can give and recap a presentation highlighting what I like and dislike about a particular city.

LISTENING	listening for signposts
VOCABULARY	using the dictionary
GRAMMAR	types of sentences
PRONUNCIATION	intonation in different types of sentences
SPEAKING	agreeing and disagreeing

LEARNING OUTCOME

Participate in a group discussion evaluating the influence money has on happiness.

Unit QUESTION

Can money buy happiness?

PREVIEW THE UNIT

A Discuss these questions with your classmates.

How much money do you think people really need to be happy? Explain.

Do you think more money would make you happier? Why or why not?

Look at the photo. Do you think the people living in this house are happy? Why or why not?

B Discuss the Unit Question above with your classmates.

Listen to *The Q Classroom*, Track 13 on CD 3, to hear other answers.

167

C Complete the questionnaire.

One Million Dollars

Imagine someone gives you one million dollars. Rank the following expenses in order of their importance to you, from 1 (most important) to 10 (least important).

☐ more education

☐ a new car

☐ a new house

☐ new clothes

☐ travel

☐ giving money to charity

☐ helping friends or family

☐ a flat-screen TV

☐ a vacation home

☐ paying off debt

D Now compare your answers with a partner. Discuss the similarities and differences in your choices.

E Write the three things that make you the happiest. Then compare this list with the three things you chose in the questionnaire in Activity C. With your partner, discuss which list of things makes you happier and why.

_____

_____

_____

LISTENING 1 | Sudden Wealth

VOCABULARY

Here are some words and phrases from Listening 1. Read the definitions. Then complete the paragraphs below with the correct word or phrase.

> **acquire** *(v.)* to get or obtain something
>
> **circumstances** *(n.)* the facts that are true in a particular situation
>
> **complicated** *(adj.)* difficult to understand
>
> **destructive** *(adj.)* causing a lot of harm or damage
>
> **dramatic** *(adj.)* very significant
>
> **get used to** *(phr.)* to become familiar with
>
> **immediate** *(adj.)* happening or done without delay
>
> **inherit** *(v.)* to receive property or money from someone who has died
>
> **pleasure** *(n.)* a feeling of being happy or enjoying something
>
> **wear off** *(phr. v.)* to go away a little at a time

A Lucky Winner?

William "Bud" Post never believed he would _____ millions of dollars by chance, but in 1988 he suddenly received $16.2 million. He didn't _____ the money from a relative; he won it. He told reporters that at the time he had only $2.46 in his bank account. Bud's sudden wealth brought him a lot of _____ because he could buy whatever he wanted. But this _____ improvement did not last long. He started to change his life in significant ways. These _____ changes were hard for Bud to deal with because everything in his life became so different. Within three months, Bud was $500,000 in debt after buying a restaurant, a used-car lot, and an airplane. His _____ had changed, but he still had trouble managing his money.

Over the next eight years, many things started happening that Bud didn't understand. His life, which once seemed simple, was becoming more and more _____ . The effects of his wealth soon became

7

_____ as he increased his debt and damaged many of his

8

relationships with friends and family members. Like many people who

_____ spending a lot of money, Bud couldn't stop even after

9

he had lost so much of it. He continued to buy houses, cars, motorcycles, and boats. The good feeling he got from spending money started to

_____ as time passed. Bud told people later that he was

10

happier before he got the money.

PREVIEW LISTENING 1

| Sudden Wealth

You are going to listen to a podcast that helps people learn to handle their money wisely. The article discusses people who suddenly become rich and the difficulties they face.

Which topics do you think the article will discuss? Check (✓) your ideas.

☐ how sudden wealth makes people happy
☐ how sudden wealth causes problems
☐ the advantages and disadvantages of sudden wealth

LISTEN FOR MAIN IDEAS

CD 3
Track 14

Read the statements. Then listen to the article. Write _T_ (true) or _F_ (false).

_____ 1. At first, acquiring a lot of money has a positive effect on our brains.

_____ 2. For most people, acquiring sudden wealth increases happiness.

Tip for Success

A question and answer early in a talk often indicates the speaker's main topic.

_____ 3. Sudden wealth can cause many different problems.

_____ 4. People can feel more alone after they become suddenly wealthy.

_____ 5. Inheriting money is easy to deal with.

_____ 6. Getting rich suddenly often reduces stress.

LISTEN FOR DETAILS

Listen again. Write two examples for each main point. Compare your ideas with a partner.

Effect on our brains

1. _____

2. _____

Effect on relationships

1. _____

2. _____

Effect on emotions

1. _____

2. _____

 ## WHAT DO YOU THINK?

Discuss the questions in a group.

1. Which of the effects mentioned in Listening 1 do you think are the most difficult to deal with? Why?

2. Has sudden money made anyone you know about happier or unhappier? Explain.

3. Under what circumstances do you think money could make someone happier?

Signposts are words and phrases that can tell you the order in which things happened. Listen for signposts to help you follow the order of events and the logic in a text.

CD 3
Track 16

Listen to these examples of signposts from Listening 1.

> **First**, it affects how our brains work, at least for a while.
> **In the beginning**, when we get the money, our brain identifies it as pleasure.
> **Then** that feeling wears off.

Here are some words and phrases which are used as signposts.

At the start	In the middle	At the end
At first,	After (that),	Finally,
First,	Before (that),	In conclusion,
In the beginning,	Later,	In summary,
	Next,	
	Second,	
	Then,	

CD 3
Track 17

A. Listen to a reporter interview a secretary who suddenly acquired a lot of money. Complete the interview with the signposts you hear.

Reporter: You are one of many people in this town who suddenly acquired a lot of wealth when your company was purchased by a large software company. How has that affected your life?

Laura Green: Well, _____ it was pretty incredible. It took a
1
while for me to believe it. But _____ I began to realize what
2
it could actually do to my life. Things have changed dramatically.

Reporter: In what way?

Laura: I paid off all of my credit card debt. And sent my son to college. Receiving this money was just fantastic! _____, I was
3
worried all the time.

Reporter: So your financial circumstances have improved. What else has changed?

Laura: You know, I was a secretary at that company for 20 years. I had gotten used to just working to pay the bills. I always wished I could do more with my life. _____ I can do that.

4

Reporter: And what do you want to do?

Laura: _____, I'm going to go to Paris. I've always dreamed of

5
going there. _____, I'm thinking of going back to school. I'd

6
like to study gardening. I love flowers. _____, maybe I will

7
open my own business.

Reporter: We hear stories in the news all the time about people who get a lot of money suddenly and have many problems. How do you think those problems can be avoided?

Laura: It's about staying true to your values and remembering what's really important in life. You don't need to let money complicate things.

B. Answer the questions using signposts and complete sentences. Then take turns asking and answering the questions with a partner.

1. What did Laura do before she received the money?

   Before that, she worked as a secretary.

2. How did Laura feel about the money in the beginning?

   _____

3. What is one of the first things she did with the money?

   _____

4. What did she do after that?

   _____

5. What is Laura going to do in the immediate future?

   _____

6. What will she do next?

   _____

VOCABULARY

Here are some words and phrases from Listening 2. Read the sentences.
Then write each bold word or phrase next to the correct definition.

1. The **analysis** of the research shows that money doesn't make people happier.

2. Sudden wealth is **associated with** stress. Many people who become rich quickly experience a lot of stress.

3. I have been working too much lately. I'm afraid I'm going to **burn out**.

4. The researchers are going to **conduct** a study on money and happiness. The study will involve fifty people.

5. Mia likes a job with **independence**. She doesn't like someone telling her what to do.

6. Researchers used the results of their study to **demonstrate** that more money does not make people happier.

7. One **outcome** of sudden wealth is a change in relationships. Others include stress and loneliness.

8. The salesman was very **persuasive**. I bought the first car he showed me!

9. I'm **somewhat** unhappy at work, but not so much that I plan to quit my job.

10. I was **wholly** to blame for the argument. You did nothing wrong.

a. _____ *(n.)* the state of being free and not controlled by another person

b. _____ *(adv.)* completely; fully

c. _____ *(v.)* to show clearly that something exists or is true; to prove something

d. _____ *(n.)* the careful examination of something

e. _____ *(phr. v.)* to become very tired through overwork

f. _____ *(v.)* to do, carry out, or organize something

g. _____ *(adj. + prep.)* connected to; involved with

h. _____ (n.) a result or effect of an action or event

i. _____ (adj.) able to make someone do or believe something

j. _____ (adv.) a little

Sonja Lyubomirsky

PREVIEW LISTENING 2

Happiness Breeds Success…and Money!

You are going to listen to an interview with Sonja Lyubomirsky, a psychologist who does research on happiness. She is going to talk about the relationship between money and happiness.

What do you think she will say about the relationship between money and happiness? Check (✓) your ideas.

☐ Money can buy happiness.

☐ Happiness can lead to money.

☐ There is no relationship between money and happiness.

LISTEN FOR MAIN IDEAS

 CD 3
Track 18

Listen to the interview. Circle the answer that best completes each statement.

1. Lyubomirsky expected that happiness would be connected to _____.
   a. money
   b. personal relationships
   c. work

2. The factor that is most associated with happiness is _____
   a. money
   b. personal relationships
   c. work

3. Lyubomirsky says that greater happiness leads to more _____.
   a. relaxation
   b. financial success
   c. love

4. According to Lyubomirsky, how happy we are at work depends on _____.
   a. the type of job we do
   b. how old we are
   c. who we work with

5. Lyubomirsky believes that money, happiness, and a good work environment are _____.

   a. difficult to achieve

   b. what everybody wants

   c. all connected

LISTEN FOR DETAILS

CD 3
Track 19

Read the statements. Then listen again. Write *T* (true) or *F* (false).

____ 1. Lyubomirsky and her colleagues looked at the research from 300 studies.

____ 2. Lyubomirsky has changed her ideas about what makes us happy.

____ 3. Our jobs have more of an effect on happiness than our personal relationships do.

____ 4. Happy people take fewer sick days than unhappy people.

____ 5. People who are happy when they are young will have lower salaries when they are older.

____ 6. Jobs that are creative and productive make people happier than jobs that are boring.

WHAT DO YOU THINK?

A. Discuss the questions in a group.

1. Which do you think comes first, happiness or money? Explain.

2. What qualities of a happy person do you think lead to better employment and financial outcomes?

Tip Critical Thinking

Question 1 of Activity B asks you to **choose** between two things. To make the best choice, you evaluate a variety of factors, including your knowledge and experience.

B. Think about both Listening 1 and Listening 2 as you discuss the questions.

1. What is the difference between sudden wealth and earning more money from a better job? Which would you prefer? Why?

2. Do you pay much attention to financial matters? Do you enjoy thinking about money, or does it make you feel stressed? Explain.

Definitions of similar words

Some words are similar in meaning, for instance, *creativity* and *productivity*.

> People in jobs where they can show creativity and productivity are happier than those who aren't.

Creativity and *productivity* both have to do with making things, but they are also a little different. Look at their dictionary definitions.

> **cre·a·tiv·i·ty** [AWL] /ˌkrieɪˈtɪvəti/ *noun* [U] the ability to make or produce new things, especially using skill or imagination: *teaching that encourages children's creativity*

> **pro·duc·tiv·i·ty** /ˌprɑdʌkˈtɪvəti; ˌproʊ-/ *noun* [U] the rate at which a worker, a company, or a country produces goods, and the amount produced: *More efficient methods will lead to greater productivity.*

When dealing with similar words, use a dictionary to decide which word is better to use in a particular context.

All dictionary entries are from the *Oxford American Dictionary for learners of English* © Oxford University Press 2011.

A. Use your dictionary to compare the definitions of these pairs of words. Then match each word with its definition.

1. ___ financial   ___ economical
   a. not costing much money, time, or fuel
   b. connected with money
   c. having a great deal of money

2. ___ fun   ___ amusement
   a. pleasure and enjoyment
   b. hopefulness about the future
   c. a feeling caused by something that makes you laugh

3. ___ sudden   ___ immediate
   a. at high speed
   b. happening or done without delay
   c. happening quickly or when you don't expect it

B. Complete each sentence with the correct word from Activity A.

1. I think the car that uses less gas is the more _____ choice.

2. You can get advice from an accountant about _____ issues.

3. If you need _____ help, go to the emergency room of the hospital.

4. Some think that you can only find _____ in your relationships with people, but you can also find it through work.

5. We all thought Lisa liked her job, so her _____ decision to leave was a big surprise.

6. John and Tom had a lot of _____ playing soccer with their new neighbors.

C. Choose five words from Activity B. Write a sentence using each word. Then read your sentences aloud to a partner.

_____

_____

_____

_____

_____

Grammar | Types of sentences

In English, there are four main sentence types in normal speech.

Declarative sentence (a statement):	I am trying to save money.
Interrogative sentence (a question):	How do you save money?
Imperative sentence (a direction or command):	Save your money.
Exclamatory sentence (an exclamation):	I saved so much money!

Punctuation at the end of sentences

Use periods with declarative sentences, question marks with interrogative sentences, and exclamation marks with exclamatory sentences.

Imperative sentences can end with either a period or an exclamation mark. An exclamation mark shows more emotion.

A. Read the conversation. Write the sentence type (declarative, interrogative, imperative, exclamatory) next to each sentence. Then practice the conversation with a partner.

_____ 1. **Hong:** There are so many cars here!

_____ 2. **Nan:** Yeah, I know. It's hard to believe we can finally afford a new one.

_____ 3. **Hong:** I just wish we had gotten the money a different way than we did.

_____ 4. **Nan:** Me, too. I didn't even know your uncle very well.

_____ 5. **Hong:** Didn't you meet him at the wedding?

_____ 6. **Nan:** Yes, but I only had a short conversation with him.

_____ 7. **Hong:** I had no idea that he was going to leave us so much money.

_____ 8. **Nan:** Speaking of money, hold my purse for a minute. I can't find my wallet!

B. Work with a partner. Read the situations below. Choose one situation and write a short conversation. Include each of the four sentence types at least once. Then practice your conversation with your partner.

1. Two friends are arguing. One friend wants to borrow a large amount of money from the other, who does not want to loan it.

2. A person is telling a family member that she or he just got a new job with a much higher salary. Both are very excited.

3. A married couple is discussing what to do with a large amount of money they just inherited. One person wants to save it; the other wants to spend it.

Pronunciation | **Intonation in different types of sentences**

Intonation varies according to **sentence type**. Learning intonation patterns can help you understand if a speaker is asking a question, giving a command, or making a statement.

Declarative and imperative sentences:

Declarative and imperative sentences have a falling intonation.

I am going to purchase a new home.

Please give me some advice.

Exclamatory sentences:

Exclamatory sentences have a rise-fall intonation.

This is fun!

Interrogative sentences:

Remember that interrogative sentences or questions have two intonation patterns. *Yes/no* questions have a rising intonation pattern.

Are you coming with me?

Wh- questions have a falling intonation pattern.

Why did you leave?

A. Listen to the sentences. Check (✓) the type of sentence for each according to the intonation you hear.

1. a. ☐ statement ☐ *yes/no* question
   b. ☐ statement ☐ *yes/no* question

2. a. ☐ command ☐ *wh-* question
   b. ☐ command ☐ *wh-* question

3. a. ☐ statement ☐ exclamation
   b. ☐ statement ☐ exclamation

B. Listen again. Repeat the sentences using the same intonation that you hear.

Speaking Skill | Agreeing and disagreeing

There are certain phrases used for **agreeing and disagreeing**. It's important to know which phrases and expressions are appropriate for formal and informal situations. An informal conversation is very different from a formal discussion at college or at work.

Here are some phrases you can use when you want to agree or disagree in different situations.

Agreeing		Disagreeing
I agree (completely).	formal	I disagree.
That's exactly what I think.		I don't agree (at all).
That's a good point.		Sorry, but that's not my opinion.
That's right.		I don't feel the same way.
I think so too.		I don't think so.
Absolutely!		No way!
Yeah, I know!	informal	Oh, come on!

A. Listen to the conversations. Complete each conversation with the phrases you hear.

Ellie: What are you going to do with the money your grandfather gave you?

Sam: I'm not sure. I think I'm going to take an expensive vacation.

Ellie: Really? Don't you have a lot of school loans to pay?

Sam: _____. Maybe the vacation's not such a good idea.
                    1

Ellie: _____. Vacations are fun, but it's much more important
                    2
to pay off your debt.

Monica: I think raising the average income in countries around the world is

the best way to increase the level of happiness.

Patricia: I _____. More money might make the very poor
                       3

happier, but not everyone.

Monica: I _____. I think everyone except perhaps the very
                     4

wealthy will benefit from a higher income.

Patricia: Well, I can see we'll just have to agree to disagree.

Unit Assignment **Take part in a group discussion**

 In this assignment, you are going to take part in a group discussion about money and happiness. As you prepare for the discussion, think about the Unit Question, "Can money buy happiness?" and refer to the Self-Assessment checklist on page 184.

For alternative unit assignments, see the *Q: Skills for Success Teacher's Handbook.*

CONSIDER THE IDEAS

Work with a partner. Discuss the questions about money and happiness. Be sure to use the correct intonation when you ask each other questions.

What is money's influence on happiness?

What kind of person do you think would be happier with more money? Why?

Would your life be different if you had more or less money? How?

Is it more enjoyable to give or receive money? Why?

PREPARE AND SPEAK

Tip for Success

When disagreeing with someone, you can sound more polite by starting with *I know what you mean, but…* or *I see your point, but…*

A. **GATHER IDEAS** Take notes on your discussion with your partner. Use these questions to guide you.

1. What were the main points of your discussion?

   _____

   _____

   _____

2. What did you agree on?

   _____

   _____

   _____

3. What did you disagree on?

   _____

   _____

   _____

B. **ORGANIZE IDEAS** Choose one question from the Consider the Ideas activity. Use the outline to help you prepare for a group discussion. Do not write exactly what you are going to say. Just write notes to help you organize your ideas.

Question: _____

Ideas that I agree with:

_____

_____

_____

Ideas that I disagree with:

_____

_____

_____

My answer to the question:

_____

_____

Reasons for my answer:

_____

_____

_____

Examples:

_____

_____

C. **SPEAK** Work in a group. Take turns presenting your ideas on the questions you chose in Activity B. Refer to the Self-Assessment checklist below before you begin.

CHECK AND REFLECT

A. **CHECK** Think about the Unit Assignment as you complete the Self-Assessment checklist.

SELF-ASSESSMENT		
Yes	No	
☐	☐	I was able to speak easily about the topic.
☐	☐	My group understood me.
☐	☐	I used vocabulary from the unit.
☐	☐	I used different types of sentences when speaking.
☐	☐	I used different intonation patterns.
☐	☐	I used phrases to agree and disagree.

B. **REFLECT** Discuss these questions with a partner.

What is something new you learned in this unit?

 Look back at the Unit Question. Is your answer different now than when you started this unit? If yes, how is it different? Why?

Circle the words and phrases you learned in this unit.

Nouns
analysis 🔑 AWL
circumstances 🔑 AWL
independence 🔑
outcome AWL
pleasure 🔑

Verbs
acquire 🔑 AWL
associated (with) 🔑
conduct 🔑 AWL
demonstrate 🔑 AWL
inherit

Adjectives
complicated 🔑
destructive
dramatic 🔑 AWL
immediate 🔑
persuasive

Adverbs
Absolutely!
Finally, 🔑 AWL
First, 🔑
Later, 🔑
Next, 🔑
Second, 🔑
somewhat 🔑 AWL
Then, 🔑
wholly

Phrasal Verbs
burn out
wear off

Phrases
After (that),
At first,

Before (that),
get used to
I agree (completely).
I disagree.
I don't agree (at all).
I don't feel the same way.
I don't think so.
I think so too.
In conclusion,
In summary,
In the beginning,
No way!
Oh, come on!
Sorry, but that's not my opinion.
That's a good point.
That's exactly what I think.
That's right.
Yeah, I know!

🔑 Oxford 3000™ words
AWL Academic Word List

Check (✓) the skills you learned. If you need more work on a skill, refer to the page(s) in parentheses.

LISTENING	○	I can listen for signposts. (p. 172)
VOCABULARY	○	I can use the dictionary to find the definition of similar words. (p. 178)
GRAMMAR	○	I can use different types of sentences. (p. 180)
PRONUNCIATION	○	I can use correct intonation in different sentence types. (p. 181)
SPEAKING	○	I can use phrases for agreeing and disagreeing. (p. 181)
LEARNING OUTCOME	●	I can participate in a group discussion evaluating the influence money has on happiness.

UNIT

10

Keeping in Touch

LISTENING	recognizing and understanding definitions
VOCABULARY	idioms
GRAMMAR	comparatives
PRONUNCIATION	unstressed connecting words
SPEAKING	expressing emotions

Role-play a phone call discussing an emotional event you have experienced.

Unit QUESTION

Do we need technology to communicate long distance?

PREVIEW THE UNIT

(A) **Discuss these questions with your classmates.**

What methods of communication do you use regularly and why?

Does the method of communication you use depend on the person? On the situation? Explain your reasons.

Look at the photo. Do you think this is a good way to communicate? Why or why not?

(B) **Discuss the Unit Question above with your classmates.**

Listen to *The Q Classroom*, Track 23 on CD 3, to hear other answers.

C Look at the different methods of communication in the chart. Then write the advantages and disadvantages of each.

Method of Communication	Advantages	Disadvantages
Body language or gestures		
Talking on the telephone		
Writing emails		
Writing letters		
Texting		
Using social networking websites		

D Discuss your answers from Activity C in a group. Do you agree on the advantages and disadvantages?

LISTENING 1 | An Unusual Language

VOCABULARY

Here are some words from Listening 1. Read the sentences. Circle the answer that best matches the meaning of each bold word.

1. Although it is very short, this guide to communicating online **adequately** covers all the basic skills you might need. I found it quite useful.
   a. well enough
   b. in detail
   c. too quickly

2. In many cities, buildings are very tall because of space **constraints**. There isn't enough land to build wide, flat houses.
   a. limits
   b. regulations
   c. preferences

3. Sorry I didn't call. The cell phone **coverage** up in the mountains wasn't good.
   a. design quality
   b. customer support
   c. service

4. Sending text messages over the phone is a very **efficient** way to communicate. I think it's faster and easier than calling.
   a. professional
   b. effective
   c. slow

5. You can **interpret** the painting of the Mona Lisa in different ways, because the reason she is smiling is unclear.
   a. believe
   b. argue
   c. understand

6. The **landscape** in the western part of United States is very dry and mountainous.
   a. summer weather
   b. physical environment
   c. highway system

7. My new computer can **process** information faster than my old one could.
   a. handle
   b. understand
   c. remember

8. For my vacation this year, I want to go to a **remote** island and relax on the beach. I really need to get away from all of the noise and stress.
   a. distant
   b. popular
   c. beautiful

9. The ability to speak a second language well **requires** practice. You have to speak a little every day.
   a. needs
   b. allows
   c. wants

10. The piano can be bright and lively, but if you press the soft pedal, it produces a much gentler **tone**.
    a. song
    b. touch
    c. sound

communicating in Silbo

PREVIEW LISTENING 1

An Unusual Language

You are going to listen to a lecture on Silbo. Silbo is a special language used in the Canary Islands, which are off the coast of North Africa.

How do you think Silbo might be different from other languages?

LISTEN FOR MAIN IDEAS

CD 3
Track 24

Listen to the lecture. Circle the answer that best completes each statement.

1. Silbo is a language that uses _____ to communicate.
   a. spoken words
   b. hand signs
   c. whistling

Tip for Success

When you are listening to a lecture, pay attention to questions the speaker asks. A question often introduces a change in topic.

2. It was brought to the Canary Islands by _____ several hundred years ago.
   a. Africans
   b. Spaniards
   c. birds

3. Silbo developed because the island has many _____ that cause communication problems.
   a. native languages
   b. hills and valleys
   c. weather conditions

4. The professor says that conversations in Silbo _____.
   a. have to be simple
   b. are usually short
   c. are just like ordinary conversations

5. People who use Silbo process the whistling and ordinary speech in _____ of the brain.
   a. the same part
   b. two different parts
   c. a similar part

LISTEN FOR DETAILS

CD 3
Track 25

Listen again. Check (✓) the characteristics you hear.

____ 1. It is a spoken language.

____ 2. It consists of whistles that can make words.

____ 3. It has many different accents.

____ 4. It is the only language used in the Canary Islands.

____ 5. It is taught in schools.

____ 6. It can be used to express complex sentences.

____ 7. It has vowels and consonants.

____ 8. People use only their mouths to make the whistling noises.

 **WHAT DO YOU THINK?**

Discuss the questions in a group.

1. Is it important to save languages like Silbo from dying out? Why or why not?

2. What disadvantages do you think there might be in using Silbo to communicate instead of a language that uses words?

3. What languages can you speak? What are some advantages of speaking more than one language?

| Listening Skill | Recognizing and understanding definitions | |

 CD 3
Track 26

The definition of an unfamiliar word or phrase often comes immediately after it. When you hear an unfamiliar word, listen carefully for a pause, which often introduces a definition. Recognizing when a speaker is going to give a definition can help you learn new words and better understand the information you hear.

Listen to this excerpt from the professor's lecture and notice the definition.

> The language is named Silbo, after the Spanish word *silbar*, **which means** "to whistle," and it is used in the Canary Islands.

Listen for these words and phrases which can introduce definitions.

> or
> that is (i.e.),
> which means
> in other words,
>
> Our brains are hard-wired to use speech. **In other words**, the ability to use speech is built into our brains. (*Hard-wired* means that an ability is built in.)
>
> Some problems are solved and others created by the proliferation of social networking sites, **that is**, the rapid increase in social networking sites. (*Proliferation* means "rapid increase.")

CD 3
Track 27

A. Listen to the sentences. Write the definitions you hear.

1. phonetic system: _____

2. gestures: _____

3. syntax: _____

4. Braille: _____

B. Choose three vocabulary words from the Listening 1 vocabulary on pages 189–190. Write a sentence with each word in context. Include a definition in each sentence.

Our brains can interpret, or understand, whistling as speech.

1. _____

2. _____

3. _____

C. Work with a partner. Take turns reading your sentences and asking questions to confirm the definitions.

A: Our brains can interpret, or understand, whistling as speech.

B: So interpret means "understand?"

VOCABULARY

Here are some words and phrases from Listening 2. Read the paragraphs. Then write each bold word or phrase next to the correct definition.

Twenty-One Years Later

In 2008, a man named Merle Brandell was walking along a beach when, **out of the blue**, he noticed an old glass bottle at the water's edge. It looked almost **ancient** because so much dirt had **built up** on the outside. He could see there was something written on a piece of paper inside. Merle opened the bottle and read the message. It came from an elementary school student in Seattle, Washington. The fact that the letter had traveled 1,735 miles without any **assistance** from the U.S. Postal Service is unusual, but that's only part of the story.

Emily Hwaung had put the message in a soda bottle in 1987. Emily was a fourth-grade student at a school in Seattle at the time, and her class was doing a project to **observe** the ocean currents. The idea was to put messages in **sealed** bottles, throw them into the ocean, and see where the replies came from. Unfortunately, the students didn't receive many replies to their messages, and Emily's teacher soon realized her project was **fighting an uphill battle**.

For Emily, the communication had been completely **one-sided** for 21 years, but when Merle found her message, he decided to get in touch. Emily was very surprised that someone had finally found her bottle, and Merle was happy to locate the sender of the message, but they did not become **pen pals**. They were just pleased to have completed the communication. After such a long wait, Emily may have **sympathy** for all the other people who put messages in bottles and hope for an answer.

1. _____ (n.) a person you become friendly with by exchanging letters

2. _____ (adj.) very old; connected with the distant past

3. _____ (n.) an understanding of other people's feelings, especially their problems

4. _____ (idiom) unexpectedly

5. _____ (v.) to collect or form

6. _____ (v.) to notice or watch someone or something carefully

7. _____ (adj.) tightly closed

8. _____ (n.) aid; help

9. _____ (adj.) one way; in one direction only

10. _____ (idiom) to struggle in difficult circumstances

PREVIEW LISTENING 2

Message in a Bottle

You are going to listen to a report about how children in two different schools use different forms of communication to stay in touch.

How do you think the children communicate with each other? Check (✓) your ideas.

- ☐ through email
- ☐ through social networking sites
- ☐ by writing letters
- ☐ on the telephone

LISTEN FOR MAIN IDEAS

 CD 3 Track 28

Read the statements. Then listen to the report. Write *T* (true) or *F* (false).

____ 1. The two groups of students are now pen pals.

____ 2. A student found a message in a bottle.

____ 3. The students from the two schools communicate by sending letters.

____ 4. The first messages put in the bottle were thank-you notes.

____ 5. The students have learned a lot about friendship.

LISTEN FOR DETAILS

CD 3 Track 29

Read the questions. Then listen again. Circle the correct answer.

1. Who wrote the messages in the bottle found in Virginia?
   a. a sick teacher
   b. a woman who worked at a school
   c. some students

2. What happened to the messages?
   a. No one could read them.
   b. Second graders read them.
   c. Meteorologists found them.

3. Why did students write the messages in a bottle?
   a. Their teacher was sick.
   b. They wanted to meet other students.
   c. They wanted to follow weather patterns.

4. Where do the pen pals live?
   a. in Virginia and New York
   b. in Virginia and North Carolina
   c. in North Carolina and Maine

5. How far did the messages in the bottle travel?
   a. 100 miles
   b. more than 200 miles
   c. more than 1,000 miles

 ## WHAT DO YOU THINK?

A. Discuss the questions in a group.

1. Why do you think people put messages in bottles when there is so little chance of receiving a reply?

2. Have you ever had a pen pal? If so, how did you become pen pals? How often did you write each other?

B. Think about both Listening 1 and Listening 2 as you discuss the questions.

1. Why do you think forms of communication like Silbo, messages in bottles, and becoming pen pals developed?

2. Many people don't write letters these days, because they prefer to use email or social networking sites. How do you think this is affecting language and communication?

Idioms are phrases that have a different meaning than the literal meanings of the individual words. Look at these examples from Listening 2.

> **Out of the blue**, Pauline found a plastic bottle.

Out of the blue means "unexpectedly." For example, storms from a clear blue sky are unexpected.

> Communicating with a new friend from another state **is a snap** these days, thanks to the Internet and e-mail.

To *be a snap* means "to be really easy." For example, making a *snapping* noise with your fingers is really easy.

Learning idioms is an important way to increase your vocabulary. English speakers use them often. As you become more familiar with idioms, you will be able to understand conversations, television programs, radio broadcasts, and movies better.

A. **Work with a partner. Read the sentences. Then match each bold phrase with the correct definition.**

____ 1. I hope you have a great summer. **Drop me a line** sometime and tell me how you are doing.

____ 2. Mark seems very upset. I think he has something he needs to **get off his chest**.

____ 3. **Off the top of my head**, I don't have any ideas about what we should do.

____ 4. Sometimes I can't **hold my tongue**. I always want to say what I'm feeling.

____ 5. I'm **all ears**. How did your conversation with Professor Elliot go? I want to hear every detail!

a. listening carefully

b. without thinking first

c. to keep quiet; not to say anything

d. to talk about a problem

e. to write someone a letter

Tip for Success

If you know all the words in a phrase, but still don't understand the meaning, the phrase might be an idiom. Idioms have to be learned by experience.

B. Complete the conversations with the idioms from Activity A. Then practice the conversations with a partner.

1. **A:** I have to do a report. Where can I find out about languages that are dying out?

    B: Hmm. I don't know _____ but we can look online.

2. **A:** I can't _____ anymore. I just have to say something.

    B: That's probably not a good idea. I think you should keep quiet.

3. **A:** I can't wait for my vacation. I've never been to Australia.

    B: Oh, you'll have a great time. _____ when you can, so I know how your trip is going.

4. **A:** I have something really interesting to tell you.

    B: What is it? I'm _____ .

5. **A:** Listen, I've got something I've got to _____ . I'm really upset about it.

    B: What is it? Tell me what's wrong.

Uluru, Australia

SPEAKING

Grammar | Comparatives

Comparatives *(faster than, more intelligent than, busier than, less interesting than, not as interesting as)* are used to describe the differences between two people, things, or ideas.

There are several ways you can describe the differences between two things.

Use **adjective + –er + than** with one-syllable adjectives and two-syllable adjectives ending in –*y*.

> Sending an email is **easier than** writing a letter.
> Texting is **faster than** making a phone call.

Use **more + adjective + than** with adjectives that have two or more syllables.

> I think math is **more difficult than** history.
> This recipe for banana bread is **more complicated than** my mother's.

Use **less + adjective + than** with adjectives that have two or more syllables.

> Sending a text message is **less expensive than** making a phone call.
> Silver is **less expensive than** gold.

Use **not as + adjective + as** with any adjective.

> Usually, text messages are **not as long as** emails.
> Sending a text message is **not as expensive as** making a phone call.

To describe two things that are equal or similar, use **as + adjective + as** with any adjective.

> The cell phone coverage around here is **as good as** anywhere in the country.
> Some Silbo sentences can be **as complex as** normal speech.

Remember that some adjectives are irregular.

> good   better   best
> bad   worse   worst
> far   farther   farthest

A. Write two comparative sentences for each topic. Use the adjective in parentheses. Both sentences should have the same meaning.

text messages/letters (formal)

Text messages are not as formal as letters.

Letters are more formal than text messages.

1. making a phone call/sending a text message (efficient)

   _____

   _____

2. driving a car/riding a bicycle (dangerous)

   _____

   _____

3. putting a message in a bottle/making a phone call (reliable)

   _____

   _____

4. speaking English/ (your idea)

   _____

   _____

B. Think about the situations. Which method of communication would you use for each and why? Tell a partner. Use comparatives.

I'd call them on the phone because phone calls are more personal than email.

1. You just got a new job and want to tell your parents. (phone call or email?)

2. You want to tell your friends you lost your job. (phone call, email, or in person?)

3. You are meeting a friend for lunch, and he is late. (text or call?)

4. You are going to miss class tomorrow and need to inform your teacher. (call or email?)

5. You just went to a friend's wedding and want to show and tell your friends about it. (any)

Short words that are used to connect ideas are often unstressed. The words are called **connecting words**.

CD 3
Track 30

Listen to the sentences. Notice that the bold connecting words are not stressed.

> Hugo is taller **than** Edmundo.
> My computer isn't **as** fast **as** yours.
> The letters **that** I sent last month just arrived.
> Liang's favorite ways to communicate are texting **and** emailing.

CD 3
Track 31

A. Listen to the sentences. Write the connecting words you hear.

1. My sister is better at staying in touch _____ my brother.

2. You need a user name _____ a password to use the

   computer network at the school.

3. Most languages don't have _____ many words

   _____ English.

4. The homework _____ the teacher assigned last night was

   very difficult.

5. We didn't know _____ texting was more expensive

   _____ speaking on the phone. We need to change cell

   phone plans.

CD 3
Track 32

B. Listen again. Repeat the sentences. Do not stress the connecting words.

When you express **emotions**, use adjectives for feelings, such as:

afraid	angry	bored	concerned
excited	happy	sad	worried

We're excited about the trip tomorrow.
I'm worried about next week's exam.

You can also use specific phrases to show your feelings about what someone else says.

Happiness or approval
That's great!
That's terrific!
I'm so glad/happy (about)…

Surprise or interest
Really?
That's interesting/amazing!
You're kidding!

Sadness or sympathy
Oh, I'm so sorry!
That's terrible!
That's too bad.

Frustration or anger
I'm fed up with…
I've had it!
It bothers me when…
I'm upset about…

Tip for Success

You can also use intonation to help express emotions.

CD 3
Track 33

A. Listen to the conversation between two sisters. Then work with a partner. Discuss how you think the sisters feel.

Hannah: Guess what? You'll never believe what happened!

Sarah: What?

Hannah: Dad bought me a car.

Sarah: _____! Why did he do that?
                        1

Hannah: He said it was a graduation present.

Sarah: _____ the way he treats you. It's not fair.
                        2

Hannah: Well, he said he was going to buy you one, too.

Sarah: _____? I didn't know that. _____!
                        3   4

B. Work with a partner. Read the situations. Then choose one situation and create a conversation about it. Use phrases from the Speaking Skill box.

1. Two brothers are talking about a car accident. One brother crashed the other brother's car and caused a lot of damage.

2. A young person is telling a parent that he or she got a great job, but it's in another country.

3. Two roommates are talking about cleaning their apartment. One roommate is very neat and organized. The other roommate is lazy and messy and never cleans.

Unit Assignment | Role-play a phone call

 In this assignment, you are going to role-play a phone call about an emotional event. As you prepare for the role play, think about the Unit Question, "Do we need technology to communicate long distance?" and refer to the Self-Assessment checklist on page 204.

For alternative unit assignments, see the *Q: Skills for Success Teacher's Handbook.*

CONSIDER THE IDEAS

Tip Critical Thinking

This assignment asks you to **create** a conversation or a role-play of a situation. **Creating** this role-play requires you to put together, or synthesize, what you have learned about expressing emotion with reporting a specific event.

Read the statements about long-distance communication. What do you think of these people's opinions? Discuss your ideas with a partner.

"Long-distance phone calls are too expensive. I use email, whatever the situation is."

"My brother always wants to talk for hours, but I just don't have the time. I usually email instead."

"The only thing better than a phone conversation is being there in person. I rarely use email for important personal communications."

"Email is not very good if you are upset or angry. It's easy to give people the wrong idea when they can't hear your voice."

PREPARE AND SPEAK

A. **GATHER IDEAS** Think about some things that have happened recently in your life. Include events that have made you happy, sad, angry, frightened, or amused. List them in your notebook.

B. ORGANIZE IDEAS Choose one event from your list. Prepare to talk about it on the phone to someone you know. Decide who you will call. Make notes describing the event, including how you felt and why.

What was the event? _____

Who will you call? _____

What happened? _____

_____

_____

How did you feel? Why? _____

_____

_____

C. SPEAK Work with a partner. Role-play a phone call to someone you know about the event you chose in Activity B. Refer to the Self-Assessment checklist below before you begin.

CHECK AND REFLECT

A. CHECK Think about the Unit Assignment as you complete the Self-Assessment checklist.

SELF-ASSESSMENT		
Yes	No	
☐	☐	I was able to speak easily about the topic.
☐	☐	My partner understood me.
☐	☐	I used vocabulary from the unit.
☐	☐	I used comparatives.
☐	☐	I practiced not stressing connecting words.
☐	☐	I used phrases to express my emotions.

B. REFLECT Discuss these questions with a partner.

What is something new you learned in this unit?

Q? Look back at the Unit Question. Is your answer different now than when you started this unit? If yes, how is it different? Why?

Circle the words and phrases you learned in this unit.

Nouns
assistance 🔑 AWL
constraint AWL
coverage
landscape 🔑
pen pal
sympathy 🔑
tone 🔑

Verbs
interpret 🔑 AWL
observe 🔑
process 🔑 AWL
require 🔑 AWL

Adjectives
ancient 🔑
efficient 🔑
one-sided

remote 🔑
sealed

Adverb
adequately 🔑 AWL

Phrasal Verbs
build up

Phrases
I'm fed up with…
I'm so glad/happy
   (about)…
I'm upset about…
I've had it!
It bothers me when…
Oh, I'm so sorry!
Really?
That's great!

That's interesting/
   amazing!
That's terrible!
That's terrific!
That's too bad.
You're kidding!

Idioms
all ears
be a snap
drop someone a line
fight an uphill battle
get something off your
   chest
hold your tongue
off the top of my head
out of the blue

🔑 Oxford 3000™ words
AWL Academic Word List

Check (✓) the skills you learned. If you need more work on a skill, refer to the page(s) in parentheses.

LISTENING	○	I can recognize and understand definitions. (p. 192)
VOCABULARY	○	I can use idioms. (p. 197)
GRAMMAR	○	I can use comparatives. (p. 199)
PRONUNCIATION	○	I can pronounce unstressed connecting words. (p. 201)
SPEAKING	○	I can use phrases to express emotions. (p. 202)
LEARNING OUTCOME	○	I can role-play a phone call discussing an emotional event I have experienced.

Audio Scripts

Unit 1 First Impressions

The Q Classroom Page 3

Teacher: OK everyone, let's start. Every unit in Q begins with a question. As we go through the unit, we will continue to discuss this question. Our answers may change as we explore the topic, or they may stay the same. The Unit Question for Unit 1 is "Are first impressions accurate?" So let's think about our first impressions of people in this class. Look around the room at your classmates. Who made a good first impression on you? Yuna?

Yuna: Sophy.

Teacher: Why did she make a good first impression on you?

Yuna: Well, she's always smiling. She looks friendly.

Teacher: And is she friendly?

Yuna: Yes, she is!

Teacher: So that's an accurate first impression. Do you think first impressions are always that accurate? Marcus, what do you think?

Marcus: No, I don't think so. Sometimes you might think someone is unfriendly, but they're just in a bad mood that day.

Teacher: Good point. Maybe someone can give you the wrong impression because they are having a bad day. What else might cause the wrong first impression? Sophy?

Sophy: Mmm. A person might be dressed differently than they usually dress. If someone met me on the way home from the gym, they wouldn't know that I'm usually very formal.

Teacher: OK, so your mood and the way you are dressed can lead to wrong first impressions. What do you think about this, Felix? Are first impressions usually accurate?

Felix: I think most of the time they are right in some way. I can usually tell right away if someone is friendly or quiet or if they're smart or funny. But I can't tell other things about a person, like if they're honest or what kinds of things they believe in.

Teacher: Interesting.

LISTENING 1 The Psychology of First Impressions
Listen for Main Ideas Page 6

Speaker: First impressions don't tell the whole story.

Good morning. Thank you so much for inviting me here today. As promised, I'm going to talk about how we **form first impressions** and how they work.

We all form impressions of other people every day. So picture this: you're waiting in line at your favorite coffee shop. The line is long, but it's moving quickly. The person in front of you in line is complaining about the wait. He's loud and rude. He makes comments about the service and the employees. When he finally gets to the counter, he yells at the person who takes his order. You **assume** "This is not a nice person," and you hope you never meet him again.

From this short **encounter**, you have formed an impression of this person. You were with him only **briefly**, but you may think you know a lot about him. One mistake people often make in forming first impressions is to think that a small example of someone's **behavior** can give us a complete picture of the person. If you see a friendly, smiling young woman taking your order at the coffee shop, you may think she is friendly and smiling all of the time.

In addition to thinking she is always friendly, you may also think she has other **positive traits**. This is the second error people often make. Because she is friendly, you assume that she is also intelligent, happy, and good to her parents. Of course, the opposite is also true. The rude customer in front of you in the coffee line did not make a good impression on you. You saw an example of his poor behavior, his rudeness, and you assumed he had other **negative** traits. You thought "This is not a nice person."

OK, so if our first impression of someone is positive, we think the person is always that way and we think that all of her traits are positive. We think that small **sample** of behavior shows us her true personality. But we don't think that way about our own behavior. Let me explain what I mean. When we see someone else acting in a negative way, we think it is because he is a negative person. But when we act in a negative way, we say it is because of the situation.

Let's go back to the coffee shop again. If I am rude to the person taking my coffee order, I will find reasons for my bad behavior—the service is too slow, my mother is very sick, or my boss just yelled at me. In other words, when I act badly, I think it's because of the situation, not because I am a bad person. But if another customer is rude, I don't look for reasons—I think it is his personality. In other words, he acted badly because he is not a nice person.

First impressions can tell us a lot. They help us make sense of new information, and form relationships with new people. But, as you can see, we can make **errors**, so sometimes we need to take a second look.

Listen for Details Page 6

[Repeat Main Ideas track]

LISTENING SKILL Making Inferences
Example. Page 8

When I first met my professor, he shook my hand firmly and then asked me questions about myself. He was very polite. He also was relaxed and seemed interested in what I was saying.

A. Page 8

I remember the first time I met Lee. It was the first day of classes my freshman year. I was on my way to my history class and had no idea where I was going. He smiled and asked me if I needed help. I must have looked really lost! Anyway, he gave me directions to the building where my history class was, which I don't think I would have found on my own. After he gave me directions he introduced himself and gave me a firm handshake. He wished me luck with my classes and then headed off across campus. So he was probably late for his own class. My first couple of weeks of college were pretty difficult and lonely. I remember hoping I would see Lee again on my way to classes. About a month or so later I did. I was eating lunch in the cafeteria. I waved to him and asked him to sit at my table with me and a couple of my new friends.

C. Page 8

When I first met Lee, I knew instantly he was the type of person I could be friends with. He was so friendly. I mean, I couldn't believe he made himself late for class to help me, a freshman he didn't even know. The fact that he helped me and made me feel welcome made a really great first impression on me. We've been good friends ever since.

LISTENING 2 Book review of *Blink* by Malcolm Gladwell
Listen for Main Ideas Page 10

Host: There is a saying: "Don't judge a book by its cover." This tells us that first impressions may be wrong. Writer Malcolm Gladwell has a different idea. In *Blink: The Power of Thinking Without Thinking*, Malcolm Gladwell argues that first impressions are usually **reliable**. This is Wednesday Book Talk. Here's critic Hannah Smith.

Hannah Smith: An **expert** in an art museum takes one look at a very old Greek statue. He is **suspicious**. The museum has just paid millions for this statue. The first word that he thinks of is "fresh." According to *Blink*, a new book by Malcolm Gladwell, whenever this expert takes a look at something new, he writes down the first word he thinks of.

This habit of writing down first impressions supports the argument of Malcolm Gladwell's book. We often know more than we think we know. And we know it faster than we can explain. That Greek statue, for example, turned out to be about 2,000 years "fresher," or newer, than the museum thought. It wasn't really an old statue at all. It was a **fake**.

Gladwell says we have two ways we make decisions. First, we can make decisions slowly and carefully with our **conscious** minds. Or, we can make decisions very quickly and **unconsciously**, or without even thinking. Our unconscious minds are using information we already know to make judgments within a second or two.

Gladwell's book looks at examples of when our first impressions turn out to be very accurate, as well as when they do not. For example, students in college classrooms have very accurate first impressions of instructors. In one study, students were shown only several seconds of a videotape of a teacher in the classroom. Then they predicted how **effective** the teacher would be. After only that quick first impression, they judged the teacher's effectiveness very accurately. They did as well as other students did after an entire term. In another study, people could tell a lot about a student's character just by looking at his or her bedroom for a few minutes.

Gladwell also looks at marriages, wars, marketing, and police actions. Sometimes, our first impression, our ability to make **snap judgments**, is very accurate. Sometimes it is very wrong. So when should we trust our **instincts**? In a section added to the new edition, Gladwell writes about some recent research. This research suggests conscious, careful decision-making works best for easy choices like buying a pot for the kitchen. However, our first impressions are best in difficult situations when we are handling many pieces of information. An example is when a coach is **selecting** a player for a soccer team. If you want a book that gets you thinking about how we think, read *Blink*.

Host: Thank you, Hannah. Now stay with us, we'll be back after the break with news of two more titles that have just reached the stores.

Listen for Details Page 11

[Repeat Main Ideas track]

PRONUNCIATION Contractions with auxiliary verbs
Page 16

She's eating now.

They're watching TV.

Lisa's already left.

We've finished our work.

What's it cost?

Where'd you go?

Why'd he arrive so late?

A. Page 16

1. Who's your favorite movie star?
2. Where'd you go on your last vacation?
3. Mary's going to the store.
4. Jack's gone already.
5. We've usually eaten by 6:00.
6. What'd you do after class yesterday?
7. The girls've been here before.

SPEAKING SKILL Taking conversational turns
Examples. Page 17

What do you think?

Do you agree?

Right?

How about you?

You know?

Okay?

Unit 2 Food and Taste

The Q Classroom Page 23

Teacher: The question for Unit 2 is "What's more important: taste or nutrition?" So how did you choose your breakfast this morning? Did you eat something you really like or something that's good for you? Sophy?

Sophy: I ate fruit for breakfast. It's good for me and I like it!

Teacher: Would you eat something for breakfast that tasted good, but wasn't nutritious?

Sophy: No, I wouldn't. Eating healthy food is important to me.

Teacher: How about you, Marcus? What's more important to you, taste or nutrition?

Marcus: Um, I'm not sure. Food that tastes good makes me happy. Happiness is important for good health!

Teacher: Good point! Yuna, what do you think? Marcus says food that tastes good makes people happy, so is taste or nutrition more important?

Yuna: Nutrition is more important. You need good nutrition to be healthy.

Teacher: OK, we need good nutrition, but good taste can make us happy, which is also important. What do you think, Felix? Taste or nutrition?

Felix: Well, nutrition is important, but I would say that for most of us, taste is important, too. If something doesn't taste good, most people won't eat it no matter how nutritious it is. So really we need food like Sophy's fruit—delicious and nutritious.

Teacher: Yes. Unfortunately, a lot of food isn't that perfect!

LISTENING 1 You Are What You Eat
Listen for Main Ideas Page 26

Andy Patterson: Greetings, and welcome to today's edition of "Your World" with me, Andy Patterson. And with me in the studio I have nutrition expert Dr. Maureen O'Ryan. Welcome, Doctor.

Maureen O'Ryan: Thanks, Andy. It's great to be here.

AP: So, it's time to listen up, people, for some top health tips. Remember, you may like the taste, but did you ever wonder about the *effect* on your body of what you eat and drink?… Doctor?

MO'R: Well, let me start by saying this isn't a lecture on healthy eating. We all know that we should drink lots of water, and eat plenty of fruits and vegetables, and so on, but in the real world, most of us prefer soft drinks to water, and we all eat food we know is bad for us. My point is, it's OK—

AP: What! It's OK? Great! I'll have a double cheeseburger!

MO'R: It's OK to eat any food you want as long as your **diet** is **balanced**. And what I want to say today is that we can all enjoy good health, but we have to know the effects that the food and drink we **consume** have on our bodies.

AP: That makes sense. So, let's look at some of the things we enjoy most…Now, I love a **spicy** beef burger or a juicy steak. Of course, I know red meat's supposed to be bad…

MO'R: Well, that's exactly my point. Red meat isn't bad for you, unless you eat too much. It actually gives us healthy bones and skin. But obviously you shouldn't eat a huge steak every night!

AP: White meat is healthier, though, right?

MO'R: Yes, white meat, such as chicken or turkey, is definitely good for you. In fact, because it contains a natural substance which makes us feel calm, eating turkey can actually change your **mood**. Have a turkey sandwich for lunch, and you'll feel more relaxed.

AP: OK, but what about a *cheese* sandwich? I love cheese, but people say it's bad for you.

MO'R: Well, cheese has calcium, so it's good for your teeth, but since it's high in fat and salt you shouldn't eat it every day. We need salt to survive, but too much salt can cause high blood pressure.

AP: OK, but I'm a coffee man, too, and I *know* that's bad for you.

MO'R: Well, coffee gives you energy due to the caffeine, and that's all right. But if you drink too much coffee it can make you feel stressed and give you problems sleeping. Coffee before lunch is OK, but I suggest drinking tea in the afternoon.

AP: Ah, but tea has caffeine, too, Doc. I read about it.

MO'R: Yes, but only a small amount, and green tea, for example, also helps fight cancer and improves your ability to **concentrate**. Tea is fine, and lots of green tea is even better!

AP: Hmm. But when I'm tired I usually **rely on** a soda.

MO'R: Well, a soda might give you energy for a short period, but one can contain up to 15 teaspoons of sugar! All of that sugar has a big effect on your body, Andy! And the **calories** in soda are what we call "empty" calories, since they have no nutrition at all. As a result, a couple of hours after you consume the soda, you'll probably feel more tired, and depressed as well.

AP: Hmm…and what about chocolate lovers? Bad again, right?

MO'R: Well, a little chocolate from time to time isn't so bad, but not milk chocolate—that's bad—it has to be dark chocolate. Dark chocolate can lower your blood pressure and is good for your heart…I guess all I'm really saying is that by making **wise** food choices, you can basically eat what you like…you just need to **mix** the good and the bad. What's so hard about that?

AP: Sounds great! Now, let me ask you one more thing…

Listen for Details Page 26

[Repeat Main Ideas track]

LISTENING SKILL Listening for causes and effects
Examples. Page 28

I rarely cook because I am tired when I get home.

We usually eat at home since it's so expensive to eat out these days.

I never buy fish as I don't know how to cook it.

The burger tasted terrible, so we didn't eat it.

Due to her healthy diet, Keiko lived to be 110 years old.

Because of the high calories, I never eat chocolate.

A. Page 28

1. Since Dr. O'Ryan is a nutrition expert, Andy interviewed her on his radio show.

2. Eating a lot of cheese isn't good because of the large amount of salt.

3. Because Andy stopped drinking soda, he feels much healthier now.

4. Andy also wants to lose weight, so he's following Dr. O'Ryan's suggestions.

B. Page 29

1. Because it contains a natural substance which makes us feel calm, eating turkey can actually change your mood.

2. Cheese has calcium, so it's good for your teeth.

3. Coffee gives you energy due to the caffeine.

4. The calories in soda are what we call "empty" calories since they have no nutrition at all.

LISTENING 2 Food Tasters
Listen for Main Ideas Page 31

Stuart: Hi, my name's Stuart Andrews, and I'm a chocolate taster. I've always loved chocolate, so this is the dream job for me. I work for a big department store. We develop our own chocolate…I also train staff, um, visit chocolate factories, and deal with suppliers. I organize volunteer "tasting sessions." Of course, since everyone loves chocolate, there's never a problem getting volunteers! It's not a job you can just walk into, though—I studied for a degree in nutrition and then worked for an ice cream manufacturer for a few years first. I started here six years ago, and I still love every day. The best thing is that when I go to work, my desk is covered in chocolate! The worst is probably **keeping an eye** on my weight because of all the calories. You know, it's easy to put on weight, so I try to eat healthily whenever I'm not working. I go to the gym, and I make sure I see my dentist every six months! I live and work in London, but I travel a lot because you have to keep up with the latest **trends**, you know—Belgium, France, Switzerland. I was in New York last week to see what's selling there. It's not just the taste that makes people buy one bar of chocolate rather than another, but the appearance and the advertising, too.

Marie: Hello, this is Marie Lavoisier. Tasting cheese, for me, uh, it's not a job at all, really. I'm a cheese buyer for a large supermarket. On what I call a "taste day" I taste maybe ten to twelve different cheeses. Because they all taste different you can't taste everything at once—you need to take your time. I check for flavor, **texture**, and especially the smell of the cheese, since smell is the most important. Some people think strong-smelling cheeses are **disgusting**, and **occasionally** they are, but in general they're my favorite! We keep cheeses for many months, some for over a year, and so I also need to check the cheese we have, and decide when each cheese is ready, you know, to go out on sale. I live just outside Paris, which is convenient because I need to meet farmers regularly, mainly to help them develop new products, since people always like to try new **flavors**. To get this job, I studied for a degree in food science and then waited for the chance to be a cheese taster. As soon as I saw the job, I was there! You have to love cheese, of course, because it's "cheese, cheese, cheese" all day, every day. Some people get tired of it from time to time, but I never do!

Enrique: Hi there, my name's Enrique Martinez. I started work as a manager in a coffee shop and gradually I began to, you know, uh, enjoy the taste. There are degrees you can get, and courses you can take, but I worked my way up through experience and now I'm the head coffee taster for a large importing company. I only taste in the mornings because that's when my sense of taste is at its best. I check the quality. Um, people can pay a lot for coffee, so they want to enjoy it. I check the smell, the taste. You know, is it sweet or bitter? Some taste of chocolate, others are spicy. Some are very **complex**. I make it, taste it, but I don't **swallow** it. I **estimate** I taste up to 100 coffees, so I don't actually drink them because of all the caffeine, right! In the afternoons I email suppliers or do paperwork. Um, I live here in downtown Los Angeles, so I walk to work, which is great. Yeah, I love this job. It can be hard work, trying to **distinguish** between so many different coffees, but I wouldn't want to do anything else!

Listen for Details Page 32

[Repeat Main Ideas track]

PRONUNCIATION Links with /j/ and /w/
Examples. Page 37

I think Marco must be Italian.

I can't see you tonight, but Tuesday is fine.

I ate salmon for dinner last night.

Do you eat a balanced diet?

Do you want to go out for lunch?

How is your steak?

A. Page 37

1. We all eat things we know we shouldn't.

2. "Empty" calories have no nutritional value at all.

3. I can't drink coffee, but tea is fine.

4. Cheese has calcium, so it's good for your teeth.

5. Sometimes in the evening I'm too tired to cook.

6. Marie makes sure the cheese is ready to go out on sale.

7. Stuart thinks the appearance of chocolate can be as important as the taste.

8. Enrique thinks people pay a lot for coffee, so they want to enjoy it.

B. Page 37

1. We all eat things we know we shouldn't.

2. "Empty" calories have no nutritional value at all.

3. I can't drink coffee, but tea is fine.

4. Cheese has calcium, so it's good for your teeth.

5. Sometimes in the evening I'm too tired to cook.

6. Marie makes sure the cheese is ready to go out on sale.

7. Stuart thinks the appearance of chocolate can be as important as the taste.

8. Enrique thinks people pay a lot for coffee, so they want to enjoy it.

SPEAKING SKILL Giving advice
Examples. Page 38

According to Dr. O'Ryan, Andy should drink less coffee.

He shouldn't drink a lot of soda.

He ought to eat more fish.

Perhaps you should eat more fruit and vegetables.

You really ought to eat more fruit and vegetables.

Unit 3 Success

The Q Classroom Page 45

Teacher: Unit 3's question is "What can we learn from success and failure?" Let's start by talking about ways that people can be successful. Sophy, what are some types of success?

Sophy: People can be financially successful, or successful in school, or they can have a good family life.

Teacher: OK, let's take success in school. Yuna, what can we learn from success in school?

Yuna: We learn which habits are important. We study hard and pass the test. This teaches us to keep studying. If we don't study and we fail, we learn the same thing.

Teacher: True! Success and failure can teach the same kinds of lessons. How about success or failure in our personal lives? What can we learn from that? Felix?

Felix: Well, you can learn from your relationships with people. If I have a good friendship with someone, it teaches me about what I value in a friendship, like honesty. If I lose a friend because I lied to him, it teaches me not to lie to my friends in the future.

Teacher: What do you think we can learn from success and failure, Marcus?

Marcus: I think we learn more from failure. When I fail at something, I know I need to learn a lesson, so I really pay attention. If I'm successful, I might not think about why I am successful.

Teacher: Good point.

LISTENING 1 Chasing Your Dreams
Listen for Main Ideas Page 48

Professor: OK. So, last week we looked at various definitions of success, and common ways people **measure** success—through **status**, fame, money, possessions, and so on. Now this week I want to expand on this and ask you to question the importance of success, and what it *really* means to be successful.

We learn from an early age that success is good…something we should try to **achieve** through a combination of hard work and **determination**. You all know the expression "If at first you don't succeed, try, try again." Well, some research suggests that trying really hard to achieve something might actually be the *wrong* thing to do. It all depends on whether your **goal** is achievable. To give you an example, imagine a short, thirty-year-old man who smokes forty cigarettes a day. Should he **give up** his job to take up basketball in the hope of becoming a major basketball star? I don't think so! So, the first point I'd like to make is that you need to be **realistic** about what it is you want to achieve. Chasing an impossible dream, one that you can never reach, is a **frustrating** waste of time and energy. Make sure the success you're aiming for is achievable. If it isn't, then readjust your goals to something more reasonable, something that you can achieve.

The second point I want to make is that of course success is good, but trying to become successful shouldn't take over your life. You shouldn't become so determined to succeed at something that it causes you stress or anxiety. People who put too much importance on succeeding at something, and then *fail*, can have serious psychological problems.

This brings me to another point, which may shock you. Success isn't always a good thing. Success in one area can bring problems in others—for instance, a successful career might result in the end of a marriage. Good relationships take time and effort, and if someone is working hard at developing their career all the time, then their family life and relationships can suffer as a result. Take for example, all the famous people we hear about getting divorced in the media. These actors, pop stars, and so on are at the top of their profession, but they pay a price with their personal lives. A close friend of mine from my high school days is a successful businessman, but he got divorced last year. He says his career **ruined** his marriage. So, be careful what you wish for, and make sure you know the **downside** as well as the up.

The final point I want to make in this introduction is that we need to remember that our definition of success changes with age. What people want to achieve in high school is different from what they want to achieve when they are 20, or 40, or even 70. So, for example, success for my grandfather is getting out of bed in the morning! Be aware that our goals change over time. You may want a sports car now, but when you have three children maybe you'll want a big family car instead! It's important to recognize that our goals can change, as our lives change.

Listen for Details Page 49

[Repeat Main Ideas track]

LISTENING SKILL Listening for examples
A. Page 50

[Repeat Main Ideas track]

B. Page 50

Paul: After I graduated from college, the only thing I wanted was to make money. I was money hungry. For example, I only chose jobs that paid well! I guess that's kind of natural, to want to earn lots of money. But I was also really concerned about my status at work. I mean, I felt the best way to measure my success—apart from my salary—was by my job title. So, to give you an example, I left one company to work for another because the job title sounded better! Amazing now that I think about it, but true! … Well, then, about a year ago, I found out I had cancer. I spent six months in and out of the hospital. I'm better now, but being successful these days, for me, is not about being a multimillionaire—it's about being healthy. For instance, jogging in the park is a success, to me. I love it, and it doesn't cost anything! I also value my friendships more. I got back in touch with my old college classmates, and we get along really well…So for me, for example, I see reconnecting with my old college friends as a great success. It's really made me a lot happier.

LISTENING 2 The Benefits of Failure
Listen for Main Ideas Page 53

Carl Simmons: Hello everyone, my name is Carl Simmons, and I would like to talk to you about the other side of success… failure. Just as success is something we all want, failure is something that we all **fear**. Yet failure is an important stage on the road to success, and I'd like to illustrate this with some examples. You've all heard of the Beatles…well, perhaps you also know that Decca Records **turned down** the Beatles, saying that their kind of music "would never be popular." Michael Jordan—the basketball superstar—was cut from his high school basketball team because he "**lacked** skill." Walt Disney was told he had "no **creativity** or original ideas." John Grisham, the **top** novelist who's now a multimillionaire, was turned down by sixteen agents and publishers before he had his first book published. All these are examples of people who experienced failure but then went on to succeed.

I think there are two points I'd like to **emphasize** here. The first is that we shouldn't be afraid of failure, because we can learn from it. Being successful is great, but it doesn't always teach you a lot. You can learn a lot more from your failures than you

can from your successes. Take Michael Jordan, for example. He learned from his mistakes. He **worked out** what he was doing wrong, changed his game, and improved to become the best basketball player in the world! The same goes for Akio Morita, the founder of Sony Corporation. The first product he made was a rice cooker that didn't work; it burned the rice, rather than cooking it! He sold fewer than one hundred of them and lost a lot of money. But he learned from the experience, and of course today everyone knows the name Sony!

The second point I want to make about failure is that you must not **permit** failure to defeat you. Failure is something to be encouraged by. Don't give up too easily! Remember John Grisham…his first book, *A Time to Kill*, wasn't a success when it was published. Only 5,000 copies were printed, and he ended up buying a lot of them and selling them himself! But he didn't give up. He continued to **develop** his writing, and his next novel, *The Firm*, was a great success and became a Hollywood movie starring Tom Cruise. So, what I'm saying is believe in yourself and never give up. Did you know that Thomas Edison tried more than 9,000 times before he managed to make the first light bulb work? He learned from his mistakes, and so must we all.

I'd like to suggest that it is because of their failures that these people became such great successes. You need to experience failure and learn from it, in order to really succeed. Failing is a good **preparation** for life. It makes you stronger and more able to overcome life's problems. Don't be scared of failure! It might sound strange, but letting go of your fear of failure may help you to succeed.

Listen for Details Page 53

[Repeat Main Ideas track]

PRONUNCIATION Stress on Important Words
Examples. Page 56

You can learn a lot more from your failures than you can from your successes.

Success for my grandfather is getting out of bed in the morning.

Failing is a good preparation for life.

A. Page 56

Failure is an important stage on the road to success.

We shouldn't be afraid of failure, because we can learn from it.

Failure is something to be encouraged by.

Don't give up too easily!

B. Page 57

Failure is an important stage on the road to success.

We shouldn't be afraid of failure, because we can learn from it.

Failure is something to be encouraged by.

Don't give up too easily!

C. Page 57

You need to experience failure and learn from it in order to really succeed. Failing is a good preparation for life. It makes you stronger and more able to overcome life's problems. Don't be scared of failure!

D. Page 57

You need to experience failure and learn from it in order to really succeed. Failing is a good preparation for life. It makes you stronger and more able to overcome life's problems. Don't be scared of failure!

SPEAKING SKILL Asking for and giving clarification
A. Page 58

1. **Professor:** So you need to make sure the success you're aiming for is achievable.
   Student 1: Sorry, I don't get what you mean.
   Professor: What I'm trying to say is be realistic with the goals you set for yourself.

2. **Professor:** Success in one area can bring problems in others.
   Student 2: What do you mean exactly?
   Professor: Well, to give you an example, someone can be at the top of her career, but her family life might be in crisis as a result.

3. **Professor:** Keep your desire for success in proportion.
   Student 3: Do you think you could say a bit more about that?
   Professor: Yes. I mean don't let your desire for success become greater than other important areas in your life.

4. **Professor:** Our definition of success alters with age.
   Student 1: Can you give an example, please?
   Professor: Sure. Someone of twenty might view success as being rich, but at fifty that same person might think of success as a happy family life.

Unit 4 New Perspectives

The Q Classroom Page 65

Teacher: The Unit 4 question is "Is change good or bad?" So what are some of the big changes you've made in your life recently? Marcus?

Marcus: Uh, I moved here and started college.

Teacher: Has that been a good change or a bad change for you?

Marcus: A good change. I'm more independent now.

Teacher: What about change in general? Have the changes in your life been good for you or bad for you? Yuna?

Yuna: Good. I lost my job and was very sad. But now I am here, going to school full time, and happy.

Teacher: So sometimes a change that seems bad at first turns out to be a good thing. Do you agree, Sophy? Is change usually a good thing?

Sophy: Well, changes in my life have usually been good, like moving or starting a new school, but sometimes changes in society aren't good, like when the crime rate goes up or the environment becomes polluted.

Teacher: OK, let's talk about changes in society. The world has changed a lot since your parents were your age. Have most of those changes been good or bad? What does that say about change in general? Felix?

Felix: I think most changes have a good side and a bad side. My mom would say that people today spend too much time sitting at the computer and not enough time talking face-to-face or getting out. But it's also true that I can stay in touch with my friends all over the world in a way she never could. So there are really two ways to look at most changes.

LISTENING 1 Changing Expectations
Listen for Main Ideas Page 68

Gary McBride: Hello everyone. My name's Gary McBride, and I'm here to talk to you today about the benefits of downshifting. By "downshifting" I mean getting out of the rat race and living a simpler life, one with less power and responsibility—and, of course, less money—but with more free time and opportunity to enjoy life. It's something we probably all think about from time to time, but I've actually done it…so thank you for giving me this opportunity to tell you about my experience.

A few years ago I worked on Wall Street for a big bank. I was a typical city trader, buying and selling stocks day after day…and it was very well-paid. I mean, I earned hundreds of thousands of dollars. I wore designer clothes, drove a luxury sports car, lived in a huge apartment downtown. I felt like I was king of the world. But there was a price to pay. I couldn't really **handle** all the stress. I had headaches and stomach problems the whole time. My personal life also **suffered**, as I was never home to build a **steady** relationship…and then the financial **crisis** came along. You remember that, right? Like many others, I lost my job. But instead of looking for work in other companies, retraining, or starting my own business, I felt I needed to do something different. I was **curious** about the world out there and I needed to **justify** my place in it. I needed a change.

So…for six months, I traveled around Mexico, then South America, and over to Europe. It gave me the time and space I needed to think about what I wanted to do…and when I got back…I decided to leave Wall Street. I sold my car, and my apartment, and went to live in a small town in Iowa, to be near my parents. After a couple of months, I started looking for work. I earned a lot as a city trader, but I also spent a lot… so I didn't have any savings. I wanted to try something new, something different. The first **position** I was offered was a home-care assistant in the local hospital. It seemed a friendly place, so I took it!

These days I'm still a home-care assistant. I go to the homes of sick or elderly people who need help, and I help them wash, I do their housekeeping, prepare their meals. I talk to them.

Being a home-care assistant is a very different job from what I was doing before. Of course, the salary is **considerably** lower, so I don't eat out often, I can't buy a new car, and I certainly can't afford an overseas vacation anymore…but you know what? I've **adapted**, and now I'm very **fulfilled**. Living life at a slower speed means I have time to make friends…*real* friends! I have a better relationship with my family, and I feel healthier too!

As a city trader, I was always busy. I only thought about myself. But now, my job is to care for other people, and helping other people has helped me to be a better person. I've achieved the goal I set for myself when I came back from traveling—I finally know what it is to be happy…Now, are there any questions?

Listen for Details Page 69

[Repeat Main Ideas track]

LISTENING SKILL Taking notes using a T-chart
Example. Page 70

A few years ago I worked on Wall Street for a big bank. I was a typical city trader, buying and selling stocks day after day…and it was very well-paid. I mean, I earned hundreds of thousands of dollars. I wore designer clothes, drove a luxury sports car, lived in a huge apartment downtown. I felt like I was king of the world. But there was a price to pay. I couldn't really handle all the stress. I had headaches and stomach problems the whole time. My personal life also suffered, as I was never home to build a steady relationship…and then the financial crisis came along. You remember that, right? Like many others…

A. Page 70

Being a home-care assistant is a very different job from what I was doing before. Of course, the salary is considerably lower, so I don't eat out often, I can't buy a new car, and I certainly can't afford an overseas vacation anymore…but you know what? I've adapted, and now I'm very fulfilled. Living life at a slower speed means I have time to make friends…*real* friends! I have a better relationship with my family, and I feel healthier too!

LISTENING 2 An Interview with Barbara Ehrenreich
Listen for Main Ideas Page 72

Interviewer: So, Barbara. Welcome to *Life and Times*. It's great to have you here.

Barbara Ehrenreich: Great to be here, Jack. Thanks for inviting me.

Interviewer: Now, you're famous as a journalist, and of course, you've written several books based on your **research**. We'll get to those in a minute, but could you start by telling our listeners some of the reasons why you go "undercover" for your research?

BE: Sure. Well, interviews are fine, but sometimes you need to experience something **firsthand** to understand it. So I guess what I'm saying is that being an undercover reporter is a good way to find out what's really going on. By putting yourself in the situation you're investigating…you can then write about your experience from a more **informed** point of view.

Interviewer: I see. So, for *Nickel and Dimed*, where did you go undercover?

BE: Well, the aim was to see if I could **support myself** in low-paid jobs, so I worked as a waitress, a hotel housekeeper, a maid, a nursing home assistant, and a supermarket clerk. I spent a month in each job, working in Florida, Maine, and Minnesota.

Interviewer: Wow. That's a lot of different jobs, and places! I guess your life changed completely during that period, right?

BE: It sure did…and boy, I learned a lot! It was amazing.

Interviewer: Really? What exactly did you find out?

BE: Well, first, that it was very difficult indeed to **cope**, you know, financially, on such low **wages**. The rents were very high and the wages were so low. You know, these people really **struggle**. Also, you have to be a hard worker! I mean, some of the jobs I was doing left me feeling physically **exhausted**— especially when I had to work two jobs in a day. Interviewing people is one thing, but actually doing the job day to day shows you exactly how hard these people's lives are.

Interviewer: Hmm. And of course, *Nickel and Dimed* went on to be a very popular book. It was a *New York Times* best seller.

BE: Yes. I was really surprised at all the interest. I think it really opened people's eyes, a firsthand account like that. You know, people in low-paid jobs like those aren't lazy. They work long, hard hours, just to survive.

Interviewer: Did you change your name when you went undercover?

BE: For *Nickel and Dimed* I didn't change my name, but I did for my next project, *Bait and Switch*. I wanted to see how easy it was for people with pretty good jobs—who became **unemployed**—to find another job at the same level. So, I went undercover as a white-collar public relations executive looking for work. I tried really hard, with a great resume that told everyone that I had lots of experience and all that, but I couldn't find any work.

It really highlighted to me how hard life can be for people at all levels…from unskilled manual workers to white-collar management.

Interviewer: Hmm. So, I guess in both cases, for *Nickel and Dimed* and *Bait and Switch*, you were pleased that the changes you made weren't **permanent**? I mean, you didn't ever want to carry on in one of those jobs.

BE: No way. I just got a brief look at people's lives there, and by the time I finished, I realized how lucky I was. I was so relieved not to be in that kind of situation long term.

Interviewer: Hmm. Well, listeners, we're going to take a short break, but if you have a question for Barbara, now's the time, so get on the phone and call…

Listen for Details Page 73

[Repeat Main Ideas track]

PRONUNCIATION Variety of intonation to show interest
Examples. Page 78

1. **Interviewer:** Really? What exactly did you find out?
   Interviewer: Really? What exactly did you find out?
2. **Man:** I've never tried horseback riding.
   Woman 2: You haven't? That's too bad. It's great!
3. **Man:** Carol went to Australia for a month last year.
   Woman: Did she? That sounds wonderful!

A. Page 78

1. **Man 1:** I hear you're looking for a new job?
   Man 2: I hear you're looking for a new job?
2. **Woman 1:** Julie and Frank just had a baby.
   Woman 2: Julie and Frank just had a baby.
3. **Man 1:** Michelle started at a new school on Monday.
   Man 2: Michelle started at a new school on Monday.
4. **Woman 1:** James has been retired for over a year.
   Woman 2: James has been retired for over a year.
5. **Man 1:** You went to London last month.
   Man 2: You went to London last month.
6. **Woman 1:** Have you ever been to Europe?
   Woman 2: Have you ever been to Europe?
7. **Man 1:** So, you learned to scuba dive as a child?
   Man 2: So, you learned to scuba dive as a child?
8. **Woman 1:** I've never lived abroad.
   Woman 2: I've never lived abroad.

B. Page 78

[Repeat of Activity A. track]

SPEAKING SKILL Asking for and giving reasons
Example. Page 79

Man: You know, I really don't think fishing is for me.

Woman: Oh yeah? Why do you say that?

Man: Well, first of all, it's boring! Also, it's expensive to buy all the equipment, and another thing I hate is the smell of fish!

A. Page 79

Jez: Hi, Lisa. I haven't seen you for ages. How was your vacation in Spain?

Lisa: It was great! I tried lots of new things—horseback riding, scuba diving…I even went to a bullfight in Madrid.

Jez: What? You went to a bullfight? I'm surprised.

Lisa: Really? Why do you say that?

Jez: Because it's cruel, isn't it? Why would you want to watch that?

Lisa: Well, first of all, it's an important part of the culture… you know? Another reason is it's really popular. Lots of tourists

were there. It's also good to experience something different for a change…I think.

Unit 5 Responsibility

The Q Classroom Page 85

Teacher: The Unit Question for Unit 5 is, "Are we responsible for the world we live in?" So let's talk about what that means. First, how can people be responsible in their communities?

Marcus: They can recycle.

Sophy: They can volunteer in their neighborhood. They can vote.

Teacher: Good examples. Let's take recycling. Do you recycle, Yuna?

Yuna: Yes, I do.

Teacher: Why?

Yuna: Um, it's important for the environment.

Teacher: How about you, Marcus?

Marcus: I recycle when it's convenient—like in the cafeteria where there are separate bins for glass and cans. But otherwise I don't have time for separating paper and plastic and taking it somewhere for recycling.

Teacher: OK, but should we be responsible for the world we live in? Is it important to make time for things like recycling and volunteering in the community and learning about the issues so you can vote?

Felix: It's important, but it's not realistic to expect everyone to do those things. People have to work and study. Lots of people don't have time to do other things. I think the government needs to take over some of the responsibility for people—like making recycling easy and setting up volunteer programs so it's easy to participate.

Teacher: Do you agree with that, Sophy? Should we be responsible as individuals or should we have the government take over some responsibility?

Sophy: Well, I think we all need to be responsible. But we can make it easier if we work together.

LISTENING 1 Corporate Social Responsibility
Listen for Main Ideas Page 88

Professor: This morning I'd like to talk to you about CSR, or corporate social responsibility. That is, the belief that companies need to be responsible for the economic, social, and environmental **impact** of their actions. Of course companies want to make money. There's nothing wrong with that. However, increasingly people are asking, at what cost? What is the cost to us, the planet, and the society we live in? It is this balance between **profit** and social responsibility in the corporate world that I want to look at today.

Believe it or not, this issue affects everyone—including you— directly. We are all happy to buy our clothes more cheaply, but do we stop to think where they were made, and who made them? Do you know who made your jeans, your shirt, or your running shoes? There are over 150 million children around the world in employment today. They are working often in dangerous and difficult conditions. Some of these children might have produced the clothes you are wearing right now. How does that make you feel? Worried?

Well, you should be concerned, because the fact is, there are companies that show little or no interest in social responsibility. They employ children because they learn quickly and they're cheap. They don't care about their safety. They don't provide health care. They save money by **polluting** our rivers and oceans. Yes, these companies may make their products in countries in the developing world. But they are owned and managed by companies in the United States, Europe, and elsewhere; countries that claim to have higher standards of social and environmental care. What's more, people living in **developed** countries seem quite happy to **ignore** these standards when they want to buy products cheaply.

But things are changing. Corporate social responsibility is becoming a big issue these days. **Consumers** are starting to take a greater interest in the companies they buy products from. More and more consumers are **demanding** that companies pay their workers a **fair** wage. As for workers, they also expect companies to protect their safety, and perhaps provide health care and other **benefits**. In addition, governments are starting to demand that companies reduce the pollution they cause. They are beginning to stop companies behaving in a way that harms the health of local residents and the environment. Thanks to pressure from all of these sources—consumers, workers, and governments—things are changing for the better.

This brings us to an important part of responsibility: the question of who is responsible. Imagine a company is polluting the environment. Who is responsible? Is it the company itself, or the individual manager that is to blame for allowing the pollution? It's not an easy question to answer. Take another example. A big brand-name clothes company uses a local manufacturer in a developing country to produce their running shoes. The local company employs children in terrible conditions. They work for less than a dollar a day, up to sixteen hours a day in dirty and dangerous conditions. Who is responsible this time? Is it the local manufacturer, or the big brand-name company that buys from them? Or are we responsible, as consumers who are happy to buy the running shoes at a cheap price? And exactly how can you force any company to be responsible? Huge **fines** will help, and the negative effect on public opinion of media reports…but it's not easy.

Nevertheless, some companies are socially responsible in the way they run their business. We shouldn't forget that. As consumers demand higher standards, more companies are trying to improve the lives of their workers and the society they live in. These companies show that profit and social responsibility can go together. I'd like to consider a few important case studies now, beginning with the example of

the cooperative movement that goes back to 19th-century Britain…

Listen for Details Page 89

[Repeat Main Ideas track]

LISTENING SKILL Inferring a speaker's attitude
Examples. Page 90

1. We are all happy to buy our clothes more cheaply, but do we stop to think where they were made, and who made them?

2. **Man 1:** It's the neighbor again. What does he want this time?
   Man 2: Excuse me. Would you mind turning down the music, please?
   Man 1: Yeah, sure.

A. Page 90

1. Did you know that this is a nonsmoking area?

2. I don't know why Simon's always late for work.

3. Yeah. That garbage has been there for a week.

B. Page 90

1. **Man:** Guess what. I have to work overtime, all next week.
   Woman: No! You mean you won't be home for dinner?
   Man: I won't be home until nine.
   Woman: That's crazy. They can't force you to work overtime, can they?

2. **Man:** It says here that the chemical company polluted the river again last week.
   Woman: Right. That's the third time this year, isn't it?
   Man: Hmm. I think so.

3. **Man:** City Hall. How may I direct your call?
   Woman: Uh…I'd like to speak to Environmental Services, please.
   Man: And the reason for your call?
   Woman: Uh, well…The park in our neighborhood is terrible. I mean, there's litter everywhere and nobody has picked it up.
   Man: I see. One moment please…

LISTENING 2 Personal Responsibility
Listen for Main Ideas Page 92

Professor: So, you're all ready to discuss this week's assignment, I hope…"Individual responsibility." I'd like to start with our personal experiences, and focus on home life. Naomi, would you like to begin?

Naomi: Sure. Well, speaking for myself, I live with my parents and so I think it's important to help out as much as possible. For example, I'm **in charge of** taking out the garbage, and sorting all the bottles, papers, and plastic things for recycling.

Professor: Hmmm. How important do you think that **obligation** is?

Naomi: Recycling? It's really important. I mean, my mom and dad don't really care, so that's why I do it all.

Professor: And Michael, how about you?

Michael: Oh, I **help out** around the house. I do the dishes after meals, and wash the car every weekend, on Saturday mornings. Those are my main responsibilities.

Professor: And you, Neil?

Neil: Oh, um, I have to look after my little sister when my parents aren't around. They both work. She's seven, so when I get back home, I usually make her dinner and help her with her homework, that kind of thing.

Professor: Maria? What are you responsible for at home?

Maria: I take care of our pets. We have two rabbits and a cat, and they are quite a lot of work.

Professor: So it seems as if you all feel responsible for helping out at home in some way…OK, let's widen this out a little now, and think a little more about parents and children. How many of you have parents who always want to know where you are? …I see. Quite a few! How do you feel about that…Maria?

Maria: Well, I know they worry about me when I go out. I guess that means they feel responsible for me, but I wish they would, you know, like, relax. They should just **trust** me to be **sensible**. They don't need to **check up on** me, where I go, or the friends I have, but they do. They phone me all the time when I'm out. It makes me really angry sometimes.

Professor: It's not always easy for parents, is it? Do any of you sometimes **lie** to your parents? Maybe tell your parents you're going to one place when in fact you go somewhere else? Neil?

Neil: Uh, sometimes, yeah.

Professor: Can you give an example?

Neil: Well, I mean, they don't like me playing computer games at home so sometimes I say I'm going to the park, when I really go to Jason's house and play games. I feel kind of **guilty**, but…

Professor: Why do you think your parents don't like you playing computer games, Neil?

Neil: They say they're too violent, you know. And they think there's too much bad language. All that.

Professor: Are they right?

Neil: Yeah, I guess so. But playing those games doesn't mean I become violent and use bad language all the time! They should trust me more. Trust me to be responsible. I'm old enough to make my own decisions.

Professor: How do the rest of you feel about that? So you want your parents to trust you to be responsible. Does age have something to do with it? The amount of responsibility your parents think is **appropriate** might depend on how old you are. Yes, Naomi?

Naomi: Yes, I think that's right. But by the age of sixteen, you're old enough to know the difference between right and wrong.

Professor: Neil? Do you agree with that?

Neil: Yes, I'd say around fifteen, sixteen. You should be responsible for what you do by then.

Maria: I don't agree at all.

Professor: Really, Maria. Why not?

Maria: You're still too young at sixteen. People can **influence** you in the wrong way. I know people who changed a lot in high school, in a bad way, because they met the wrong people, had the wrong friends. I think you have to be twenty before you're really responsible.

Professor: Michael?

Michael: I think you can be responsible from a much younger age. I mean, from the age of five or six your parents can teach you what is right and wrong, how to behave, how to respect other people and…

Listen for Details   Page 92

[Repeat Main Ideas track]

PRONUNCIATION   Intonation in tag questions
Examples.   Page 97

Telling a lie is always wrong, isn't it?

We can trust Jeff, can't we?

Telling a lie is always wrong, isn't it?

We can trust Jeff, can't we?

A. Page 97

1. You're responsible for this, aren't you?
2. It's not my fault, is it?
3. The government should do something, shouldn't they?
4. Tina's late again, isn't she?

B. Page 97

1. You don't really believe that, do you?
2. Mike hasn't given us any help, has he?
3. The company accepted responsibility for the accident, didn't it?
4. Taxes have gone up again, haven't they?

SPEAKING SKILL   Leading a group discussion
A. Page 99

Leader: OK, so today we're going to look at recycling, and exactly who should be responsible. Brad, what's your opinion?

Brad: Well, I think that basically as individuals we can't change much. It's the government that has to take action.

Leader: I see. What do you think, Seline?

Seline: I don't agree. We all need to do what we can. I mean, just one person can't do much…but everyone in the world acting together can change a lot! It's the same with raising money for charity. When everyone gives a little money, you can raise millions!

Brad: Yes. My brother ran a marathon for charity last year and…

Leader: Sorry, but can we keep to the topic? Susan, do you have anything to add?

Susan: Well, I probably agree with Brad. Recycling is such a big problem—you need the government to act, really.

Leader: OK, so to sum up then, Susan and Brad feel the government should take responsibility, while Seline thinks individuals should lead the way.

Unit 6 Advertising

The Q Classroom Page 105

Teacher: The Unit Question for Unit 6 is "How can advertisers change our behavior?" So let's talk about how advertisers have changed our behavior. Yuna, have you ever bought something because you saw an ad for it?

Yuna: I don't think so. I don't pay attention to ads.

Teacher: Sophy, how about you?

Sophy: Well, maybe if I've seen ads for it and friends have liked it. I don't think I've bought anything just because of the ad.

Teacher: If we don't always buy things because of ads, why do advertisers make them? Can advertisers really change our behavior?

Marcus: You may not buy the product when you see the ad, but maybe it stays in your mind and one day you see it in the store and you buy it because it seems familiar.

Teacher: Do you agree with that, Felix? Can advertising change your behavior without you noticing it?

Felix: Sure. You hear the name of a company over and over, and you start to feel that that name is famous and trustworthy. For example, maybe I'm looking for an insurance company, and I'm nervous about choosing some place I've never heard of. But if I've heard the name a lot, I think, "This is a well-known company. I can trust them." And ads can also make you want things you never wanted before. Maybe your old phone works fine, but then you see an ad for a fancy new one that can do different things, and you think, "Oh, I need that!"

LISTENING 1 Advertising Techniques
Listen for Main Ideas Page 109

Professor: OK, everyone. So, this week we're looking at ways advertisers try to persuade us to buy products. I gave each group some techniques to research. Are you ready to begin your presentations? OK, so Leon, your group first, please.

Leon: Hello, everyone. Um, we had five techniques to research. I looked into ways advertisers try to reach us through our feelings. You know, like ads with babies and children. They're popular because we **relate to** them emotionally. This technique is called "emotional **appeal**." But I also found that many emotional appeal ads depend on negative emotions,

like fear. For example, no-smoking ads warn of the terrible things smoking does to your body. I found this example, too.

Is your home safe when you go out at night? Who's watching *your* house when you're not there? You work hard for the things you have. Don't let someone just take them! At Seattle Security, our locks are the best in the business. We will come to your home and give a free…yes, free…security check. We can fit locks on all your windows and doors. Keep safe. Keep your family safe. Call us at 1-888-555-8880. Don't delay.

Leon: Scary, right? Anyway, that's emotional appeal. Maria-Luz, you're next.

Maria-Luz: OK. Well, I looked into something called "association of ideas." That's when advertisers encourage us to make a link between a particular product and certain ideas. So, driving a particular car will make us happy and lucky in love. Wearing a certain type of running shoes will mean we win every race! That kind of thing. Here's an example I found.

Man 1: The wonderful aroma. The superb taste. Nothing can compare with the **memorable** experience of a bar of Robertson's Black. Made from the finest Swiss-style dark chocolate right here in California. Impress your friends any time of year with this delicious chocolate.

Man 1: Robertson's Black—When only the best is good enough.

Maria-Luz: So, in this **campaign**, advertisers are telling us that eating this **brand** of chocolate will make us appear cultured, and impress our friends. Over to you, Miguel.

Miguel: Thank you, Maria-Luz. I investigated something called the "bandwagon" technique. That's when advertisers **claim** that everyone is buying a product, so we should too. We're told that a product is the world's number one choice, or 80% of people use it. They want us to buy it so we don't feel, you know, left out. Here's an example.

Woman: Say, where is everybody? Why, they've all gone to Arizona Rodeo, of course! The biggest rodeo event of the year at Arizona Rodeo. Next Saturday, come and join the fun. Thousands of people will be there. Watch the bull riding, enjoy the fantastic barbecue, and dance to live music from the state's top country bands. Action starts at 11a.m. Fun for the whole family. Everybody will be there. Don't miss it! Buy your tickets now. Don't be the only person left behind.

Miguel: Joanna, it's your turn.

Joanna: Oh, my technique is really easy. It's repetition. That's when you see a company **logo** everywhere, or hear the name of a product all the time. Advertisers hope that by repeating key information it will be planted in our heads, so when we go to buy something we recognize it and choose it. This is why some ads also feature catchy **jingles** and **slogans**. They're really annoying because they stick in our heads.

Woman: This weekend only, at Ben's Diner, enjoy a fantastic family evening for only $10 per person. That's right. All you can eat for just $10 at Ben's Diner. Try our famous Ben's Diner homemade pizza, or a big, juicy steak and fries. And there's more…Kids under five eat free! Ben's Diner. 225 Mills Drive, Chicago. Bring the family. Bring your friends. Ben's Diner—The best value in town!

Joanna: Really annoying, right? Anyway, Brian, you're last.

Brian: Mine was a bit more fun. I looked at ads involving humor. Making people laugh is a great way to grab attention, and advertisers know that. They also know that a funny ad is more memorable. I found loads, and some are funnier than others, but here's one example:

Man 1: Hey, Terry! Come over here. I'd like you to meet… Whoa! What's that smell?

Woman 1: Ugh. What is it?

Man 2: Arrgh! I can't breathe!

Man 1: Terry, did you shower before you came out tonight?

Woman 2: Oops! Don't let embarrassing body odor affect your social life. Buy Sparks Body Refresher today. Leaves your skin feeling fresh and smooth. Oh, and did I mention you can choose from three great fragrances?

Professor: OK, that was great. Now, next group…

Listen for Details Page 109

[Repeat Main Ideas track]

LISTENING SKILL Identifying fact and opinion
A. Page 110

1. Kids under five eat free!
2. Ben's Diner—the best value in town!
3. At Seattle Security our locks are the best in the business.

B. Page 110

1. We have the best range of personal computers in the state.
2. The MX5 is the latest personal computer from XP Systems.
3. It has a 380 Gigabyte memory.
4. It is very easy to use.
5. This is the most important purchase you will make all year.
6. This offer is available for this week only.

LISTENING 2 Advertising Ethics and Standards
Page 112

Interviewer: Mary Engle, can I start by asking a simple question? What exactly does the FTC do?

Mary Engle: Well, we basically keep an eye on the world of advertising, and make sure that advertisers keep to the "truth-in-advertising" laws. That is, that their ads have to be truthful, and that they shouldn't **mislead** anyone—

Interviewer: Hmm. I see.

ME: —so of course any claims have to be based on **evidence**.

In the early days of advertising, companies could say what they wanted! I mean, ads for weight loss products, for example, were making claims that simply weren't true. Things are different now, though. These days advertisers have to be very careful when giving facts and statistics.

Interviewer: So, what areas do you focus on in particular?

ME: Health…claims that are hard to prove such as the benefits of health products. And safety, of course. If a product says it's safe, then it has to be safe! Also things like beauty products, and environmental claims. Oh, and any ads **aimed at** children, especially now that healthy eating is such a big issue. We just want to make sure that advertisers act in a responsible way, in these areas especially.

Interviewer: OK. But there's no national code, is there?

ME: No, there isn't. The **regulations** are different for TV, radio, and so on. Basically, they are all aimed at the same thing; ads can't be unfair. That means they shouldn't cause physical **injury** to the consumer, or financial injury, you know, where consumers lose money.

Interviewer: And how do you find ads that break the rules?

ME: Well, mostly people tell us! You know, members of the public, **competitors**…They contact us about ads they think are misleading. And we **monitor** ads ourselves, of course: TV, radio, magazines, newspapers, posters, leaflets, and so on. We don't see ads before they come out, though. We can only act afterwards. And we just deal with national advertising, so any local matters we refer to the state.

Interviewer: Right. Are there any famous cases where advertisers broke the rules?

ME: Plenty! A few years ago a fast food chain actually claimed its food was a *healthy* choice! This clearly wasn't true, so we took action.

Interviewer: And what happens to advertisers who break the rules?

ME: Sometimes we ask them to **withdraw** the ad, as we did with the fast food chain. Uh, if they continue false advertising we can give fines of up to $11,000 a day. Sometimes more. There was a company selling weight loss vitamins a few years ago—they continued to make false claims after we told them not to, so in the end they paid $2.6 million in fines. Other times advertisers may have to give customers a **refund**, or put another ad out to correct anything misleading. We call that "corrective advertising."

Interviewer: Hmm. And how have new forms of advertising affected your work?

ME: Oh! It's a lot tougher these days. Well there's the Internet, of course. That's really challenging. It's so cheap and easy to advertise on the net. We find a lot of companies that don't know the rules about advertising. We're also getting ads in video games now, although that's mainly product placement rather than advertisers making claims.

Interviewer: What's product placement?

ME: That's when a product appears in a movie, game, or TV program. You know…a billboard in the background or where the star wears a watch or drives a car and it's **deliberately** very visible. It's very common here in the States.

Interviewer: I've also heard of something called sub-viral marketing that's becoming popular.

ME: Oh yes. That's where a company will put a funny video or something on the Internet, which features their product, and they hope people will send it to their friends. More and more big companies are doing that, but they need to make it clear that it's an ad, or they're misleading people.

Interviewer: That's interesting. Well, thanks very much, Mary, for telling us about standards in advertising. It's been great.

ME: You're welcome.

Listen for Details Page 112

[Repeat Main Ideas track]

GRAMMAR Modals expressing attitude
A. Page 116

Yvonne: Oh, look at that ad. Those poor animals. How can they show them suffering like that? I think it's terrible!

Martin: Really? I think it's quite effective. They're trying to get your attention, you know.

Yvonne: Well, they don't have to do it that way! It's not necessary, and it's upsetting.

Martin: You don't have to look at it if you don't want to.

Yvonne: That's not the point. That kind of advertising makes me really angry. I'm sure there's a law that says they can't use animals like that.

Martin: Maybe you should complain, then.

Yvonne: Yes, I think I will. They shouldn't be allowed to do that!

PRONUNCIATION Part 1: Intonation in questions
Examples. Page 117

Is there an advertising standards code?

Are the rules the same in other countries?

How do you find ads that break the rules?

What areas do you focus on in particular?

A. Page 117

1. Do you spend a lot of money on advertising?
2. What do you think of that ad?
3. Is that ad misleading?
4. Does it have a special offer?
5. Why is there so much hype these days?

B. Page 117

1. Do you spend a lot of money on advertising?
2. What do you think of that ad?
3. Is that ad misleading?
4. Does it have a special offer?
5. Why is there so much hype these days?

PRONUNCIATION Part 2: Intonation in questions
Examples. Page 118

There are no federal regulations.

There are no federal regulations?

They're going to withdraw the product.

They're going to withdraw the product?

C. Page 118.

1. There are no federal regulations?
2. The company is giving a refund to all its customers.
3. You're going to withdraw the product?
4. That ad is really annoying.
5. There used to be no controls?
6. The rules aren't the same in other countries?
7. Viral marketing is becoming more popular.

D. Page 118

1. There are no federal regulations?
2. The company is giving a refund to all its customers.
3. You're going to withdraw the product?
4. That ad is really annoying.
5. There used to be no controls?
6. The rules aren't the same in other countries?
7. Viral marketing is becoming more popular.

SPEAKING SKILL Giving and supporting your opinions
Page 119

Hugo: Hey. Look at this ad. It's got six famous people in it!

Beatrice: So what? If you ask me, they should spend less on these expensive ads and lower the price of their clothes.

Hugo: Hmm. But I like seeing famous people in ads because it makes it kind of cool.

Beatrice: As far as I'm concerned, there are better ways to advertise things. For instance, they could have some facts and statistics or something. You know, some information…

Hugo: But it's an ad, right? In my opinion, an ad should get people's attention, and using famous people does that.

Beatrice: Well, I guess it's eye-catching, but I'm not sure how effective it is.

Unit 7 Risk

The Q Classroom Page 125

Teacher: Here we are at Unit 7. "What risks are good to take?" is our question. So what are some risks that people take that can be good? Felix?

Felix: Well, there are social risks—for example, introducing yourself to new people.

Teacher: Definitely risky! Is it good to take social risks? Marcus, what do you think?

Marcus: Yes, it's good. You need to take those risks to meet new people. If you don't, you might not make any new friends. It might take a few tries, but that's OK. You can learn from your mistakes.

Teacher: What other kinds of risks are there? What kinds of risks do people take with their jobs? Yuna?

Yuna: Um, getting a new job?

Teacher: Sure. Changing jobs or careers can be a big risk. Is it a good risk to take? Sophy?

Sophy: Maybe. You might lose money or cause problems for your family. But if the new job or career makes you happy in the long run, it could be a good risk to take. You need to think carefully before you take that kind of risk, though. You shouldn't just jump into it.

Teacher: OK, so you believe in being careful about taking risks. I can understand that.

LISTENING 1 Financing a Dream
Listen for Main Ideas Page 128

Host: Independent filmmakers have always had a hard time getting their movies made. Michael Andrews talks about the risks filmmakers have taken and will continue to take to make a dream come true.

Michael Andrews: In the 1980s, Hollywood was spending millions on special effects for movies like *Top Gun*. At the same time, Spike Lee made his first movie for the very low cost of a hundred and eighty thousand dollars. He used his own savings. Back then, the average Hollywood film cost about 100 times that amount—nearly eighteen million. A year later, another African American filmmaker, Robert Townsend, made a hit comedy called *The Hollywood Shuffle*. He spent even less, about a hundred thousand. He said he had charged almost half of that on his **credit** cards.

Independent filmmakers have even won Oscars by going into personal **debt** to make their movies. This has become a new **model** for either independent success or **financial** failure. There are other models. Some moviemakers have taken out second mortgages on their homes. Many shoot on video rather than film to save a lot of money. Independent moviemakers try to keep the costs as low as possible.

In the 1990s, when Kevin Smith made a comedy, he did it for just twenty-seven thousand dollars. And then Robert Rodriguez made *El Mariachi*, a movie about a singer, for only seven

thousand. Rodriguez risked more than his money to raise the **funds** for the film. Rodriguez raised a lot of the seven thousand by taking part in drug testing trials for drug companies. Taking these new drugs could have **threatened** his health. But the risk was worth it. *El Mariachi* made millions at the box office. After that, a movie studio provided the funds for his second and third movies. Peter Jackson, the director of *King Kong* and other successful movies, took four years to make his first film. He used his **income** from a full-time job to produce the movie. He and his friends worked for free on weekends. They acted all the parts and worked with the equipment. Near the end, the New Zealand Film Commission gave Jackson about two hundred and fifty thousand dollars to help him finish.

Independent filmmakers have often had to take financial risks to make movies. Now they may have new help. Some filmmakers are putting their work on the Internet. With a video camera and a little time, anyone can make and show a movie to thousands of viewers. Matt Harding is a good example. He quit his job. He used his savings to travel around the world. Someone took videos of Matt as he danced in places around the world, and Matt put them on the Internet. A chewing gum company saw Matt's videos, and decided to sponsor him. Matt still travels around the world dancing, but now he gets paid.

The Internet **exposes** a filmmaker's work to a huge **audience**. But that may not be such a good thing. Although the moviemaker does not risk much money, he or she does risk something else. A film on the internet can **embarrass** the filmmaker if it is not done well. And everyone can see it. I'm Michael Andrews.

Listen for Details Page 129

[Repeat Main Ideas track]

LISTENING SKILL Part 1: Identifying amounts; cardinal and ordinal numbers
Example 1. Page 130

five hundred dollars

one thousand pounds

ten thousand euros

two hundred thousand dollars

five million pounds

twelve billion euros

Example 2. Page 130

In the 1990s, when Kevin Smith made a comedy, he did it for just twenty-seven thousand **dollars**. And then Robert Rodriguez made *El Mariachi*, a movie about a singer, for only **seven** thousand.

Example 3. Page 130

It was a fifty-dollar shirt.

The three-hundred-pound football player needed a larger uniform.

The four-hundred-seat theater was too small for the crowd.

It's a fifteen-minute bus ride to my office.

A. Page 130

1. Spike Lee made his first movie for the very low cost of a hundred and eighty thousand dollars.
2. The cheapest tickets are ten dollars.
3. The five-pound bag of sugar is three dollars.
4. The four-hundred-seat theater was too small for the crowd.
5. That store sells five-hundred-dollar shoes.
6. We took a ten-question survey online.
7. My suitcase weighs over sixty pounds.
8. Maria found a fifty-dollar bill on the sidewalk

LISTENING SKILL Part 2: Identifying amounts; cardinal and ordinal numbers
Examples. Page 131

one; first

two; second

three; third

five; fifth

seven; seventh

twenty; twentieth

thirty-four; thirty-fourth

forty-six; forty-sixth

C. Page 131

1. The seventh test can be taken this week.
2. The nine students left an hour ago.
3. I ate the fifteen cookies.
4. Did you receive the sixth email I sent you?
5. Push the fourth button.

D. Page 132

1. The seventh test can be taken this week.
2. The nine students left an hour ago.
3. I ate the fifteen cookies.
4. Did you receive the sixth email I sent you?
5. Push the fourth button.

LISTENING 2 The Truth about the Loch Ness Monster
Listen for Main Ideas Page 133

Reporter: For centuries, people have believed in **mysteries** such as the Loch Ness Monster. One such believer is Bob Rines, a lawyer, an inventor, a war hero, and a scientist and professor at the Massachusetts Institute of Technology (MIT). Why would a famous man of science risk his **reputation** trying to prove Nessie, or the Loch Ness Monster, exists? Because Bob Rines has seen the monster himself. In June of 1972, Bob Rines

was visiting Loch Ness. Loch Ness is the largest freshwater lake in Scotland. He'd been to the lake on a **previous** visit to **investigate** the reports of a large, strange animal that lived in the deep water. He hadn't believed the reports at first. Then he met many people who had seen the monster. By the time Rines came back on the second visit, he'd started to change his mind.

On that June night in 1972, Rines and his companions saw a large gray shape move across the surface of the lake. That event changed Bob Rines' life. He made a promise to **prove** the monster existed, no matter how it threatened his reputation. Until Rines **retired** in 2008, he'd taught classes at MIT. His classes focused on discovery and invention. Through his work as an inventor and lawyer, Rines **solved** problems and found new ways to do things. Unfortunately, even with this background, he hasn't found enough evidence of the Loch Ness Monster to satisfy most scientists. And this may threaten the way people think about Rines. They may remember him only as a *crazy* person who believed in monsters. They may not remember him as a well-known scientist. He worked on the technology that **discovered** the famous ship the *Titanic* on the ocean floor.

In his efforts to find the monster, Rines has been creative. He asked a perfume company to make a chemical that would attract the monster. He also trained two dolphins to carry cameras. He wanted to take the dolphins to Loch Ness so they could photograph the monster. Although these ideas didn't work, Rines has been successful in other ways. In trying to **locate** Nessie, he and a friend **invented** a device with an underwater camera. The camera took pictures when it detected something nearby. The device hasn't taken any pictures of Nessie, however. Rines thinks this is because Nessie is dead.

What do Rines' efforts to find the monster tell us about human nature? Maybe that people need to believe in mystery. And that we want to discover something new, no matter the cost.

Listen for Details Page 134

[Repeat Main Ideas track]

PRONUNCIATION Contraction of *had*
Examples. Page 139

1. I'd already finished the test when the teacher collected our papers.
   He'd eaten at that restaurant before.
   We'd often talked about getting married.
   You'd left when we got there.
   She'd written her email before she received mine.
2. Had you heard from him by the time you left?
   Had everyone finished the test by two o'clock?
3. I hadn't finished my phone call by the time the train arrived.
   They hadn't gone to the movies before they ate dinner.

A. Page 139

1. He'd worked at a bookstore.
2. We left when it started raining.

3. They answered the questions.

4. I'd eaten my lunch.

5. You'd already taken the test.

6. She hadn't worked there.

7. It hasn't started to rain.

8. Had he found it?

9. Have you called Alex?

B. Page 140

1. He'd worked at a bookstore.

2. We left when it started raining.

3. They answered the questions.

4. I'd eaten my lunch.

5. You'd already taken the test.

6. She hadn't worked there.

7. It hasn't started to rain.

8. Had he found it?

9. Have you called Alex?

SPEAKING SKILL Giving a short presentation
Page 141

Man: I'm going to talk about a time I took a risk and it turned out well. I'd always wanted to learn to speak Japanese. When I was in high school, I started to take classes in Japanese. By the time I graduated from college, I had studied the language for eight years, but I still couldn't speak it very well, so I decided to go to Japan to study. I didn't know anyone there. My grandmother had died the year before, so I used the money she had left me for the trip. Before I left, I'd done some research on language schools. I stayed in Japan for three months and met some great people there. My Japanese improved a lot. By the time I finally returned to my country, I had become fluent.

Consider the Ideas Page 142

Woman: Some risks are worth taking. I took one huge one, but it turned out to be the best thing I think I've ever done in my life. I lived in Reading in England and after several failed attempts at backpacking through Europe (Amsterdam, Paris...) I was starting to give in. I took a 9 til 6 office job in an accounts department, spent most of my money on shopping and going out, and basically led a "normal" life.

Something was missing, though, and I couldn't work out what. I had a nice house, a good job, a good social life with lots of friends. I decided that to work out what was missing I needed to leave what I had. I chose to leave it to destiny and got out a world map. I closed my eyes and moved my hand over the map, put my finger down, and opened my eyes. It had landed on Italy. I decided that if I was going to go to Italy, the best place to start was the capital. Two weeks later, I was on a plane to Rome. I couldn't make up my mind whether I was brave or stupid...or maybe both.

Unit 8 Cities

The Q Classroom Page 147

Teacher: The Unit 8 question is "What do our cities say about us?" So let's talk about this city. How would you describe it? Big or small? Noisy or quiet? Relaxed or exciting? Yuna?

Yuna: It's big, noisy, and exciting.

Teacher: Do you like living here?

Yuna: Yes.

Teacher: OK, Yuna likes living here. What does that say about her? What kind of people like living in a city like this? Marcus?

Marcus: We like excitement. We like to see lots of different kinds of people and eat different kinds of food. We like to go out a lot.

Teacher: And what about people who choose to live in a small town? What does their city say about them?

Sophy: Um. They like things to be quiet. They like to know their neighbors and not be surrounded by strangers all of the time.

Teacher: But there are some other kinds of differences among cities besides size. What else do our cities say about us?

Felix: Well, in this city, everything is close together and people walk around a lot. I think people here have a lot of energy. In some cities, people mostly live in the suburbs and drive. So they're more slow-moving and less energetic. Maybe they're more relaxed. I guess it depends on your point of view.

LISTENING 1 Do Cities Have Personalities?
Listen for Main Ideas Page 150

Commentator: This is Ellen Coyle with *Talk About the News*. In today's world, some might argue that it doesn't really matter where you live. That's not true, according to Richard Florida. He believes the world now has **regions** known for particular jobs and certain types of people. In his book *Who's Your City?* Richard Florida says the decision about where to live may be the most important one you make. He says the place we choose to live affects the income we earn, the people we meet, the friends we make, and the partners we choose. So how do we end up living in the cities we live in?

Florida thinks that people tend to collect in certain cities according to the work they do and even the type of personality they have. Some cities, such as Boston, San Francisco, and Seoul, lead the way in technology and **innovation**. New York and London are financial centers. Cities like Los Angeles and even Wellington, New Zealand, produce quality films. Others such as Sydney, Dublin, and Toronto **attract** many types of companies and skills, and still others like Guadalajara and Shanghai are known primarily for manufacturing. Why are some cities centers of creativity while others are more likely to focus on producing things? Richard Florida uses recent research about the United States to suggest that personality may play a role.

Cities like Boston and San Francisco are home to people who are open to experience. They like high levels of activity, and new ideas. These cities are magnets for people who are curious, but who may also like to work alone. The location may spark their **innovation**. Most technology companies are in or near these centers of creativity. The people in cities like Chicago, or perhaps Sydney, on the other hand, **tend to** be much more social, and like to play sports and get together with friends. Many people in these cities are in sales or jobs that deal with people directly. In cities like Atlanta or Pittsburgh, residents are both **conscientious** and **agreeable**. They tend to follow rules and work well on teams, qualities that are important in manufacturing. Many of the German and Japanese auto companies are located in these areas, where they have a workforce that meets their needs.

So why might we see similar people living in certain places? Richard Florida suggests a couple of explanations. First, people may move to the place that will **satisfy** their psychological needs. A very social person may be happier near Chicago and so chooses to live there. A second explanation is that our **surroundings** affect our personalities. Someone who moves to Atlanta or Dallas may become more agreeable because of the people nearby. Third, research suggests that those people who are creative and seek new experience are more likely to pack up and leave one place for another. So someone good at developing software or writing may move to a place like Vancouver or Seattle for the risk as well as to be near others of a similar mind.

The geography and history of a place and the personalities of its people work **hand in hand** to create centers that seem to be particularly good at certain things. People tend to be happier in places that suit them psychologically. During good economic times, when the population is more **mobile**, people can choose to live in a city that matches their personalities and interests. Of course, bad economic times can cause different shifts in cities. Long-term financial centers like London and New York can become less important as centers in other parts of the world, such as Hong Kong, become more important. But creative people will probably continue to move to places where they know innovation is important.

Let us know what you think. Tell us: do you agree with Richard Florida? If your city had a personality, what is it? And does it match your own? Who's your city? Go to our website and tell us about the city where you live and also a little about yourself…

Listen for Details Page 151

[Repeat Main Ideas track]

LISTENING SKILL Understanding figurative meaning
Example. Page 152

These cities are magnets for people who are curious, but who may also like to work alone. The location may spark their innovation.

B. Page 153

1. My mother is the heart of our family.

2. I'm not sure what I am going to do, but I have the seed of an idea.

3. The vending machine ate all of my money.

4. I can't believe it's so late. The time just flew by.

LISTENING 2 Buenos Aires, Beijing, and Dubai
Listen for Main Ideas Page 154

1. Buenos Aires

Marcos Aguinis: Many people compare Buenos Aires to Paris. I know what they mean. Indeed, the stamp of Europe is difficult to miss in this city of boulevards, palaces, opera houses, and monuments. But Buenos Aires is so much more.

I was born outside of Buenos Aires, but was attracted to the city by the cafés that satisfy the thirst and spirit of every hopeful writer: Writers, journalists, musicians, and politicians met here. Sipping the strong coffee, listening to the mix of ideas, I developed ideas for my novels.

My favorite square is the Plaza de Mayo, and standing there today for me is like entering a time machine. It was here that the seeds of independence were planted; where Argentinean president Juan Perón and his wife Evita shouted from the balcony of their residence, the Casa Rosada.

The arts and music scene in Buenos Aires was always a center of cultural innovation. Ideas and **values** still considered strange elsewhere were often accepted here. Filmmakers Luis Buñuel, Ingmar Bergman, and Woody Allen were **celebrated** in my city when they were still almost unknown in Europe and the United States. The writer Jorge Luis Borges used the **lively** neighborhood where I live as a setting for many of his stories. The most celebrated singers and conductors not only came to Buenos Aires, but also toured dozens of opera houses throughout the country. And the dance, the tango—born in the streets of our neighborhood—soon captured the world.

There are some people who feel embarrassed by the European aspects of Buenos Aires and believe we should be more "Latin American." But Europe's influence was never a limitation for the city, more a launching pad. European and Latin American **characters** live together, creating uniqueness. Those of us who live here, and even visitors who allow the city to **reveal** itself to them, know Buenos Aires to be like no other.

2. Beijing

Peter Hessler: The city of Beijing—busy and huge, home to some 15 million people—was originally designed along the simple lines of a body. According to traditional Chinese stories, the god Nezha tamed the rivers of the country, and the layout of the city's buildings reflected his physical form. The Gate of Heavenly Peace, Tiananmen, was his brain and the Zhengyang Gate was his head. Today, Beijing's largest map publisher has to **update** their Beijing diagrams every three months to try to keep up with changes. Sometimes they even try to draw tomorrow: On the wall of their office hangs an enormous map of Beijing, future-tense. There are new streets, new buildings, new bus lines. The only thing that isn't new is the feeling of change, because for the past century Beijing has been a city which has been constantly changing.

The people, though, will always tell you what they think. In modern times, that's become the heart of Beijing; the city's construction is changing quickly, but the local character can still be drawn in clear, **precise** lines. The typical Beijinger is **direct**, practical, and has opinions. He knows politics and culture better than business. The Beijinger usually expresses his opinions through humor rather than anger. Mostly, he remembers. He remembers the clear blue skies of the pre-pollution capital. This is Beijing pride. There is no other part of the country where memories are so long.

3. Dubai

Paul Coelho: On a recent trip to Dubai, I took a quick walk through the narrow roads of the Bastakiya Quarter, an old village that **provides** a look at a slower-paced time. In the village of Bastakiya, you cannot take a walk on your own, because its roads were designed in such a way that only the people who lived in the village knew the way through it, making it a safer place to live. The roads were a place for people to get together over dinner and special feasts, to share news, and to discuss common village issues. High wind towers grow from houses, bringing cool air throughout the home. The more I walked around the Bastakiya, the more I felt the greatness of the people who once lived in them.

I left old Dubai for new Dubai, on the west side of the city. New Dubai has fancy modern buildings—the luxury hotel built on an **artificial** island, and the world's tallest skyscraper. In Dubai's central business district, locals say that you can buy anything that comes to mind. In new Dubai, young people pursue their dreams, trying to achieve the impossible. This is a city that has been working for the past two decades, with no rest at all. Its residents all share one goal: to win at all times, even if they have to race time itself. Although they may not share a common language, they know they will succeed, because they all speak the language of success.

Listen for Details Page 155

[Repeat Main Ideas track]

PRONUNCIATION Links between consonants and vowels

Examples. Page 160

Please put away your books.

I hope you get over the flu soon.

Can you look after my camera for a moment?

Did you find out what happened?

Can you come over this evening?

A. Page 160

1. Can you look after my apartment when I'm in Paris?

2. I'd like to bring up a topic for discussion.

3. I need to look up some information about Cape Town.

4. Would you point out my mistakes?

5. The plane is about to take off.

SPEAKING SKILL Recapping a presentation

A. Page 161

Woman: A number of years ago, I moved from Boston to Charlotte. It took some time for me to get to know my new city. One of the first things I noticed was how pretty the city was. It has many trees and nice neighborhoods. Charlotte is also very clean. You don't see garbage on the streets. Like many cities in the southern part of the United States, the people are very friendly and like to talk to new people. That's a very good thing because so many people have moved to Charlotte in recent years, from other parts of the United States and from other countries. Twenty years ago, the people were similar to each other, but now the city is more interesting. You can find Chinese, Mexican, and Vietnamese restaurants. However, Charlotte still doesn't have as many good places to eat as Boston does. Boston also has more cultural opportunities and activities such as museums and concerts, although Charlotte is providing more each year. I also think that Charlotte is still too quiet. There aren't as many places to go out in the evening. One thing I miss about Boston is the number of creative people who live there. Perhaps because there are so many universities in Boston, it's a center of innovation.

C. Page 161

Woman: To summarize, on the positive side, Charlotte is pretty and clean and the people are friendly. It is also becoming more interesting because of the different people who are moving there. On the negative side, Charlotte is too quiet, with not as much to do as in Boston. It also has fewer cultural activities, places to eat, and creative people.

Unit 9 Money

The Q Classroom Page 167

Teacher: Unit 9's question is, "Can money buy happiness?" What do you think, Marcus? Would you be happier with more money?

Marcus: Yes. If I had lots of money, I wouldn't have to worry about getting a job. I could just do the things I like to do all day, so of course I would be happy.

Teacher: What about you, Yuna? Would you be happy with more money?

Yuna: Yes, I would.

Teacher: Why?

Yuna: I could help my family.

Teacher: So Yuna and Marcus want more money. Does this mean money can buy happiness?

Felix: No, it doesn't. Money can't buy health. And being healthy is the first step to being happy. No matter how rich you are, you won't be happy if you're sick. And money can't buy friends and family, either, and you can't be happy without good relationships in your life.

Teacher: What do you think, Sophy?

Sophy: Well, I couldn't be happy with *no* money, but being rich doesn't mean you will be happy. There are lots of rich people who are unhappy. I think some people are just unhappy no matter what they have, and some people are just happy.

LISTENING 1 Sudden Wealth
Listen for Main Ideas Page 170

Speaker: Have you ever dreamed of winning a large amount of money, or inheriting millions from a distant relative? Me, I don't really care where the money comes from, as long as it comes, because the money will solve all my problems, right?

The reality is that people who **acquire** a sudden fortune, whether they earn it or **inherit** it, experience a lot of stress. I know. It doesn't make sense. Who would believe that an enormous amount of cash would be hard to handle? But sudden money is not always a good thing. It's easy to forget that a large quantity of money can have several **destructive** effects on our lives.

First, it affects how our brains work, at least for a while. Sure, if you give someone money, there will be an **immediate** effect on his brain, similar to the way his brain would respond to food or medication. But that **pleasure** goes away quickly. Similarly, people think they will enjoy something they buy much longer than they actually do. The problem is that our brains **get used to** positive experiences. In the beginning, when we get the money, our brain identifies it as pleasure. Then that feeling **wears off**. The same thing happens when we spend the money on something we think we really want. And to get the same amount of pleasure the next time, we need to buy something even bigger and better. It's not a surprise that many people who acquire a lot of money they didn't expect, lose it all within a few years.

Second, sudden wealth can also affect our social relationships. Interestingly, sudden wealth and the sudden loss of money can have quite similar effects. It's the **dramatic** change in **circumstances** that causes the problems. In the case of sudden wealth, too many other people want something from their newly rich friend or relative. And they may not understand the stress the rich person is experiencing, thinking, "Oh, too bad. I wish I had your problems." Most people get a lot of pleasure from being with other people, but a sudden change in your financial picture can make you feel alone. If you move because of changing circumstances, you won't have your usual sources of support. That expensive house on a private island somewhere may not be quite as wonderful as it sounds if no one is with you.

A third effect of sudden wealth is emotional. People who acquire huge amounts of cash very quickly can experience many negative emotions, such as fear, shame, guilt, and anxiety. These feelings can lead to making bad decisions. *How* you get the money can also contribute to negative feelings. If someone dies and leaves you a fortune, the relationship you had with that person can make things more **complicated**. If you loved him, you may feel sadness. If you never visited her, you may feel guilt. If you didn't get along, you may feel uncomfortable. And none of these feelings will make you happy.

So if sudden wealth buys just as much stress as it does happiness, what good is it? Probably not much, unless you are very sick and it buys you needed health care. Or you are very poor and it provides you with food and shelter. For most of the rest of us, people who are getting along okay without it, sudden wealth is often more trouble than it's worth.

Listen for Details Page 171

[Repeat Main Ideas track]

LISTENING SKILL Listening for signposts
Examples. Page 172

First, it affects how our brains work, at least for a while.

In the beginning, when we get the money, our brain identifies it as pleasure. Then that feeling wears off.

A. Page 172

Reporter: You are one of many people in this town who suddenly acquired a lot of wealth when your company was purchased by a large software company. How has that affected your life?

Laura Green: Well, in the beginning, it was pretty incredible. It took a while for me to believe it. But then I began to realize what it could actually do to my life. Things have changed dramatically.

Reporter: In what way?

LG: I paid off all of my credit card debt. And sent my son to college. Receiving this money was just fantastic! Before that, I was worried all the time.

Reporter: So your financial circumstances have improved. What else has changed?

LG: You know, I was a secretary at that company for 20 years. I had gotten used to just working to pay the bills. I always wished I could do more with my life. Finally, I can do that.

Reporter: And what do you want to do?

LG: First, I'm going to go to Paris. I've always dreamed of going there. Next, I'm thinking of going back to school. I'd like to study gardening. I love flowers. After that, maybe I will open my own business.

Reporter: We hear stories in the news all the time about people who get a lot of money suddenly and have many problems. How do you think those problems can be avoided?

LG: It's about staying true to your values and remembering what's really important in life. You don't need to let money complicate things.

LISTENING 2 Happiness Breeds Success…and Money!
Listen for Main Ideas Page 175

Host: …Welcome back, you're listening to *Pause for Thought* with Brian Thompson. Today's subject is money, money, money, and in this next part of the show I'm going to be talking to Sonja Lyubomirsky, an experimental social psychologist who has been studying the causes of happiness for almost 20 years. It's wonderful to have you in the studio, Sonja.

Sonja Lyubomirsky: Thanks, Brian, it's a pleasure to be here.

Host: Now, Sonja, let me ask you the obvious question first: what have you discovered in all those years of research? What is it that makes people happy…could it be money?

SL: Well, Brian, not money exactly, but I'll get to that in a minute. Until a few years ago, if you had asked me what makes people happy, my answer would have been, "It's relationships, stupid." That is, I always responded that our personal relationships—the strength of our friendships, family, and other close connections—have the greatest influence on happiness.

So, I was very surprised when two other researchers and I **conducted** an **analysis** of 225 studies of happiness. I **wholly** expected to discover that social relationships, more than anything else, would be both causes and consequences of being happy. However, what I found was something rather different. There is something much more important than relationships—work.

Host: Work makes us happy? That *is* surprising. How?

SL: The evidence, for example, **demonstrates** that people who have jobs with **independence** and some variety—and who show creativity and productivity—are significantly happier than those who don't. And, of course, the income that a job provides is also **associated with** happiness. However, we all know that money has more of an impact when we don't have very much.

Host: Okay, so work—at least some kinds of work—can make us happy. Why?

SL: Because work provides us a sense of identity, structure to our days, and important goals in life. Perhaps even more importantly, it provides us with close colleagues, friends, and even marriage partners.

But that's not all. Studies reveal that the relationship between happiness and work goes both ways. Not only do creativity and productivity at work make people happy, but happier people are better workers. And they are less likely to take sick days, to quit, or to **burn out**.

The most **persuasive** data regarding the effects of happiness on positive work **outcomes** come from scientific studies that follow the same people over a long period of time. These studies are great. For example, people who report that they are happy at age 18 have better jobs by age 26. And the happier a person is, the more likely she will get a job offer, keep her job, and get a new job if she ever loses it. The same people who are happy at age 18 have more financial independence later in life also.

Host: Could you tell us more about the financial side of happiness?

SL: Well, not only does greater wealth make people **somewhat** happy, but happy people appear more likely to acquire greater wealth in life. For example, research has demonstrated that the happier a person is at one point in his life, the higher income he will earn at a later point. In one of my favorite studies, researchers showed that those who were happy at age 21 had higher incomes 16 years later, when they were about 37!

But before we find yet another reason to wish we were very happy, consider what the research on happiness and work suggests. The more successful we are at our jobs, the higher income we make, and the better work environment we have, the happier we will be. This increased happiness will contribute to greater success, more money, and an improved work environment, which will lead to greater happiness, and so on, and so on.

Host: So what you're saying, Sonja, is that if we are happy, we are more likely to get a job we like, and if we have a job we like, we are likely to make more money. I wonder if our listeners find that to be true in their own lives. Let's go to our first caller this evening, and find out: Joanna in Chicago. Joanna, welcome to *Pause for Thought*…

Listen for Details Page 176

[Repeat Main Ideas track]

PRONUNCIATION: Intonation in different types of sentences
A. Page 181

1a. Is this your new coat?

1b. This is your new coat.

2a. Tell me what you want to buy.

2b. What do you want to buy?

3a. Saving money can actually be fun.

3b. Saving money can actually be fun!

B. Page 181

1a. Is this your new coat?

1b. This is your new coat.

2a. Tell me what you want to buy.

2b. What do you want to buy?

3a. Saving money can actually be fun.

3b. Saving money can actually be fun!

SPEAKING SKILL Agreeing and disagreeing
A. Page 182

1. **Ellie:** What are you going to do with the money your grandfather gave you?

   Sam: I'm not sure. I think I'm going to take an expensive vacation.

   Ellie: Really? Don't you have a lot of school loans to pay?

   Sam: That's a good point. Maybe the vacation's not such a good idea.

   Ellie: You can say that again! Vacations are fun, but it's much more important to pay off your debt.

2. **Monica:** I think raising the average income in countries around the world is the best way to increase the level of happiness.

   Patricia: I don't feel the same way. More money might make the very poor happier, but not everyone.

   Monica: I disagree. I think everyone except perhaps the very wealthy will benefit from a higher income.

   Patricia: Well, I can see we'll just have to agree to disagree.

Unit 10 Keeping in Touch

The Q Classroom Page 187

Teacher: "Do we need technology to communicate long distance?" This is our question for Unit 10. Yuna, how do you communicate with your long-distance friends and family?

Yuna: Through the Internet, mostly—Internet phone calls or video chat. I text my friends a lot.

Teacher: How about you, Sophy? Do you text and chat like Yuna, or do you use email or the telephone?

Sophy: Well, I don't use email much to talk to family and friends, but I use it for other things, like communicating with teachers. And I make telephone calls to have a long conversation with a friend or when I'm talking to my mother.

Teacher: So do we need technology to easily communicate long distance? What did people do before? Marcus?

Marcus: They wrote letters mostly. It was very slow and you couldn't be in touch like you can now. So I would say that to communicate as much as we do now, you definitely need technology.

Teacher: Does anybody write letters anymore? Why would you write a letter?

Felix: Businesses write letters. People notice something more if it comes in the mail. Also, when something is very important, like a wedding announcement or a sympathy card, people usually send it in the mail. The method you choose just depends on who you are communicating with and what you want to say. In the old days, you didn't have a choice.

LISTENING 1 An Unusual Language
Listen for Main Ideas Page 190

Professor: Today I'm going to talk about one of the most unusual forms of language. As you know, humans have a natural ability to learn languages, and there are many different spoken languages in the world—actually over 6,500 total. But are there any languages that are *not* spoken? Raise your hand if you know of any other types of language.

OK, I see a couple of hands in the air. Don, give us an example of a language that is not spoken.

Don: Sign language.

Professor: Yes, that's a great example. Sign language is used to communicate but does not **require** speaking. Instead, it uses hand motions. Any other ideas?

What if I told you there is a language that uses whistling to communicate? It's true! The language is named Silbo, after the Spanish word *silbar*, which means "to whistle," and it is used in the Canary Islands.

This language was brought to the islands by Africans back in the 15th century. When the Spanish came, the whistling was adapted, or changed, to be closer to Spanish in its grammar. During the 20th century, it nearly became extinct because there were so many other methods of communication. But the people and the government didn't want to lose this language and now it is taught in elementary schools on the islands. Surprisingly, the very technology that threatened to make Silbo extinct is now helping to bring it back. The Internet offers ways for people to learn this language online.

So why did this language develop? Silbo is a very useful language because the whistles can be heard more than two miles away. The islands have many hills and valleys, which make it difficult for people to communicate with each other from one hill to the next. Whistling is more **efficient** than face-to-face communication because it saves people the time of traveling over to the other hill. Silbo is even useful for people with cell phones. Because the islands are **remote**, cell phone **coverage** is not reliable there.

Silbo can be used to have a "normal" conversation, and can handle complex sentences **adequately**. So it's possible to say: "How was your weekend?" or "I am going to the store to buy potatoes for dinner." Individual names can be whistled, and numbers can be whistled. Animals can even be taught some simple Silbo phrases. Yes, Cho?

Cho: What does the language sound like?

Professor: That's a good question. Well, it doesn't sound like a song, as you might imagine. It sounds more like short, sharp whistles mixed with longer whistles. The key to understanding the whistles is understanding these different sounds.

Scientists have studied Silbo and found that this language, even though it is not spoken, is **processed** in the same part of the brain that is used for spoken language. Therefore, people who understand Silbo use the language part of their brain, but people who don't understand Silbo **interpret** it as whistling.

Of course, the phonetic system, that is, the system of sounds, is very different from regular speech. The whistling actually has four vowels and four consonants. People also use different **tones** to create different words.

Nico, do you have a question?

Nico: Don't their lips get tired?

Professor: Actually, people who speak Silbo use their hands to make the whistles. So it's similar to playing a flute—they use their fingers to make the different sounds as they blow air into their hands.

Silbo is a great example of the creative and unique ways people have discovered to communicate with one another. It also shows us how environmental **constraints** affect language. In this case, the islands' **landscape** encouraged people to use something other than their voice—something louder that would travel farther—to communicate with each other. It shows us that nothing can stop people from trying to keep in touch with each other—not even long distances, hills, and valleys…Any questions?

Sandra: Is that why they call the islands the *Canary* Islands—because people whistle like birds there?

Professor: No—that was the islands' name long before Silbo was used. But I agree that there couldn't be a better language on islands named after a bird!

Listen for Details Page 191

[Repeat Main Ideas track]

LISTENING SKILL Recognizing and understanding definitions

Examples. Page 192

1. The language is named Silbo, after the Spanish word *silbar*, which means "to whistle," and it is used in the Canary Islands.

2. Our brains are hard-wired to use speech. In other words, the ability to use speech is built in to our brains.

3. Some problems are solved and others created by the proliferation of social networking sites, that is, the rapid increase in social networking sites.

A. Page 193

1. Of course, the phonetic system, that is, the system of sounds, is very different from regular speech.

2. When two people who don't know the same language try to communicate, they often use gestures, or hand movements, to represent a word or idea.

3. Different languages also have different syntax, which means the rules for forming grammatical sentences.

4. Blind people can't read words with their eyes so they use books in Braille. In other words, they read words that are made with raised dots, using their fingers, not their eyes.

LISTENING 2 Message in a Bottle
Listen for Main Ideas Page 195

Reporter: The second graders at Nansemond Suffolk Academy in Suffolk, Virginia, have some very special long-distance friends. They communicate with other second graders in North Carolina as "**pen pals**." The students write letters to each other the old-fashioned way, with pen on paper. Then, they mail their letters at the post office. A week or two later, they get replies from their friends over 200 miles away.

But perhaps the most interesting thing about this pen pal relationship is how it began. It all started with an even more **ancient** method of communication: a message in a bottle. Starting as far back as the 3rd Century BC, people have put written messages in **sealed** bottles and thrown them into the ocean. They hope that someone, somewhere, will receive them. This form of communication is **one-sided**, but it is a unique and rewarding way of observing the power of chance. It has also been a useful tool for scientists and meteorologists, who have used messages in bottles to **observe** weather and wind patterns.

The letters between the pen pals in Virginia and North Carolina began with a message found in a bottle on the beach. Pauline Warren was looking for seashells along the Cape Henry Shore in Virginia. **Out of the blue**, she found a plastic bottle among the sticks and other stuff that often **builds up** along the Virginia Beach coastline. Pauline walked over, and saw pieces of paper neatly placed inside the sealed bottle. She opened the bottle, which was covered with a hard layer of salt and dirt, and found messages from elementary school students in the small town of Kannapolis, North Carolina, over 250 miles away. The students were sending get-well wishes to a favorite teacher, Ms. Parker, who had been **fighting an uphill battle** against cancer. The fact that the messages traveled over two months and two hundred miles without help from the U.S. Postal Service is unusual, but that's only the beginning of the story.

Coincidentally, Pauline worked in the office of an elementary school herself: Nansemond Suffolk Academy in Suffolk, Virginia. She decided the best thing to do with the bottle was to give it to the second graders at *her* school. She thought that the students would be interested in responding to the North Carolina students and to Ms. Parker. With the **assistance** of their teacher, Ms. Perry, the NSA second graders wrote two sets of their own letters. The first set was put back into the bottle and sent up the coastline, and the second set was sent directly to Ms. Parker in North Carolina.

Friendships grew as the two groups of second graders from different schools began to write and exchange letters as pen pals. Now, the students enjoy carefully hand-writing their letters. They can't wait for the mail to arrive in case they get a delivery. "Communicating with a new friend from another state is a snap these days, thanks to the Internet and email, but for these students, it is so much more than that," commented Ms. Perry. "They've relied on the ordinary mail and have had the opportunity to learn good writing techniques. They've developed their map skills, and experienced the feeling of **sympathy**. They've shared how it feels to know and care about someone who is very sick. And, more importantly, they've learned that friendships can be made in many ways: even through a message in a bottle."

Listen for Details Page 195

[Repeat Main Ideas track]

PRONUNCIATION Unstressed connecting words
Examples. Page 201

Hugo is taller than Edmundo.

My computer isn't as fast as yours.

The letters that I sent last month just arrived.

Liang's favorite ways to communicate are texting and emailing.

A. Page 201

1. My sister is better at staying in touch than my brother.

2. You need a user name and a password to use the computer network at the school.

3. Most languages don't have as many words as English.

4. The homework that the teacher assigned last night was very difficult.

5. We didn't know that texting was more expensive than speaking on the phone. We need to change cell phone plans.

B. Page 201

[Repeat of Activity A. track]

SPEAKING Expressing emotions
A. Page 202

Hannah: Guess what? You'll never believe what happened!

Sarah: What?

Hannah: Dad bought me a car.

Sarah: You're kidding! Why did he do that?

Hannah: He said it was a graduation present.

Sarah: I'm fed up with the way he treats you. It's not fair.

Hannah: Well, he said he was going to buy you one, too.

Sarah: Really? I didn't know that. That's terrific!